PHILOSOPHICAL ESSAYS

PHILOSOPHICAL ESSAYS

BY

A. J. AYER, M.A., F.B.A.

*Grote Professor of the Philosophy of Mind
and Logic in the University of London*

LONDON
MACMILLAN & CO LTD
NEW YORK · ST MARTIN'S PRESS
1954

Phil.

MACMILLAN AND COMPANY LIMITED
London Bombay Calcutta Madras Melbourne

THE MACMILLAN COMPANY OF CANADA LIMITED
Toronto

ST MARTIN'S PRESS INC
New York

PRINTED IN GREAT BRITAIN

TO
JULIAN AYER

PREFACE

WITH a few minor alterations, the essays which are collected in this volume are reprinted in their original form. Since many of the problems with which they deal are inter-connected, there is a certain amount of repetition, but I hope that it will not be thought excessive. I do not think that there are any serious inconsistencies, though the short paper on 'The Identity of Indiscernibles' raises doubts about the thesis of the paper on 'Individuals': this is, indeed, my reason for including it. While I have not reprinted anything that I now believe to be false, I should certainly not claim that all the questions treated had been satisfactorily disposed of. In particular, I think that there is still much work to be done on the subject of 'Basic Propositions' and on that of 'Freedom and Necessity'. I am more confident about the results obtained in the essay on 'Statements about the Past', and I have used them in making yet another attack on the vexatious problem of 'One's Knowledge of Other Minds'. In both these cases I am much indebted, at least as regards the manner of approach, to the writings of Professor Wisdom.

In the second edition of *The Philosophy of G. E. Moore*, Professor Moore has written an addendum to his 'Reply to my Critics', in which he raises some strong objections to the criticisms that I make of certain of his views in my paper on 'The Terminology of Sense-data'. I have added two long footnotes to this paper in an attempt to rebut Professor Moore's argument, as well as the similar arguments which were used by Mr. Lewy in a note on the same subject in *Mind*, vol. lv, no. 218.

It will be seen that three of these essays are concerned with questions of logic, in a broad sense of the term, five with the theory of knowledge, one with ontology, and three with questions of moral philosophy. I have chosen to reprint them in this order, rather than in the chronological order in which they were published.

The essays first appeared in the following books and periodicals:

(1) 'Individuals', in *Mind*, vol. lxi, N.S., no. 244, 1952.

(2) 'The Identity of Indiscernibles', in *Proceedings of the XIth International Congress of Philosophy*, vol. iii, 1953.

(3) 'Negation', in *The Journal of Philosophy*, vol. xlix, no. 26, 1952.

(4) 'The Terminology of Sense-data', in *Mind*, vol. liv, N.S., no. 216, 1945.

(5) 'Basic Propositions', in *Philosophical Analysis*; a collection of essays edited by Max Black. Cornell University Press, 1950.

(6) 'Phenomenalism', in *Proceedings of the Aristotelian Society*, 1947–48.

(7) 'Statements about the Past', in *Proceedings of the Aristotelian Society*, 1950–51.

(8) 'One's Knowledge of Other Minds', in *Theoria*, vol. xix, 1953.

(9) 'On What There Is', in *Supplementary Proceedings of the Aristotelian Society*, 1951.

(10) 'On the Analysis of Moral Judgements', in *Horizon*, vol. xx, no. 117, 1949.

(11) 'The Principle of Utility', in *Jeremy Bentham and the Law*; a symposium edited by G. W. Keeton

and G. Schwarzenberger.   Stevens & Sons Ltd.,
    1948.
(12) 'Freedom and Necessity', in *Polemic*, no. 5, 1946.

I have to thank the editors and publishers in question for allowing these essays to be reprinted.

A. J. AYER

2 WHITEHORSE STREET
   LONDON, W.1
   October 1953

CONTENTS

I

INDIVIDUALS

THE distinction between individuals and properties is
a commonplace of logic; but it is easier to illustrate
than to define. For instance, I am an individual, so is
the after-image that I saw a moment ago, so is to-
morrow's sunrise, so is the French Revolution and the
British Army, so is the collection of all the sheets of
paper in this room. These entities are by no means all
of the same logical type, but they are all contrasted with
such things as being human, being extended, being
combustible, redness, generalship, preceding, father-
hood, being further from a given place than two other
places are from one another, which, as qualities or
relations, come under the heading of properties. It
may be indeed that this distinction is not exhaustive.
It would appear strange, for example, to speak of the
liberal tradition, or the American Constitution, or the
theory of relativity either as properties or as individuals.
What might be claimed is that the statements which
referred to such doubtful things as these could always
be reformulated in such a way that everything that they
mentioned fell clearly into one or other category; but,
for the present, at least, this must be treated as an open
question. Neither is it certain that our distinction is
exclusive. There are some philosophers who, without
denying that redness is a property, would yet wish to

say that in making the statement that redness is a property, one is actually using the word 'redness' to designate an individual. And here again it might be argued that we can always eliminate such doubtful individuals by giving suitable translations of the statements in which it might appear that they were mentioned. Thus, in the example chosen, the statement that redness is a property might be replaced by the statement that if anything is red it follows that it has some property. But perhaps not everyone would admit that this was a fair translation; and even if this were admitted, it might still be thought to be an open question whether a similar procedure could be carried out in every case.

I shall not, however, press this matter here. It is enough for my purpose that there is a large number of cases in which it can be clearly recognized whether a particular expression is being used to stand for an individual or for a property. My problem is to discover in what the distinction consists. When we say of something that it is an individual or that it is a property, what is it exactly that we are saying? This may indeed be a question to which there is no informative answer. It may be that the distinction between individuals and properties is one that it is futile to try to explain in terms of anything else, a point which is sometimes made in a more dignified way by saying that particularity and universality are ultimate categories. But even if this be true, it is not so obviously true that the question will not bear a little more investigation.

The traditional view that individuals are the logical subjects of discourse, or, to put it more precisely, that they are entities which enter into discourse only as logical subjects, and never as attributes, does not seem to me very helpful. I do not mean by this that it is not correct, but that it is not illuminating. For it amounts to saying that individuals are not themselves properties but the things to which properties are ascribed. And to say this is to do hardly more than reaffirm the distinction which we are required to elucidate.

Another well-known answer to our problem is that individuals can be in only one place, that is, occupy one continuous region of space, at a time, whereas properties can be in many places at once. But this is not at all a satisfactory answer, as it stands. For, in the first place, it is not true of every individual that it occupies one continuous region of space at any given time. It is not true of most of the examples that I gave. And even if it were true, it would not be the answer we are seeking. For being in one or many places at a time is itself a relation between individuals, or a relation between properties, or a relation between individuals and properties, according as you interpret it : and this itself needs further clarification. Nevertheless, the spatial criterion does play a part in this question, as we shall see later on.

It might be thought that we could discriminate individuals from properties by saying that only individuals existed. This would not be to say that all individuals existed, since the ascription of existence to a given individual might be false, nor yet that other things might exist but happened not to. The suggestion must be that it always makes sense to say of an individual that it exists but never makes sense to say this of a property. But one objection to this is that it is still a matter of dispute whether all the things that are commonly reckoned as individuals can significantly be said to exist. Spatio-temporal points are individuals, and so are biological species and unconscious minds ;

but not everyone would allow it to be said that they existed. Once again, it might be claimed that the statements which referred to such individuals could always be translated into statements in which no individuals were mentioned but those that had an undisputed candidature to existence; but even if this is so we are hardly justified in making the question whether something is an individual depend upon the question whether such a translation is possible. Even if it were shown, for example, that statements about spatio-temporal points could not be so translated, we might still wish to say that points were individuals. It may be indeed that they are reducible to properties, but then it is a question whether all individuals are not. That is one of the main issues that needs to be decided. Furthermore, it is by no means common ground that properties do not exist. A great many philosophers have held that they do, and I do not see how they can very well be refuted. On the contrary, a way to draw the sting from the problem of universals is to show that there need be no harm in saying that universals are real, that the philosopher who insists on ascribing existence to properties as well as to individuals need not be saying anything that anyone would want to disagree with; a concession which is not so friendly as it looks, since once a philosophical statement has been shown to be harmless there is seldom much point in making it. Of course no one maintains that properties exist in the same manner as individuals, but if we admit the possibility of their existing after their own fashion, which is merely to allow a certain liberality in the use of the word 'existence', then the most that we can claim is that only individuals exist in the way that individuals exist. And even this will be inaccurate if it is true that not all individuals exist in the same way. It does not seem, therefore, that this suggestion takes us very far.

Perhaps we can make more progress if we cease to conceive our problem as one of differentiating between different categories of objects, and approach it instead from the standpoint of language. In short, I propose to do what is described, somewhat loosely, as changing from the material to the formal mode of speech. I shall refer to predicates instead of properties, and to individual signs, to which I shall give the name of indicators, instead of individuals. I think that this substitution of statements about signs for statements about objects is a useful manœuvre, else I should not engage in it, but it needs to be handled more carefully than it used to be when Carnap and others first made it popular. Thus it is not correct to say, as I at least was once inclined to do, that a statement like 'Napoleon is an individual' is simply a misleading version of the linguistic statement '"Napoleon" is an indicator': for the two statements are not equivalent. One may be true and the other false if the 'Napoleon' which is said to be an indicator is not the name of the Napoleon who is said to be an individual; and merely to say that 'Napoleon' is an indicator is not to give any information at all about what it is used to refer to. In the same way, 'redness is a property' is not to be translated into '"red" is a predicate': for while it does follow from the statement that 'red' is a predicate that it stands for some property, it does not follow that it stands for the property of redness. Besides a statement like '"red" is a predicate' is elliptical. It is true of the English word 'red', but might not be true of the sign 'red' as it occurred in some other language. We should, therefore, say not simply '"red" is a predicate' but '"red",

B

as it is used in English, is a predicate'. But, certainly, no part of what is meant by saying that redness is a property is that 'red' is an English word. It could still be true that redness was a property, even though 'red' were not the English word for red, or there were no English word for red, or indeed there were no English language at all. Of course, propositions like 'there is no such language as English', 'there is no English word for red' are pragmatically self-refuting when they are expressed in English; but they are not self-contradictory. To assume that they are self-contradictory is to revive in a modern form the error of those idealists who argued that no object could exist without being thought of, on the ground that to specify any such object was to think of it; to which the simple answer is that if an object is not thought of it is not specified. This answer does not, indeed, dispose of the fallacy, which rests on a confusion between failing to think of something and thinking of it as unthought of, or, in its modern form, between failing to describe something and describing it as undescribed. But the full treatment of this problem would lead us into the realm of the semantic paradoxes, into which I do not propose to follow it.

What I hope to have shown is that the old-fashioned recipe for putting category statements into linguistic form was rather too simple, but I do not wish to maintain that there is no way of bringing this about. For example, instead of 'Napoleon is an individual' or 'redness is a property', we might say 'any sign that designates Napoleon is an indicator', or 'any sign that designates redness is a predicate'. But even this will not do if we interpret the second pair of statements categorically, that is as having existential import, for it does not follow from the fact that Napoleon is an individual, or that redness is a property, that any signs do designate them. There are no doubt a great many individuals and properties that never have and never will be designated by any signs, though *ex hypothesi* I cannot say which they are. Napoleon and redness happen not to be among them, but it is not inconceivable that they should have been. Accordingly, to make our translations exact we must be content to say that if any sign designates Napoleon it is an indicator, and that if any sign designates redness it is a predicate, leaving it open whether there are such signs. But even if this method of translation is correct, it is not of much service. I cannot see that anything of importance is to be gained by such straightforward transpositions from the material into the formal mode, which anyhow is a misnomer, since the statements which are said to be in the formal mode are not purely formal, or are useless if they are. What we need is a more laborious account of the ways in which indicators and predicates are used.

A part of my argument may be more concisely put by saying that the distinction between indicators and predicates is not syntactical. Or perhaps we should say that while it may be treated as a syntactical distinction, it is not thereby clarified in the way that we want. It is indeed possible to list the signs in a language, and then to bestow on the members of one such class the title of predicates and on the members of another the title of individual signs or indicators. But then in saying of a sign that it is an indicator, or that it is a predicate, one will be saying nothing about what it designates, or about the way in which it is used, but only that it is of a certain shape, the shape that it is, or that it occupies a certain position in a sentence, the position that it does. Whereas what it intended, surely, by the bestowal of these titles is to inform us not merely that a sign of a certain shape has the physical properties that it has, or even that it is one of a set of such signs, but rather that a sign of a certain shape is to function as an indicator, or that it is to function as a predicate. And this raises the question of what it is for a sign to function in these ways, which is not a question of syntax. Neither is it satisfactory to treat it as a question of semantics in the naïve way that some logicians now do, by saying that indicators stand for individual concepts, and that predicates stand for predicate concepts or attributes. For my part, I think it is a mistake to bring concepts in at all in this context : we can allow 'Napoleon' to indicate Napoleon without intercalating what is, in effect, a reduplication of the sign. But there is no need to press this objection. For this distinction between concepts, to which appeal is made, so far from explaining the distinction between predicates and indicators has itself to be explained in terms of it. Having been told that indicators stand for individual concepts, and that predicates stand for attributes, we want to know how these two sets of concepts are to be distinguished. And the only way in which this question can be informatively answered is by showing how the use of indicators differs from the use of predicates. It is to this problem, therefore, that I shall now turn.

In what follows I am going to make use of the undefined terms 'situation' and 'occasion'. I am going to use them in such a way that every expression that has descriptive content may be said to signify a situation and to apply to one or more occasions. A situation which an expression signifies will be said to be exemplified by the occasions to which it applies. It will make sense to say of situations that they occur more than once but not of occasions. Thus each repetition of a situation is, in my terminology, a different occasion. Any situation that is exemplified at all is exemplified by some occasion, but the same occasion may exemplify a number of different situations. For example, the occasion of my writing these words exemplifies the situation of a person's writing, of my hand moving, of black shapes appearing on a white background, and many others besides. Occasions need not be actual. Whether an expression has denotation or not, whether a statement is true or false, the occasions to which it applies are the same. Perhaps objection will be taken to the admission of merely possible occasions. What is an occasion, it may be asked, if it be not actual? But this is like asking what it is that an expression denotes when it has no denotation, or what is the shadow fact that a statement corresponds to when it is false. To say that an expression applies to certain occasions is just to say that it has a descriptive meaning; to say that the occasions in question are not actual is just to say that the expression has no denotation; where the expression is a descriptive statement, it is to say that the statement is not true. So long therefore as we do not regard possible occasions as objects, I do not think that this way of speaking need give rise to any trouble.

Since I am concerned here only with descriptive and not at all with logical signs, I make it necessary that occasions should be empirical. That is to say, the situation which is signified by any expression which applies directly to any set of occasions must be an observable situation. And here it may be left open what situations are to count as being observable; whether, for example, we are to treat such objects as electrons as being directly accessible to observation, or only such common-sense objects as chairs and tables, or only sense-data. Whatever decision may be taken on this point we are, however, likely to be left with some descriptive expressions which do not signify observables. And since I propose to elucidate the difference between indicators and predicates by commenting on the different ways in which they apply to occasions, it may be suggested that the admission of expressions which do not signify observables presents me with a serious difficulty. But I do not think that this is so. For if these are descriptive expressions, then even though they do not themselves signify observables they must be reducible to expressions which do. By this I do not mean that the sentences in which they occur can always be faithfully translated into sentences which contain as descriptive expressions only those that designate observables. In general, such translations will not be forthcoming. Nevertheless there must be occasions to which these expressions apply, if only indirectly : for if this were not so they would have no descriptive content. And they can be said to be reducible to those expressions which signify the observable situations that are exemplified in the occasions to which they apply. To determine which are the occasions to which they can apply is indeed not always an easy matter. But this is not a problem that concerns us here. All that our argument requires is that such determination should be possible.

At this point it may be objected that in referring, in the way I do, to situations and occasions I am covertly re-introducing the very distinction between universals and particulars that I am attempting to clarify. And this objection is well founded, inasmuch as the word 'universal' has no doubt sometimes been used in the way in which I am using the word 'situation', and the word 'particular' in the way that I am using 'occasion'. It should, however, be remarked that I do not strictly need to make any such distinction. I have introduced the word 'situation' for convenience of exposition, but it will be seen that I use it in such a way that everything that I say about situations could be rephrased as a statement about occasions. Nevertheless, the objection still remains that my use of the word 'occasion' is such that an account of individuals in terms of occasions will be circular. To which I can reply only that I do not think this matters. My contention is that we can come to understand better what is meant by an individual by examining the different ways in which expressions of different types are used. For this purpose, we require to be able not only to mention the expressions but also to mention, at least in a general way, what it is that they refer to. And it is this second function that is performed by my term 'occasion'. I do not say that a better term could not be found; but only that some such term is needed. I have indeed admitted that the word 'particular' might itself be a candidate. But even if we used the word 'particular' in talking about the references of various expressions, this would in no way prejudice an account of the distinction between particulars and universals, or individuals and properties, as it is applied to the expressions about which we were talking. It would not even prevent us from dispensing with particulars altogether by eliminating indicators in favour of predicates. And I shall in fact be saying that this is possible. In a language in which this was done there would be no means of mentioning individuals, but it would not be descriptively poorer than a language in which they were mentioned. Particulars, considered as occasions, would be referred to only at the level of the meta-language; when it was a question not of using the language, but of talking about its use.

Having tried to explain my terminology, I shall now use it to elucidate the distinction between indicators and predicates. It is characteristic of predicates that they all apply to an indefinite number of occasions. The situation which a predicate signifies may not ever be exemplified, or it may be exemplified only once, but whether or not it is in fact repeated it is essential that it should be repeatable. To take a simple example, there might have been no green things in the world, or only one, but however many things may in fact be green, it is possible that there should be any number: and here when I speak of the number of green things, I am referring to the number of occasions to which the word 'green' applies. And this is sufficient to distinguish predicates from a certain class of indicators, namely those which philosophers have called 'logically proper names'; for the function of a logically proper name is to apply only to one occasion. Just for this reason, however, logically proper names would be of very little use, and while it is possible to devise a language which would contain them, they are not to be found in any actual language that is known to me. It might indeed be thought that demonstratives like 'I', 'this', 'here', or 'now', at least in some of their uses, were logically proper names; but this would be a mistake. It is true that in particular instances of their use these words may apply to single occasions; but the same is true of many signs which are not classified as demonstratives, including many predicates. The peculiarity of these demonstratives is not that their

range of application is exceptionally narrow but that it
is exceptionally wide. Certain restrictions may be put
upon it, as, for example, that personal pronouns apply
only to occasions that satisfy descriptions of persons,
but within such limits it is indeterminate. Demonstratives of this sort acquire precision of reference only
in a context where account is taken of the situation of
the persons by whom they are being used.

But whatever may be the correct account of our use
of words like 'I' or 'this' or 'now', it is clear that not
all the signs that count as indicators are logically proper
names: and this being so, the fact that predicates
apply to an indefinite number of occasions is not
sufficient to distinguish them from indicators; for this
is true of indicators also. The name 'Napoleon', taken
as designating Napoleon, has a range of application,
just as the predicate of being a soldier has a range of
application. There is, of course, a difference in the two
ranges, although they are not entirely independent, but
so is there a difference in the ranges of different
indicators, or of different predicates. What we are
seeking is a difference in type, a difference in the way
the respective ranges are constituted, and I think that
I can see what this difference is, though I have not been
able to find a very satisfactory way of describing it. In
the case of a predicate, the ground which we have for
saying that the different occasions to which it applies
exemplify the same situation, namely the situation
which the predicate signifies, is the observation of
qualitative resemblance. It is not true, indeed, of all
predicates, as it is, for example, of the predicate 'green',
that the different occasions to which they may apply
need bear any marked resemblance to each other, but
it is, I think, at least necessary that they should be

severally associated with occasions between which this
relation does obtain. It is not required of soldiers that
they should at all times look or sound alike, but there
must be some contexts in which their behaviour is
resemblant; and it is in virtue of these resemblances
that they satisfy the predicate of being soldiers. The
occasions by which it is manifested that something is
electrically charged may be widely divergent, but it will
be found at least that occasions which resemble one of
them have often been accompanied by occasions which
resemble another. I do not claim, indeed, that this
talk of resemblances is at all an effective substitute for
the use of predicates. Instead of saying vaguely that
two occasions resemble each other, or even more
vaguely that while they do not resemble each other,
they are somehow associated with occasions that do, it
would be very much more informative to mention a
predicate which they satisfy. The reference to qualitative resemblance is introduced only to show that the
distinction between indicators and predicates depends,
in one of its aspects, upon the use of different criteria of
identity. For in the case of those indicators such as
'Napoleon' or 'The Young Pretender' which are used
in accordance with a criterion of substantial identity,
the relations of qualitative resemblance in virtue of
which different occasions may be said to satisfy the
same predicates are not sufficient. Supposing that
these names or descriptions refer to physical objects,
we require of the occasions to which they apply that
they stand to each other, directly or indirectly, in
relations of spatio-temporal continuity. And here the
possibility of there being spatially discrete individuals
need not constitute an exception; for while the parts of
such individuals are not contiguous to each other, the

criterion for the identity of the individuals as a whole
may be that the condition of spatio-temporal continuity
is fulfilled by each of the parts. On the other hand,
there are many indicators which do furnish exceptions
to this rule. 'The tallest man in the room', for
example, when construed as applying to every man
who is in a room with other men and is taller than they
are, functions in the same way as a predicate with
respect to our criterion of identity. It is to be classified
as an indicator for reasons which I shall come to later on.

At present I am making only the familiar point that
there is an important class of individuals which we
identify by tracing their paths in space and time ; and
no doubt it is because we do this that some philosophers
have regarded the ability to be in only one, as opposed
to many, places at once as the criterion by which
individuals are distinguished from properties. But
here it may be argued that this difference in our ways
of grouping occasions, in the one case on the basis of
qualitative resemblance and in the other on the basis of
spatio-temporal continuity, is only superficial. For is
not the relation of spatio-temporal continuity itself to
be explained in terms of qualitative resemblances, not
indeed between the several occasions to which a given
indicator applies, but between them and other sets of
occasions ? The point is that expressions which stand
for spatial or temporal relations are themselves predicates ; and this being so, the fact that the identity of
certain individuals depends upon spatio-temporal position in a way that the identity of properties does not,
is not, it may be said, a sufficient ground for distinguishing between them.

The argument which I am trying to develop may be
put in a form which is both simpler and more general.

Occasions can be grouped in many different ways and in particular they can be grouped in the way that certain indicators group them. But any such grouping can always be described exclusively in terms of predicates. For the occasions can be grouped only in virtue of the relations that they bear to one another, or, severally or collectively, bear to other occasions. Describing the occasions is a matter of using predicates; and so is describing the relations, which may themselves be treated as ingredients in occasions. It is a matter of using predicates, because to describe something is to say that it exemplifies a situation, that is, is a member of a set of possible occasions which are taken together as being similar in a certain respect, and this is the work that predicates do. Now the question that I wish to consider is whether it follows from this that indicators are short-hand predicates. This conclusion is indeed often drawn, although not often presented in this form. It appears rather in the form of the statement : things are bundles of qualities, or of the question : what is the thing itself apart from its properties ? — leading to the challenge : describe the thing without describing its properties, a challenge which it is evidently impossible to meet, since what is demanded is self-contradictory : or it may take the form of the threat : if you will not allow that things can be reduced to properties you are committed to believing in substance : or the lament : we can know the 'what' but never the 'that', which goes with : structure can be communicated but not content. But what is, I think, at issue in all these cases is just whether indicators are or are not short-hand predicates.

Now it may well be said that this question is itself obscure, but, as I interpret it, it can be resolved into

three questions which are reasonably clear. First, can
we find for every descriptive statement which contains
an indicator a logically equivalent statement in which
all the non-logical signs are predicates ? Secondly,
assuming, as would generally be conceded, that this is
not possible, could a language which contained only
predicates as descriptive signs describe all the facts that
our language does, that is, apply to all the occasions
that our language applies to ? It might be thought
that a negative answer to the first question entailed a
negative answer to the second, but this is not so. For
example, a language which contained no equivalents
for indefinite words like 'someone' would not be such
that all the statements that could be made in English
were translatable into it ; but it might still be rich
enough to describe all the facts, in the sense in which I
am using this phrase. For the occasion of someone's
doing some thing is necessarily an occasion of some
particular person's doing something, and the language
under consideration might have the means of designating that person. And the third question is : assuming
that indicators are not eliminable in a sense that would
give an affirmative answer to the first question, what
work do they do ?

A model for the replacement of indicators by predicates is already at hand in Russell's theory of descriptions. For the principle on which this theory works is
that the description of anything which satisfies a given
propositional function is itself associated with the
function, yielding thereby a new function the values of
which are not identified. When they are identified the
same process is repeated. The function feeds like an
insect on whatever satisfies it ; all the nourishment goes
to swell the body of the insect, while the head shrinks to

nothing. The ꓷx which stands at the head throughout has no descriptive force; it serves only to make an instantiation claim. It may be objected that this does not hold in the cases where it is claimed that the instantiation is unique : for while the individual which is said to satisfy an unique description is not otherwise identified than as something which satisfies that description, it is at least distinguished, through the use of different variables, from other individuals : the rider is added that there is no individual y which satisfies the description and is not identical with x. But since all that can differentiate x from y is their satisfying different functions, the question of their identity or difference is still a question of certain descriptions having or not having application. If a predicate ϕ is uniquely instantiated, it will not be possible to find two more complex predicates ψ and χ such that (1) ϕ is a constituent of both ψ and χ, (2) both ψ and χ are instantiated, (3) the predicate formed by combining ϕ with all the other constituents of both ψ and χ is not instantiated. Thus, let us assume that we have some indefinite description of the bank at Monte Carlo, say a bank which has a capital of so many million francs. Then it may be that being a man who broke a bank which satisfies this description, being, in short, a man who broke the bank at Monte Carlo, is a description which is itself uniquely satisfied. In that case, many complex predicates will be instantiated in which this predicate is an ingredient; for example, being a grey-haired breaker of such a bank, being a loud-voiced breaker of such a bank, being a breaker of such a bank who died in poverty and so on. It is clear also that any combination of these predicates will be instantiated, since if they are severally true of the man who broke the bank at Monte

Carlo they are also true of him collectively. But now suppose that at least one other man broke the bank at Monte Carlo. Then many other complex predicates will be instantiated, being a French-speaking breaker of such a bank, for example, or a breaker of such a bank who owns a racehorse. But it will now not be true that every combination of any two such predicates is itself instantiated. For instance, the predicate of being a loud-voiced racehorse-owning breaker of such a bank will not be instantiated if only two men have broken the bank and the one who owns the racehorse is not loud-voiced. And from this it follows according to our criterion that the description of being a man who broke such a bank is not uniquely satisfied.

If this can be taken as an adequate definition of a predicate's being uniquely instantiated, we have a basis for disposing of the other cases in which Russell appears to use the existential quantifier as something more than an instantiation sign. To say, for example, of two predicates ψ and ψ' that they apply to the same individual is to say that it is possible to find a predicate ϕ, such that ϕ is uniquely instantiated and both $\phi\psi$ and $\phi\psi'$ are instantiated. To say that just two individuals satisfy a certain description ψ is to say that one can find predicates ϕ and ϕ' such that ϕ is uniquely instantiated, ϕ' is uniquely instantiated, $\phi\phi'$ is not instantiated, $\phi\psi$ is instantiated, $\phi'\psi$ is instantiated, and one cannot find a predicate χ such that $\psi\chi$ is instantiated without either $\phi\psi\chi$ or $\phi'\psi\chi$ being instantiated. These are, indeed, fairly straightforward cases. But I hope that they may serve to show that it is possible to deal with classes on this basis and consequently also with relations. All that I am now doing is to sketch a language, arising out of Russell's, in which indicators occur only vestigially as

existence symbols, or, as I prefer to call them, instantiation claims.

Suppose now that such a language were developed.
To show that the sentences of a language such as
English were translatable into it, it would be necessary
to show, among other things, that proper names and
pronouns, as we ordinarily use them, could be replaced
by definite descriptions, and these in their turn by
indefinite descriptions of which it was said that they
satisfied the condition of applying uniquely. And for
reasons which Mr. Strawson [1] and others have already
given, I do not believe that this programme can be
carried out. Perhaps the well-known difficulties of
endowing proper names with connotations can be met
by Professor Quine's device of inventing special
predicates. Instead of saying that Mr. Truman is a
politician, we are to say that one and only one thing both
trumanizes and is a politician, where 'trumanizing' is
'an unanalysable irreducible attribute' which happens
to be uniquely instantiated.[2] This device may not
appeal to those who wish to insist, with Mr. Joseph,
that 'the son of James I and VI was not called Charles
on account of his Carolinity',[3] but considering it only
as a proposal to amend our way of speaking I cannot
find any serious objection to it. It does not, however,
enable us to dispense with pronouns, nor, I think, does
it correctly render our own use of proper names in
ordinary speech. For even if the predicate of being-
Truman is uniquely instantiated, it is contingent that
it is so. We have to allow for the possibility that
nothing trumanizes or that more than one thing does:

[1] P. F. Strawson, 'On Referring', *Mind*, vol. lix, no. 235.
[2] W. V. Quine, 'On What There Is', *Review of Metaphysics*, vol. ii,
no. 5, p. 27.
[3] H. W. B. Joseph, *Introduction to Logic*, p. 152.

and in either of these cases we have, on this interpretation, to say that all the statements that are made about
Mr. Truman are false. But, whatever may be the case
with definite descriptions, it seems to me clear that we
do not use proper names in such a way that failure to
secure unique reference would render the statements
which contained them false. As Mr. Strawson has
argued, it is rather that we assume uniqueness of
reference as a condition of treating such statements as
candidates for truth or falsehood. I allow, therefore,
that there are sentences of the English language, as it is
ordinarily spoken, for which the language I have outlined would not be able to furnish logical equivalents.

It does not follow, however, that the language
would be descriptively poorer than English, or indeed
than any other. On the contrary, since what can be
described in a language depends only on what predicates it contains, replacing indicators by predicates can
never impoverish a language descriptively. It is necessarily true that any occasion which is described with
the help of signs that are ordinarily classified as indicators can also be described exclusively by predicates.

But is there not, it may be asked, a difficulty about
individuation? There can be no description which
necessarily individuates. How then can we ever be
sure that any predicate is uniquely instantiated? The
answer is that we cannot be sure. However complex
we make our descriptions, it is always at least conceivable that we should make them more complex still:
and given a description of limited complexity, it is
always possible that it should be satisfied by more than
one set of occasions, the occasions being differentiated
by descriptions which are not included in it. No doubt
we are able to find many quite simple predicates which

c

are in fact uniquely instantiated, but there is no way of demonstrating that they are. The ground for holding that they are can be no more than the failure of a search for counter-examples. It is a contingent fact that the conditions of unique instantiation are ever fulfilled.

It does not seem to me, however, that this creates a difficulty. Certainly there can be no guarantee that any description individuates. But why should it be thought that a guarantee is needed? If I use a predicate which is not uniquely instantiated I do indeed run a risk of being misunderstood. My assertion that the predicate in question is instantiated may be found to be true by the person to whom I am speaking but he may still misunderstand me in the sense that he does not receive the information that I intended to give him. The occasion which I had in mind was correctly described by the predicates which I used, but my description was insufficient. The occasion which he correctly takes as verifying what I actually said satisfies other predicates than those for which I wished to make an instantiation claim. To achieve my object I must therefore enlarge my description. It may be that I shall thereby come to formulate a description which does in fact individuate, but it is not essential that I should. I have only to continue to the point at which he responds in such a way that I say that he has understood me, the test being that any further description that he gives is one that I acknowledge to be relevant. And this I may very well achieve without using any predicate that is in fact uniquely instantiated.

This may seem an unsatisfactory method of communication, but our current procedure is not so very different. In ordinary speech, expressions which I have classified as indicators do the work of individuating.

But they do not do it by furnishing any information which could not be given without them, nor does their use afford a guarantee against misunderstanding. The predicates which a speaker actually mentions are constituents of many more complex predicates, and many of these are likely to be instantiated : his use of an indicator, whether it be a demonstrative, a proper name, a pronoun, or a definite descriptive phrase, shows that it is only for a certain selection of them that he wishes to make an instantiation claim. In certain contexts the use of one or more such indicators, and especially of demonstratives, may even serve to show which these predicates are; it does so by directing attention to occasions to which the predicates apply. Indicative words are like signals in a game of hunt the thimble. They show the searcher when he is getting warm. They are not themselves descriptions but they do duty for descriptions. To understand how an indicator is being used is to be able to substitute for it a description which is recognized by the speaker as appropriate. Sometimes it is a matter of substituting another indicator for which one is able to substitute the relevant descriptions, as when a personal pronoun is replaced by a proper name. But this is not to say that two such indicators are logically equivalent to one another or to the descriptions which replace them. A dictionary will not tell us what is meant by 'Julius Caesar', but studying Roman history may tell us who he was, that is, provide us with a range of descriptions which it is permissible to substitute for the name. If I misunderstand the use of such a name in a given context, that is, associate it with other descriptions than those that the speaker was concerned with, I may be put right by being given further descriptions, which

will probably contain indicators that I am not likely to
misunderstand. 'The Julius Caesar that I am talking
of is not the Dulwich Hamlet footballer, but the Roman
general, the man who lived in the first century B.C.'
And at some point, it is to be hoped, no further explanations will be needed. Understanding is reached when
I can go on to provide further descriptions which are
relevant; and here it should be remarked that their
being relevant does not entail that they are satisfied, or
even that they are satisfied if the other relevant descriptions are. I can be misinformed about a person to
a very high degree, but this is not to say that I have
not identified him, so long as my misinformation is
contextually plausible. Nevertheless, I must get something right. If I am totally misinformed, I have not
caught on to the use of the indicator. I may be
describing a different person and so be mistaken only
about the conventional reference of a name. Or perhaps
I am telling a fictitious story and mistaking it for fact.
In theory, I suppose that we could manage without
indicators; we might be lucky or skilful enough to be
able to communicate solely by means of indefinite
descriptions; but, in fact, we are trained in such a way
that we should be comparatively helpless without them.

It is a common mistake in philosophy to assume, in
a case where A is different from B, that A is not really
different from B, but is only B in some disguise. And
I suspect that something of this sort has happened here.
It has been seen that there is something odd about the
suggestion that indicators function in the same way as
predicates, and this creates a situation of philosophical
discomfort, to which one party responds by saying that
of course indicators function as predicates; they must
signify properties, if they have any meaning at all, and

it is only through accidents of grammar that we are led to imagine anything else: 'things are bundles of qualities': while the other party says: they do describe, but not by signifying properties; they describe mysterious entities, substances, selves, which we are obliged to postulate but cannot say anything about: 'we can communicate the "what" but not the "that"'. But both parties are wrong. Indicators do not describe what predicates describe. They may, and indeed, to have meaning, must, be associated with descriptions, but their use *qua* indicators is not to describe anything at all. The believers in substances were seriously at fault in taking indicators to be descriptions and then having to invent something for them to stand for. But they were right in objecting to the simple identification of individuals with their properties. For this shows them at least to have been aware that our actual use of indicators is different from our use of predicates.

2

THE IDENTITY OF INDISCERNIBLES

THE principle of the identity of indiscernibles would seem, in the forms in which it is usually stated, to be at best contingently true. It does not appear that even Leibniz held it to be logically inconceivable that different things should have all their properties in common. That 'no substances are completely similar, or differ *solo numero*'[1] was established, in his view, by the principle of sufficient reason, but he conceded that 'the supposition of two indiscernibles seems to be possible in abstract terms'.[2] Indeed, it may plausibly be argued that even to ask whether things can be different without being discernible from one another is to admit that it is logically possible. For what sense could there be either in affirming or in denying that two things could have all their properties in common unless they were already distinguished? As Russell put it, 'it is a sheer logical error to suppose that, if there were an ultimate distinction between subjects and predicates, subjects could be distinguished by differences of predicates. For before two subjects can differ as to predicates, they must already be two;

[1] C. J. Gerhardt, *Die philosopischen Schriften von G. W. Leibniz*, vol. iv, p. 433.
[2] Leibniz, fifth letter to Clarke, quoted by Bertrand Russell, *The Philosophy of Leibniz*, p. 55.

26

and thus the immediate diversity is prior to that obtained from diversity of predicates. Again, two terms cannot be distinguished in the first instance by difference of relation to other terms; for difference of relation presupposes two distinct terms, and cannot therefore be the ground of their distinctness.' [1] It is true that Russell himself is prepared to disregard this argument, no doubt because he does not assume that there is any ultimate distinction between subjects and predicates; for his own definition of identity is that x and y are identical if and only if x satisfies just those predicative functions that are satisfied by y.[2] But for this he is taken to task by Wittgenstein. 'Russell's definition of " = " won't do; because according to it one cannot say that two objects have all their properties in common. (Even if this proposition is never true, it is nevertheless significant)'; [3] and in saying that this proposition is at least significant Wittgenstein means also to imply that it is not self-contradictory.

But if it is to be admitted from the outset that the principle of the identity of indiscernibles can be denied without self-contradiction, then surely it is divested of any philosophical interest. No doubt the discovery, if it could be made, that there actually were different objects which were mutually indiscernible, would come as a surprise; but so long as the bounds of logical possibility are respected, it is not for the philosopher to set any limit to the marvels of nature. Philosophically, the grounds for a denial of existence are always *a priori*. The proof that nothing does answer to a given description is that nothing could, and the proof

[1] Bertrand Russell, *The Principles of Mathematics*, p. 452.
[2] Russell and Whitehead, *Principia Mathematica*, vol. i, p. 168.
[3] L. Wittgenstein, *Tractatus Logico-Philosophicus*, s. 4302.

of this is that the description in question is meaningless
or self-contradictory. I propose, therefore, regardless
of what Leibniz may originally have meant in affirming
the identity of indiscernibles, to treat the principle as
a candidate only for necessary truth. What we have
to consider is not whether there actually are 'in nature
two indiscernible real absolute beings' [1] but whether
it makes sense to say that there are. And for this
purpose we need to reformulate the principle, in such
a way that it does not itself appear to make the purely
numerical distinction between objects which it declares
to be impossible.

The defect of the usual formulations is, as Russell
saw, that they already imply the distinction between
subjects and predicates. The question whether indiscernibles are necessarily identical is made to look as if
it were a question about the capacities of substances.
Is it, or is it not, within the power of different things
to achieve an entire community of properties? But
this way of putting it makes there appear to be no
problem. The philosopher who wishes to maintain
that things which are not discernible from one another
must be identical is represented as saying that he is
unable to distinguish what he has already recognized
to be distinct. It is easy enough, however, to see what
his difficulty is. He doubts whether there can be any
sense in talking of a plurality of objects unless it is a
way of talking about differences of properties. Accordingly, if justice is to be done to his position, the
question must be rephrased as a question about
predicates. What are the conditions which a set of
predicates must satisfy for it to count as descriptive of
a single individual? Since the criteria for the identity

[1] Gerhardt, *op. cit.* vol. vii, p. 393.

of different individuals are of various sorts, there is no simple answer to this question; but it is not here required that we should examine it in detail. It is enough that we propound a rule which has the principle of the identity of indiscernibles as a logical consequence. Thus, it may be suggested that it is a necessary, though not indeed a sufficient, condition for any two sets of predicates to apply to different things either that one set should contain at least one member which is not a member of the other, or that there should be at least one further predicate which is co-instantiated with one set but not with the other. If this rule is valid, the principle of the identity of indiscernibles becomes analytic; for it will then be necessarily true that there is no difference between things that cannot be represented as a difference between properties.

At this point, however, some indication must be given as to what is, or at any rate what is not, to be counted as a predicate. For if no restriction is placed upon the type of predicate to be admitted, our rule very easily becomes trivial. Thus if A is allowed to have the property of being identical with itself, it is clear that there will be at least one predicate which will not be included in any set of predicates applying to something other than A, namely the predicate of being identical with A. Under these conditions, if A and B are different there can be no doubt that they are discernible; for even if they share all their other properties, A alone of the two will be different from B and identical with A, while B alone will be different from A and identical with B. To avoid such trivialities it is not sufficient, and indeed not even necessary, to make the ruling that 'identity' and 'difference' are not genuine predicates. Neither is it necessary to exclude

such relational predicates as 'being spatially co-extensive with' or 'being at no distance from'. Any qualitative or relational predicate may be admitted, provided
that it has a descriptive meaning. It is, however,
essential that its meaning be purely descriptive. The
objection, in this context, to such an expression as
'being identical with A' is not that it mentions the
dubious relation of identity but that it contains the
name 'A'. If 'A' were replaced by an indefinite
description the objection would fall. The principle
which here comes into play is that descriptions are
essentially general; to describe anything is to attribute
to it a property of a certain sort, a property which is
capable, in theory, of being manifested in any number
of different contexts, whether or not it is so manifested
in fact. And the corollary of this is that a description
may contain no reference to any object which is not
itself described in this indefinite way. Consequently,
an expression is, for our present purposes, to be accounted fully predicative only if all the demonstrative
or individuating elements that it may contain are
replaced by indefinite descriptions. And when it is
claimed that objects can be differentiated only through
their properties, or rather, that to speak of different
objects can only be a way of speaking of different sets
of properties, the only expressions that are to be regarded as designating properties are those that are
fully predicative in this sense.

When it is interpreted in this way, the principle of
the identity of indiscernibles is still necessarily true, if
it is true at all; but this is not to say that its truth is
by any means obvious. The motives for holding it to
be true are the same as those that have led philosophers
to adopt, in one form or another, the view that things

are only 'bundles of qualities'. It is thought that to describe the character of any thing is to list the functions which it satisfies; these functions may themselves contain references to other things, but these things in their turn can be described only by listing the functions which they satisfy. The demand that all such descriptions be made fully explicit leads, as we have seen, to their being rendered wholly general. It may in fact be the case that a given function is satisfied by only one individual, or indeed that it is satisfied by none, but provided that it is logically capable of being satisfied at all, there can be nothing in the nature of the function to limit the number of individuals, or sets of individuals, which satisfy it. That a predicate is uniquely instantiated is always a contingent, never a necessary, fact. In our ordinary way of speaking, we do indeed appear to distinguish between functions and the individuals which satisfy them, between properties and the things which they characterize. But this appearance, so it is argued, is fallacious. For if we are asked what the thing is that has the properties in question, the only informative answer that we can give is to enumerate further properties. What remains undescribed is the thing itself, the substance, the 'unknown somewhat' in which the properties adhere. But this, it is maintained, is a metaphysical invention. And if it is a metaphysical invention, then it seems to follow that things can be differentiated only through their properties. And this, on the interpretation that we have given, is just another way of saying that things are different only to the extent that they are discernible from one another.

I confess that I am sympathetic to this argument, and therefore I am inclined to accept the principle of the identity of indiscernibles, not merely in some trivial sense but in the controversial form in which we have stated it. My difficulty is that it seems possible to devise counter-examples to it. Thus, Professor Max Black, in an interesting paper which he has devoted to this problem, invites us to imagine a 'radially symmetrical' universe in which 'everything that happened at any place would be exactly duplicated at a place an equal distance on the opposite side of the centre of symmetry'.[1] In such a universe every object would have its exact counterpart 'through the looking-glass' and every function that was satisfied by either would be satisfied by the other. They would be numerically different, but also, in our sense, indiscernible. In terms of indefinite descriptions there would be no way of differentiating them. Consequently, if such a universe is even imaginable, the principle of the identity of indiscernibles is false. A simpler example is that of an infinite series of sounds . . . *A B C D A B C D A* . . ., succeeding one another at equal intervals, with no first or last term. It is assumed that there is no qualitative difference between any two *A*s; neither do they differ in their relational properties, for each is preceded and succeeded by the same number of *B C D*s, at the same intervals and in the same order. If there is any sense at all in speaking of a plurality of *A*s in such a case, it would seem to follow that there is also sense in saying that they differ only numerically. It is, indeed, hard to conceive of a universe consisting only of such a series of sounds; some might say that it was impossible. But it does at least appear that we can describe such a

[1] Max Black, 'The Identity of Indiscernibles', *Mind*, vol. lxi, no. 242, p. 161.

series without referring to, or in any way implying, the existence of anything outside it; and this is all that the argument requires.

A possible way to meet it would be to maintain that such examples seem intelligible to us only because we tacitly introduce into them some further feature by reference to which we do in fact discern between the objects which we are supposing to be indiscernible. Thus, it might be argued that if we are able to imagine Professor Black's radially symmetrical universe, it is because we surreptitiously bring into the picture a point of observation with respect to which the two halves of the universe are differently situated. In the case of the uniform succession of sounds, it might be held that we are able to think of them, in default of any other distinction, as being separated in time, only because we envisage some other sequence of events as being correlated with them. But then it is required that this second series of events should not itself be cyclical. Suppose, for example, that the sounds were correlated with a stop-watch, marking only intervals of seconds, and that they succeeded one another at fifteen-second intervals, as defined by the movements of the hand around the dial of the watch. In that case, provided that the events consisting in the coincidences of the hand with figures on the dial themselves formed an infinite series with no first or last term, the sounds whose quality was the same would still be indiscernible from one another. Every A would be simultaneous with the hand's coinciding with the figure 60, and each of them would be preceded by a D which was simultaneous with the hand's coinciding with the figure 45, and succeeded by a B which was simultaneous with the hand's coinciding with the figure 15. It is only by bringing in some event, or pattern of events, which is not uniformly repeated that we can secure the discernibility that we are seeking. And I suppose it can be argued that this is what one always does when one constructs such examples, even though one may not be aware of it. On the other hand, it is certainly not obvious that the conception of a completely cyclical universe, however constituted, with no beginning or end in time, must be self-contradictory or meaningless. There would, of course, be no way of describing any one turn of the cycle so as to distinguish it from any other, but this, it may well be said, is no objection to their actually being, or even to their being thought to be, distinct.

It is, however, to be noticed that in framing such examples a use is freely made of the distinction between subjects and predicates. It is assumed, for instance, that one is entitled to refer to a plurality of sounds in order then to raise the question whether they are all discernible from one another. And this being so it is not surprising that these examples should appear to refute the principle of the identity of indiscernibles; for thereby, as we saw at the outset, they simply take for granted what it is intended to deny. But it is just here, it may be argued, that the mistake arises. Being accustomed to speak of objects in the plural without further qualification, we come to think that this alone is enough to differentiate them. We are led to treat numerical difference as a relation among others, which may obtain independently of anything else. But this, the argument continues, is an illegitimate extension of the concept of number. It is only where there is discernibility that it makes any sense to talk of a plurality of objects. In a wholly predicative language these fanciful universes, in which things are supposed to differ only numerically, could not even be described.

Although I attach some weight to this argument, I admit that I do not find it altogether convincing. At the same time I am somewhat disturbed by what appear to me to be the consequences of rejecting it. It may be that I am unduly suspicious of the category of substance, but I still cannot see how asserting that an individual exists can be to assert anything more than that some predicate, or set of predicates, is instantiated. No doubt there are many philosophers for whom this question presents no difficulty; but I am not of their number. And the proof of this is that, in spite of all that can be urged against it, I am still inclined to hold that the principle of the identity of indiscernibles is necessarily true.

3

NEGATION

THAT certain statements have the quality of being negative would hardly seem a matter for dispute. There may be a problem about the way in which affirmative and negative statements are related to each other, but it is commonly taken for granted that we have some adequate means of distinguishing between them. Yet to give a satisfactory account of this distinction is not altogether easy. In practice, one tends to regard a statement as negative if it is expressed by a sentence which contains such English words as *not, no, nobody, nowhere, nothing*, or the corresponding words in other languages. But an argument against taking this as a criterion is that its use would lead to ambiguous results. Thus, the statement that Mt. Everest is the highest mountain in the world is to be classified, according to this principle, as affirmative and the statement that Mt. Everest is not the highest mountain in the world is to be classified as negative. But to say that Mt. Everest is the highest mountain in the world is to say that there is no mountain in the world which is as high as Mt. Everest, a statement which we have now to regard as negative, and to say that Mt. Everest is not the highest mountain in the world is to say that there is some mountain in the world which is higher than Mt. Everest, a statement which we have now to regard as affirmative.

36

It would seem, therefore, that each of these statements is both affirmative and negative according to the means chosen for expressing it. Neither is this by any means an exceptional case. It is well known that a universal statement of fact, which we should have to count as affirmative so long as it was expressed by a sentence of the form 'all A is B', can always be rewritten in the form of a negative existential. And there are many other instances in which the same difficulty would arise.

To this it may be objected that what is proved by such examples is not that the use of our syntactical criterion allows the same statement to be both affirmative and negative, but merely that it allows certain affirmative and negative statements to be logically equivalent. According to this argument, the English sentences 'Mt. Everest is the highest mountain in the world' and 'There is no mountain in the world which is as high as Mt. Everest' do not express the same statement. The statements which they are used to make may be logically equivalent to one another, but they are not identical. But now if we ask by what criterion it is decided that these are two different statements, we find that it is again syntactical. The reason for saying that the statements, though equivalent, are not identical is just that they are expressed by sentences of different forms. And on this basis, indeed, the objection can be sustained. The use of a syntactical criterion for distinguishing between affirmative and negative statements does not lead to the conclusion that the same statement may be both affirmative and negative, if it be also understood that when two sentences are of different forms they cannot express the same statement. And if we make the further assumption, which there seems no reason to deny, that we can draw up a list of the negative

D

forms of expression that figure in a given language, then, with respect to that language at least, we can after all obtain an unambiguous characterization of negative statements. But what would be the point of this procedure ? All that we should in fact be doing would be to christen a certain form of sentence. In virtue of their forms, certain sentences will be labelled negative, and other sentences affirmative. And since it would not follow that the bestowal of these different labels reflected any differences of meaning, the distinction which they served to make would be merely grammatical. But when philosophers contrast affirmative with negative statements, the distinction with which they are concerned applies not to the grammatical form of different sentences but to the different ways in which they are used.

The attempt, which is sometimes made, to distinguish between affirmative and negative statements on psychological grounds is equally unsatisfactory. It is supposed that there is a special class of statements which are made only in rebuttal of other statements, and these statements, which are construed as expressing the mental attitude of denial, are accordingly classified as negative. But the fact is that any statement whatsoever may figure in discourse either as a rebuttal of another statement or as one that is itself rebutted. If someone says that it is raining, I may indeed contradict him by saying that it is not, but equally, if he says that it is not raining, I may contradict him by saying that it is. Bradley, who was an exponent of the view under discussion, appears to have thought that a negative form of expression was used only to mark the fact that some other statement, itself to be classified as affirmative, was discovered, or at any rate believed, to be false.

As he characteristically put it, 'What negation must
begin with is the attempt on reality, the baffled
approach of a qualification'.[1]   But once again, any
statement whatsoever which is seriously put forward
may be picturesquely described as an attempt to qualify
reality; and if the statement turns out to be false the
attempt may be said to have been baffled.   No special
class of statements is marked out in this way.   It is
indeed the case that certain pairs of statements are
mutually contradictory, and when one member of such
a pair is asserted it may be allowed that the other is
being implicitly denied.   But this is not to say that for
either to be asserted it is necessary that the other
should have been previously considered.   From the
fact that someone asserts that it is not raining one is
not entitled to infer that he has ever supposed, or that
anyone has ever suggested, that it is, any more than
from the fact that someone asserts that it is raining one
is entitled to infer that he has ever supposed, or that
anyone has ever suggested, that it is not.   No doubt
negative forms of expression are very frequently used
to deny some previous suggestion; it may even be that
this is their most common use.   But whatever the
interest of this fact it cannot be the ground of any viable
distinction between different types of statement.

What seems a more promising approach is to try
to define negation semantically, in terms of the truth-
tables.   Thus, it might be suggested that, in a two-
valued logic, in which every statement had either the
truth-value 1 or 0 but not both, the negation of a given
statement S could be defined as a statement which had
the truth-value 1 if S had the truth-value 0, and the
truth-value 0 if S had the truth-value 1.   Professor

[1] *The Principles of Logic*, vol. i, p. 115.

Quine, for example, says that the meaning of negation is summed up in the laws: 'the negation of a true statement is false; the negation of a false statement is true'.[1] But to this there is the obvious objection that if S in fact has the truth-value 1, then, according to this definition, every false statement will have to count as its negation, and if S has in fact the truth-value 0, every true statement will have to count as its negation. The familiar view that the negation of a given statement is a truth-function of the statement which is negated must, if it is to be acceptable, be taken as implying something more than that the two statements have opposite truth-values. What is required in any such case, where one statement is said to be a truth-function of another, is that its truth or falsehood shall be dependent on the truth or falsehood of the other. But this dependence cannot be construed simply as a concomitant variation, for the sufficient reason that the truth-value of a statement does not vary. It has the truth-value that it has. In a two-valued logic, either it is true or it is false.

This difficulty can, however, be avoided if we construe the dependence as logical. For, dealing with a two-valued logic, we can then define the negation of a given statement S as being any statement T which is so related to S that if either has the truth-value 1 it follows that the other has the truth-value 0, and if either has the truth-value 0 it follows that the other has the truth-value 1. Neither need we restrict ourselves to a two-valued logic. If we are interested in a three-valued logic, such as that developed by Tarski and Lukasiewicz,[2] in which every statement has one, but not more

---

[1] *Methods of Logic*, p. 2.
[2] *Vide* Lewis and Langford, *Symbolic Logic*, pp. 213 ff.

than one, of the truth-values 1, 0, and $\frac{1}{2}$, we can define
the negation of a given statement S as being any
statement T which is so related to S that if either has
the value 1 it follows that the other has the value 0, if
either has the value 0 it follows that the other has the
value 1, and if either has the value $\frac{1}{2}$ it follows that the
other has the value $\frac{1}{2}$. And this procedure can be
generalized so as to apply to systems with any number
of values. For, whatever be the number n, between
0 and 1 inclusive, which is assigned as a truth-value to
a given statement S, the negation of S can be defined as
any statement T which is so related to S that if either
has the value n it follows that the other has the value
$1\text{-}n$. For our present purposes, however, these multi-
valued systems may be disregarded, since whatever
interpretations may be found for the so-called truth-
values that figure in them, it can hardly be that they
are measurements of truth; so that what is therein
defined as negation, though the definition be entirely
legitimate with respect to the relevant system, will not
correspond to anything that would ordinarily be understood by the term. In the case of the two-valued
calculus, on the other hand, there is no difficulty in
interpreting the values 1 and 0 as truth and falsehood,
respectively, and consequently no strong reason for
objecting to the definition of negation on the grounds
of its discrepancy with ordinary usage. It may, indeed,
be doubted whether our practice is entirely consistent
in this matter. It would seem, for example, that we
usually uphold, but sometimes also disregard, the law
of the excluded middle. There are cases where we are
not, on the whole, disposed to say of two incompatible
statements that either one is true, or that either one is
false, supposing, for example, that they contain some

definite description which is not satisfied. And in such cases it might be held that our actual usage was more closely reflected in a three-valued logic, where the assignment of the value $\frac{1}{2}$ was taken as implying, not that a statement might be literally a half-truth, but that it might be a non-starter, in the sense that the question of its truth or falsehood did not arise. For the most part, however, it seems a fair reflection of ordinary usage to identify the negation of S with any statement T which is so related to S that if either is true it follows that the other is false and if either is false it follows that the other is true.

In saying that this definition of negation conforms to ordinary usage, I am suggesting only that it specifies the conditions under which it would be proper to say that two statements negated one another; and I should claim, in support of this, that the expression of negations, in the sense here defined, was one, and indeed the principle, use in any given language of what would commonly be regarded as negative signs. I am not claiming, however, that it is the only use to which these signs are put. It is easy enough to find examples, in the English language at least, where the introduction into a sentence of what is counted as a negative sign does not yield the negation, in our sense, of the statement which the sentence originally expressed. Thus, prefixes like 'un-' and 'in-' count in English, in many instances, as negative signs; but to say, for example, of someone that he is ungenerous is not to negate what is expressed by saying of him that he is generous. If it is false that he is ungenerous, it does not follow that he is generous: he may be neither the one nor the other but something between the two. Again, consider the difference between saying that one is not anxious to do something and saying that one is anxious not to do something; in the first case what is expressed is the negation, in our sense, of the statement that one is anxious to do whatever it may be, but in the second case it is not; one may be neither anxious to do a thing nor anxious not to do it. What these and other such examples show is that, while the presence in an English sentence of what is counted as a negative sign does often have the effect of negating the statement which is expressed by the remainder of the sentence, this is not always so. To assume that negative signs served only to reverse the truth-values of the statements which were expressed by the sentences into which they were introduced would be to overlook some niceties of actual usage. But this does not mean that our definition of negation is inadequate. What it does show is that when one is dealing with the sentences of a natural language, such as English, the question whether the statements which they express negate one another cannot always be settled by any such mechanical procedure as counting the negative signs which they respectively contain. The fact that two English sentences, both of which express statements, differ only in the number of negative signs occurring in them is not a sufficient ground for inferring that one statement is the negation of the other. It could no doubt be made into a sufficient ground, but only by laying down the appropriate rules for deciding what were to be regarded as negative signs.

A more serious matter is that even if our definition of negation is acceptable, it does nothing towards enabling us to delimit a class of negative statements. At best it allows us only to determine with respect to any pair of statements whether or not one is the negation of the other. The statement that London is the capital of England is not negated by the statement that Paris is the capital of France, whereas it is negated by the statement that London is not the capital of England, allowing the presupposition that there are such places. But equally the statement that London is not the capital of England is negated by the statement that it is. No doubt it is natural for us to regard the statement that London is not the capital of England as negative, if on no other ground than that the English sentence which expresses it contains the word 'not'; and for a similar reason the statement that London is the capital of England would ordinarily be treated as affirmative. But, so far as our definition takes us, there is no warrant for making this distinction between them. All that we can say is that each is the negation of the other.

But can we really go no further than this ? We have got to the point where we are able to classify a set of statements as negative, provided that we are able to classify another set of statements as affirmative. And surely, it will be argued, there is no insuperable difficulty in deciding when a statement is affirmative. Considering, for the moment, only the simplest cases, we are surely entitled to say that a statement is affirmative if it refers to some particular individual and ascribes a property to it, or if it refers to a particular set of individuals and states that they stand in a certain relationship, or if it asserts that some unidentified individual, or set of individuals, answers to a certain description. No doubt there are more complicated possibilities, the existence of which would make it a laborious matter to give a complete list of all the forms of affirmative statement, and perhaps among the statements that we counted as affirmative there would be some that it would be natural to express, in English at least, by the use of negative signs. But this, it will be said, does not raise any difficulty of principle. There is no *a priori* reason why a complete list of all the forms of affirmative statement should not be given. The fundamental distinction, which is all that concerns us here, is that between affirming and denying that a certain individual has a given property, or, to use another type of language, between saying that a given property is instantiated and saying that it is not.

Now I do not say that this view of the matter is incorrect. On the contrary, I think it will be found that there is, in the end, no better way than this of differentiating between affirmative and negative statements. At the same time the distinction, here involved, between affirming and denying that an individual has a given property is not so clear as one could wish. For the proof of this we need look no further than to the traditional problem of negation.

The difficulty felt by those philosophers who have shown themselves to be puzzled by the subject of negation has not been that they failed to understand the use of negative signs. I imagine that even Parmenides, who is supposed to have proscribed negation on the ground that not-being could not be, and so to have been led to monism, was none the less able to make use of negative expressions for the purposes of ordinary communication. So long as he relied only upon the Greek language, he could not, indeed, have formulated his own thesis without them. Neither has the problem of such philosophers been to find an adequate way of characterizing the class of negative statements. They have been at a loss, not to understand what negative statements are, but only to account for their existence. Holding that the absence of a given quality is not itself a quality, nor the absence of a given relation itself a relation, they have been unable to see how it is possible that statements which merely deny to a given individual the possession of a certain quality, or to a given set of individuals the possession of a certain relation, can yet be true and verifiable. What predicate, they ask, am I applying to someone's eyes when I say only that they are not blue? What relationship am I ascribing to my cigarette-case and to this table when I say that my cigarette-case is not on this table? How am I characterizing reality when I say only that dodos do not exist? Since many such statements are true, there must, it is thought, be positive facts that make them so, and this would suggest that they must after all be equivalent to affirmative statements, namely to such as describe the positive facts in question. Yet the attempt to establish such equivalences generally fails. Neither will those who see this as a difficulty be satisfied by the logician's device of interpreting statements of the form 'A is not B' or 'A has not got the relation R to C', not as ascribing to A the absence of B, or to A and C the absence of R, but simply as negating the statements 'A is B' or 'A has R to C'. They may agree that this delivers them from negative qualities and relations, but only, they will complain, to subject them to negative facts. For surely, they will say, the mere failure of A to be B, or the mere failure of A and C to be related by R, is no more a genuine fact than not-B is a genuine quality, or not-R a genuine relation. If I say that the Mediterranean sea is blue, I am referring to an individual object and ascribing a quality to it: my statement, if it is true, states a positive fact. But if I say that the Atlantic is not blue, though I am again referring to an individual, I am not ascribing any quality to it; and while, if my statement is true, there must be some positive fact which makes it so, it cannot, so the argument runs, be the fact that the Atlantic is not blue, since this is not positive, and so, strictly speaking, is not a fact at all. Thus it would seem either that the apparently negative statement is somehow doing duty for one that is affirmative, or that it is made true, if it is true, by some fact which it does not state. And it is thought that both alternatives are paradoxical.

If this problem has a somewhat artificial air the reason may be that it makes too much of the distinction between affirming and denying that an individual has a certain quality. Why should it not be allowed that the statement that the Atlantic ocean is not blue is as much a description of the Atlantic as the statement that the Mediterranean sea is blue is a description of the Mediterranean? Admittedly, it is not so informative a description. In saying only that the Atlantic is not blue, I am not saying what colour it is, although, as I shall argue presently, even this might be disputed if we were in the habit of using a single word to stand for any colour other than blue. But to say that a description is relatively uninformative is not to say that it is not a description at all. As for the difficulty about positive facts, I do not know how a positive fact is to be defined except as that which is described by some affirmative statement. But, if this is so, to say that negative statements do not state positive facts is merely a way of saying that they are negative, and not affirmative. It does not follow that, in the event of their being true, they are not as closely related to fact as any other true statements. No doubt reality is positive in the trivial sense that things are what they are. But then it remains to be shown that there are any true empirical statements that are not, in this sense, descriptive of reality. Surely, if we are to speak in this way, all statements become positive. To say what things are not is itself a way of saying what they are. And conversely, to say what things are is itself a way of saying what they are not.

This point can be developed further. The fact is that every significant predicate has a limited range of application. Its correct use is determined both by the fact that there is a set of occasions to which it applies and by the fact that there is a set of occasions to which it does not apply. This being so, it must always be possible to find, or introduce, a predicate which is complementary to the predicate in question, either, in the wide sense, as applying to all and only those occasions to which it does not apply, or, in a narrower sense, as applying to all and only the occasions of this sort that fall within a certain general range. In the narrower sense, at least, such pairs of complementary predicates are actually to be met with in ordinary speech. 'Odd' and 'even', 'long' and 'short', 'near' and 'far', 'light' and 'dark', 'wet' and 'dry', 'hot' and 'cold', 'well and ill' are among the more obvious examples. And if it be objected that some of these are not perfect examples, since they leave room for intermediate cases, the answer is that they can always be made so by a suitable adjustment in the meaning of the words concerned. This is not to say, indeed, that we can ever make our language so precise that we can be sure *a priori* that no further occasion will furnish another intermediate case; but whenever such a case arises, we can always deal with it by expanding the range of

one or other of the complementary predicates which
are, as it were, competing for it. It is not, therefore,
an objection to the existence of complementary predicates that the delimitation of their ranges may be a
subject of boundary disputes.

But whatever be the worth of the examples of
complementary predicates which one might claim to
have discovered in the English, or some other, natural
language, the fact which at present concerns us is that
they are likely to be rare. In the case of most words
which are used as predicates, the only means that we
have for designating the properties that would be
designated by their complementary predicates is to use
the words themselves in combination with a negative
sign. There is no English word that is related to
'blue' as 'wet' is related to 'dry'. If we want to say of
anything that it has, even in the narrow sense in which
only colour is in question, the complementary property
to blue, we have to be content with saying that it is not
blue. But this fact about the English language is
surely not a reason for regarding the property of not
being blue as any less genuine a property than its
complement of being blue. And if it is the negative
form of expression that worries us, we can very easily
get rid of it. All that we need to do is to invent a
number of new words. Thus, to adapt a suggestion of
F. P. Ramsey's, we might, in the cases where a word
which is used predicatively has no complement in our
language, make good the deficiency by writing its
letters in the reverse order. Instead of saying that
something is not blue we may decide to say that it is
eulb. And if it be objected that being eulb is still a
negative predicate, since it is merely equivalent to not
being blue, the answer may be that it is just as little, or

just as much, a negative predicate as being blue itself is. Being eulb is the complement of being blue, and being blue is the complement of being eulb.

But still, it will be argued, there is an important difference between them. Blueness is a 'true universal': its instances have something positive in common, they share the common character of being blue. Eulbness, on the other hand, is not a true universal: its instances have nothing positive in common; all that unites them is that they fail to instantiate blueness. Even if we restrict the field to colour the same objection holds; for while all the instances of eulbness will then have it at least in common that they are all coloured, this will not suffice to make eulbness a true universal. The instances of blueness themselves are instances of colour, so that if all that the instances of eulbness have in common is that they are coloured, there is no way of differentiating them from anything within the given field that is not an instance of eulbness, except, once again, their mere failure to be blue. But the answer to this is that what they have further in common is precisely that they are eulb, just as what the instances of blueness have in common is that they are blue. I know of no criterion for deciding whether things have something in common other than that some predicate applies to them, and I know of no criterion for deciding whether something is a genuine predicate other than that there is a limited range of things to which it applies. And on this count being eulb is just as good a property as being blue. It is, indeed, a less specific property, which is, perhaps, a ground for treating it as negative. But to say that what the instances of eulbness have in common is relatively unspecific is not to say that they have nothing in common at all.

Even so, it will be said, there is a difference between blue and not-blue, which is not merely a difference of meaning or of specificity, and this difference is not removed by any such whimsical procedure as simply calling what is not blue 'eulb'. The use of 'not-blue' presupposes the use of 'blue' in a way that the use of 'blue' does not presuppose the use of 'not-blue'. We can teach someone the use of the word 'blue' by pointing to instances of the property for which it stands : if the instances are numerous and varied he may come to understand what blueness is even though he has not yet learned the use of any negative signs. But we cannot in this way teach anyone the use of 'not-blue'. In order to understand what is meant by 'not-blue' he must not only have learned the use of a negative sign but also know what is meant by 'blue'. But why, I ask, must this be so? Even if, in practice, it always is so, it is not difficult at least to envisage a counter-example. Imagine a community the members of which are for some reason unconcerned with differences of colour. The only colour of special interest to them is the colour blue, to which they attach a magical significance. For all other colours they use a single word, let us say the word 'eulb'. They also have a word for blue, but because blue things are sacred, the word is never used except in the course of certain ceremonies to which only the initiated are admitted. Children are taught the use of the word 'eulb' ostensively, but not the use of the word which stands for blue. They learn to refer to blue objects, which, let us further assume, they are seldom if ever allowed to see, simply as not being eulb. Thus it is 'eulb' that they regard as the positive predicate; and if they are disposed to be philosophers and iconoclasts, it may even be imagined that when, at the initiation ceremony, they are finally taught the use of the word for blue, they protest that this property of blueness to which their elders attach so much importance is not a true universal, that it is nothing but the property of not being eulb. This supposition is fanciful, but not, I think, even psychologically, let alone logically, impossible.

A consequence of the fact that predicates such as 'eulb' are relatively unspecific is that they may comprehend predicates such as 'red' and 'green', which, though not complementary, since the non-application of one does not entail the application of the other, are nevertheless mutually exclusive, inasmuch as the application of either does entail the non-application of the other. It follows, then, with regard to any such set of merely exclusive predicates, that each is comprehended in the complementary predicates of all the others. But this, it has been argued, leads to a contradiction, on the ground, to quote Cook Wilson, that 'if a universal is a differentiation of two different universals, either the two are related themselves as true genus and species, or they mutually involve one another, so that each necessitates the others'.[1] Now, if we were obliged to hold that either of the complementary predicates to 'blue' and 'green' entailed the other, let alone that each entailed the other, we should certainly be involved in contradiction; for it can easily be shown that if this were so the same thing might be, in the one case, both blue and not blue and, in the other, both green and not green. But why should we have to make any such assumption? No reason has been given for supposing that just because the complementary predicates to 'blue' and 'green' have a number of other

[1] *Statement and Inference*, vol. i, p. 254.

predicates, such as 'brown' and 'red' and 'yellow', subsumed under them both, they must therefore stand in any relation of logical necessitation to one another. And if it be alleged that this is true of all universals that have any common specification, the answer may be that it is just such cases as these that provide a counter-example.

So far we have been considering only the case of so-called negative predicates, and have in fact taken only qualities for our examples, but the argument extends also to relations. It extends, indeed, still further, to the cases where what is understood to be negated is not a predicate but a statement as a whole. For just as every predicate has, or can be made to have, its complementary, so does every statement. Setting aside necessary and self-contradictory statements, which raise problems of their own that I shall not now go into, it is true of statements, as it is of predicates, that they are meaningful if and only if they have a limited range of application. And here I am using the word 'range' in such a way that the range of a statement is to be understood to cover every possible set of circumstances in which the statement holds. That is to say, it comprises everything which is described by any story, however long, in which the statement can consistently figure. The appearance of the word 'consistently' at this point may indeed provoke an accusation of circularity; but I should meet this by saying that I am not employing it to define my concept of range but merely to explain its use. In one sense, then, the range of a statement is indefinitely extensive, but in another sense it is limited, since there are indefinitely many sets of circumstances that fall outside it, namely all those that are described by any story in

E

which the statement cannot consistently figure. Any two statements are mutually exclusive if and only if neither can comprehend the other in any description of its range. Any two statements are complementary if and only if each comprises in its range the ranges of all the statements which are exclusive of the other. It follows that a pair of statements cannot be complementary without being mutually exclusive, although they can be mutually exclusive without being complementary.

Of any two statements which are not mutually exclusive it may be said that each is a partner in the range of the other. Clearly no statement can have as a partner any statement which is complementary to it, but it can have as partners many statements which are complementary to one another. In this sense, the range of a statement may be largely indeterminate. Suppose now that, reviewing the range of a statement S, we eliminate from its partnership all those statements of which it is true both that they do not entail S and that their complements are also partners in the range of S. What we then obtain I shall call the narrow, or determinate, range of the statement in question : and this, I think, can be identified with what the statement itself describes.

I believe that this distinction between the narrower and the wider, or more and less determinate, range of a statement may help to elucidate a question which has troubled some philosophers, the question why certain statements are mutually incompatible and others not. There is, of course, no problem once it is established that two statements are complementary, or even exclusive ; for then it follows analytically that they are incompatible. What is found puzzling is not that

statements which are mutually complementary or
exclusive should be incompatible, but that certain
statements only should be mutually complementary or
exclusive. Again, there appears to be no problem
when the fact that one statement is the negation of
another is revealed by the occurrence in the appropriate
sentence of a negative sign. The difficulty is thought
to arise in the cases where the incompatibility of different statements is due to the incompatibility of certain
predicates : for the most part these are cases in which
the statements are not complementary but only
mutually exclusive.

Now, whenever two statements are different in
meaning without being incompatible, it will be found
that each comprises in its wider range the narrow
range of the other, and the narrow range not only of
the other but of any statement which is complementary
to the other. That is to say, each is non-committal
with respect to the circumstances concerning which the
other is committed. And this may come about in two
ways. Either the reference of the two statements may
be different, or, having the same reference, they may be
concerned with different aspects of the occasion to
which they refer. In a non-referential language no
two statements to the effect that different predicates
are instantiated are ever incompatible, even though
the predicates themselves may be. Incompatibility of
statements arises only when it is said that each of two
incompatible predicates is co-instantiated with some
predicate which is itself uniquely instantiated, or when
it is said that each of two incompatible predicates is
instantiated and that at least one of them is universally instantiated; the mention of unique, or universal,
instantiation is a means, and indeed in such a language

the only means, of securing identity of reference. In a referential language, that is, a language which possesses the means of designating individuals, it is again only where there is identity of reference that statements can be incompatible; but here it is more easily secured.

What may seem curious is that the converse does not hold, that statements with different meanings but the same reference can be compatible. And the explanation of this is just that the account which they severally give of the occasion to which they refer is incomplete. If there were a language, as I suppose there might be, which was capable of expressing only such statements as were committal with respect to every property that could be assigned, in the language, to the individuals to which they referred, the statements which were made in it would not admit of any distinction between their wider and narrower ranges, other than the limitations of their reference. Within its field of reference every statement would have only its narrow, or determinate, range, and the result would be that if any two statements with the same reference had different meanings it would follow that they were incompatible. Consider, for example, a pictorial language regarding which there is a convention that every picture purports to represent every feature of the occasion to which it refers. A picture has meaning only as a whole; no section of any picture is independently meaningful. In such a case, if every picture with the same reference tells a different story, each will be incompatible with all the others, and, provided always that they do have the same reference, their incompatibility will follow simply from the difference in their meanings. If this does not obtain in our language, it is because its universe of discourse is so extensive that a statement seldom, if ever, has any pretension to describe all the features of the occasion to which it refers. It is only sections of pictures that we normally aspire to paint.

Pursuing this analogy, we can now explain why certain predicates are mutually incompatible and others not. The difficulty felt by those who regard this as a problem is that they do not see how such a statement as that the same thing cannot be both blue and red all over can be interpreted as an empirical generalization or as a truth of logic : it seems to them, in Russell's words, that 'red and blue are no more *logically* incompatible than red and round'.[1] Accordingly, they are led to the conclusion that such incompatibilities lie in the nature of things, that the statements which assert them are synthetic *a priori* truths. But the answer is that the incompatibility, whether or not we care to call it logical, is at any rate semantic. The reason why 'red' and 'blue' are incompatible is that, each meaning what it does and not what is meant by the other, they compete for the same part of the picture. The reason why 'red' and 'round', though their meanings again are different, are yet not incompatible is that each is non-committal with respect to that part of the picture for which the other competes. If there were no distinction between the wide and narrow ranges of such predicates, the anomaly would disappear; the incompatibility of any two predicates would simply follow from the difference in their meanings. Again, this can be very simply illustrated. Imagine a universe of discourse restricted to a single homogeneous individual and the four properties, red, blue, round, and square. Then the facts are either that this individual

[1] *An Inquiry into Meaning and Truth*, p. 82.

is round and red, or that it is square and blue, or that it
is square and red, or that it is round and blue; and of
the four statements that can be made about it, that it is
red, that it is blue, that it is round, and that it is square,
the first pair will be incompatible with each other but
each merely different from either of the second pair, and
the second pair will be incompatible with each other
but each merely different from either of the first. But
now suppose that the language admits no predicates
that only partially describe its universe. It will then
have as simple, unanalysable predicates, not 'blue',
'red', 'round', 'square', to which under this condition
no meaning can be attached, but 'blue-round', 'red-
round', 'red-square', and 'blue-square'. Four statements can still be made about the individual, but each
will now be incompatible with all the others, and it
will be so simply for the reason that it has a different
meaning. But why, it may be asked, should 'red-blue'
and 'round-square' not also be simple predicates in
this language? The answer is that there is nothing in
this universe of discourse for them to stand for. One
could, indeed, give a meaning to such expressions, and
a meaning not far removed from ordinary English
usage. One might, for example, decide to call something red-blue when its colour was red shot with blue,
or to describe a figure with curved sides of equal length
as a round square : more simply, one might decide to
apply the term 'red-blue' to an object one part of which
was red and another part blue and the term 'round-
square' to an object one part of which was round and
another part square. But assuming that the words
'red', 'blue', 'round', and 'square' are used as they
normally are in English, and that they are used to
characterize the colour or shape of some individual as

a whole, the combinations 'red-blue' and 'round-square' are inadmissible only because the different predicates which they combine range determinately over the same circumstances. For, to revert to our analogy, just as it is true of any picture as a whole, so is it true of every section of a picture that 'it is what it is and not another thing'. It cannot be both what it is and something different as well.

Regarding incompatibility as a logical relation and assuming, mistakenly, that if two predicates are incompatible one or other of them must be complex, logicians, such as Wittgenstein and Carnap, have held that all basic, or atomic, statements must be logically independent of one another, from which it follows that no two basic predicates which can be significantly applied to the same individual can be incompatible. Now so long as we consider only those basic statements which are true, it does indeed follow, on the assumption that none of them is complex, that they are all logically independent of one another. But the class of true basic statements is not the whole class of basic statements; we must allow also for the possibility that some of them are false. And if we insist that, whether they are true or false, all basic statements must remain compatible, we obtain the awkward consequence that no basic statement can be falsified by the verification of any other. And since it is assumed that the truth or false-hood of all higher-level statements depends upon the truth or falsehood of these basic statements, it will also follow that while the establishment of any higher-level statement, through the verification of the appro-priate basic statements, entails the rejection of its complementary, it does not entail the rejection of any statement of which it is no more than exclusive. Even

though *m* and *n* are different numbers, from the fact
that some quantity is found by observation to have
exactly the value *m*, it will by no means follow that it
does not also have exactly the value *n*; for the basic
statements which are the only means of establishing
either that it has the value *m* or that it has the value *n*
will *ex hypothesi* not be incompatible. On this view
the falsification of a basic statement will consist simply
in not finding that a certain predicate applies to a given
individual. It will never consist in finding that some
other predicate does apply to it, not even the predicate
which is its complementary. For either this complementary predicate is itself basic, which contradicts the
assumption that no two basic predicates are incompatible, or it is not basic, in which case it can apply to the
individual only if some basic predicate applies to it;
but whatever basic predicate does apply to it the predicate originally in question will *ex hypothesi* not be
excluded. A language which obeyed these rulings
could, indeed, be constructed, but it would be a poor
language, inasmuch as it would afford no means of
describing the aspect of a situation which falsified a
basic statement, in any more specific way than by saying
only that the statement was false. Correspondingly, it
may be regarded as a defect in a non-referential language that of the statements which can be made in it
only those which state that some particular property is
uniquely, or universally, instantiated can strictly be
refuted. An indefinite existence statement, to the effect
merely that some property is instantiated, cannot be
falsified. A decision may be taken to abandon such a
statement when a certain situation fails to disclose the
property in question. But since the situation which is
taken as relevant cannot be definitely referred to in the

statement, such a decision will always be to some extent arbitrary. The situation may itself be described as consisting in the instantiation of some predicate; but from the fact that one predicate is instantiated it can never logically follow that any other is not.

I hope that this discussion has thrown some light upon the question of incompatibility. It was partly with this in view that I introduced my concept of the range of statements and defined their complementarity in terms of it. I could, however, have chosen a very much simpler way of defining complementarity. Having already defined negation, we can say that two statements are complementary if and only if each is the negation of the other.

What we have still not done is to delimit a class of negative statements. On the contrary, the main tendency of the argument has been to reduce the distinction between affirmative and negative statements to a matter of emphasis. A statement is negative if it states that an object lacks a certain property rather than stating that it possesses the complementary property: a statement is negative if it states that a certain property is not instantiated, rather than stating that the complementary property is universally instantiated. The objection remains that, on this showing, the same statement may be both affirmative and negative, or, at least, that affirmative and negative statements may be logically equivalent: but perhaps this is a conclusion that we just have to accept.

If we insist on making a clear-cut distinction between affirmative and negative statements, the best course that I can see open to us is to base the distinction upon degrees of specificity. Let us say of any two singular referential statements S and S', that is,

statements which refer to a particular individual and
ascribe some property to it, that S is a specifier of S' if
and only if S' is not a component of S, S entails S', and
S' does not entail S. And let us say that a singular
referential statement S is absolutely specific, with
respect to a given language L, if there is no statement
expressible in L which is a specifier of S. Further let
us say that a statement has the first degree of specificity,
with respect to a language L, if it is not absolutely
specific but has no specifiers expressible in L which are
not themselves absolutely specific, that it has the second
degree of specificity if it is not absolutely specific, or
specific to the first degree, but has no specifiers which
are not themselves absolutely specific or specific to the
first degree, and so on. Then among complementary
pairs of singular referential statements it may happen
that one member of the pair has a higher, that is, a
lesser, degree of specificity than the other. In that case
the more specific statement may be said to be affirmative
and the less specific to be negative. Thus, while for
the members of our imaginary tribe the statement that
an object was blue would not be more specific than the
statement that it was eulb, to say in English that an
object is blue is to make a more specific statement than
to say that it is not blue ; for whereas the statement that
an object is not blue is specified by such statements as
that it is red, or that it is green, or that it is colourless,
the statement that it is blue is not specified by any
statements at this level. Accordingly the statement
that the object is blue counts, with respect to the
English language, as affirmative by this criterion, and
the statement that it is not blue as negative.

Having in this way formed the class of affirmative
singular referential statements as being all and only

those that, with respect to a given language, are more specific than their complementaries, we can extend the distinction to other types of statement. An existential statement may be said to be affirmative if and only if it is entailed by an affirmative singular referential statement. A universal, or particular, statement may be said to be affirmative if and only if the singular referential statements which are obtained from it by giving values to its variables are affirmative. The class of negative statements, with respect to a given language, may then be held to consist of all and only those statements that have affirmative statements for their complementaries.

I think that the results which are yielded by this criterion agree fairly closely with the assessment of statements, as affirmative or negative, that one would intuitively make. There are, however, certain anomalies. For example, the statement that an object is coloured will have to count as negative: for it is less specific than the statement that the object is colourless. Furthermore, not every member of every pair of complementary statements will fall under either classification. To revert to our original example, the statement that Mt. Everest is the highest mountain in the world is not, I think, either more or less specific than the statement that Mt. Everest is not the highest mountain in the world: and if this is so we shall have to allow that neither statement is either affirmative or negative. And if there are any predicates which are not excluded by predicates other than those which are complementary to them, then the statements which consist in the ascription to individuals of the properties for which these predicates and their complementaries stand will also escape the classification. They will, according to our criterion, be neither affirmative nor negative. If 'not high' were a synonym for 'low', or 'not long' for 'short', or 'not wet' for 'dry', then statements, made in English, to the effect that something was, or was not, high or long or wet would be examples.

In view of such considerations it may appear preferable not to make their comparative lack of specificity a defining property of negative statements, but merely to regard it as a property which most of them do in fact possess. The point is in any case important, as it accounts for the belief that negative statements are somehow less directly related to fact than affirmative statements are. They are less directly related to fact just in so far as they are less specific. From a psychological point of view, a negative statement may be directly verified. An observer may discover the absence of something which particularly concerns him, without noting the presence of anything else. Being interested only in the truth of the negative statement, he may not consciously apprehend the truth of any more specific statement on which the truth of the negative statement depends. But logically a negative statement, assuming it to be relatively unspecific, can be verified only through the truth of some more specific statement which entails it; a statement which will itself, by contrast, be counted as affirmative. Neither, as has often been remarked, are negative statements, when characterized in this way, reducible to affirmatives. They are not equivalent to a disjunction of the more specific statements which entail them, even though the disjunction be finite. To secure the equivalence one needs the additional statement that these are all the alternatives that there are.

In the same way we can account for the inclination

that many people have towards saying that reality is positive. The explanation is that any information which is provided by a less specific statement will always be included in the information provided by some more specific statement. Given a finite universe, we could, within the resources of the language, give a complete description of it by using only absolutely specific statements, such statements counting as affirmative. If at any point a less specific, negative, statement were substituted for one of these affirmatives, the description, though it might remain true, would cease to be complete. Some information, expressible in the language, would have been left out. It is, however, to be remarked that while, with only absolutely specific statements at our disposal, we could give a complete description of such a universe, we could not with these means say that it was complete.

4

THE TERMINOLOGY OF SENSE-DATA

1. Professor G. E. Moore's Conception of a Sense-datum

In the reply to his critics which constitutes the third part of the volume entitled *The Philosophy of G. E. Moore*, Professor Moore has given the following explanation of his usage of the term 'sense-datum'. Having taken as an example a situation in which a person 'is seeing his right hand as well as something else', he says that this person 'must be having a direct visual field which contains at least two objects',[1] and he explains that he regards this as a case not merely of a *de facto* concomitance but of a logical entailment. He is assuming that 'it is part of the very meaning of the assertion that a person is seeing his own right hand as well as something else that he has a direct visual field containing at least two objects';[2] and he refers to these objects, which are directly seen, as examples of what he means by sense-data. He explains further that the sense of the word 'see' in which constituents of the direct visual field may be said to be seen is the 'visual variety' of what he has elsewhere called 'direct apprehension', and that the objects of the other varieties of direct apprehension are also to be accounted

[1] *The Philosophy of G. E. Moore*, pp. 630-631.
[2] *Ibid.* p. 631.

sense-data according to his usage. Thus he says: 'I think I have always both used and intended to use "sense-datum" in such a sense that the mere fact that an object is directly apprehended is a sufficient condition for saying that it is a sense-datum: so that according both to my usage and my intentions directly apprehended smells and tastes and sounds are just as much sense-data as directly seen objects'; [1] and he remarks later that his usage has been such that 'a toothache which you feel is necessarily a sense-datum'.[2] It may be noted that he does not say that the fact that an object is directly apprehended is a necessary, as well as a sufficient, condition for saying that it is a sense-datum, for he would then be committed to holding that it was impossible for sense-data to exist without being perceived, in one of the senses in which Berkeley used the word 'perceived', and this is a proposition of whose validity he says that he is not wholly convinced. At the same time he would presumably make it a necessary condition of anything's being a sense-datum that it should be directly apprehensible, in the sense of being the sort of object that can be directly apprehended; and if this is so, he may be said to be defining sense-data in terms of direct apprehension in its various modes. Accordingly the question which now has to be answered is that of the meaning, in this usage, of such expressions as 'directly hear' or 'directly feel' or 'directly see'.

Before we consider this question, however, there is one incidental feature of Moore's exposition that is deserving of notice. Why is it that in giving his example of someone's seeing his own right hand he makes a point of adding that this person is also seeing

[1] *Ibid.* p. 639.   [2] *Ibid.* p. 643.

something else, if it be only a black background ? The
answer appears to be that he has in mind the directions for 'picking out' a sense-datum which he gave in
his 'Defence of Common Sense'. Using the same
example of someone's looking at his own right hand, he
there says that this person 'will be able to pick out
something (and unless he is seeing double, only one
thing) with regard to which he will see that it is, at
first sight, a natural view to take, that that thing is
identical, not indeed, with his whole right hand, but
with that part of its surface which he is actually seeing,
but will also (on a little reflection) be able to see that it
is doubtful whether it can be identical with the part of
the surface of his hand in question'; [1] and he goes on
to say that 'things of the sort (in a certain respect) of
which this thing is' are what he means by sense-data.
To this he has now added, in reply to some pertinent
criticisms by Mr. O. K. Bouwsma,[2] that it is from the
subject's direct visual field that the sense-datum is
supposed to be capable of being picked out, so that
what is left over when it has been picked out is the rest
of this direct visual field ; and accordingly that he
ought to have made it clear that the operation of picking
out the sense-datum could not be performed if the
subject were seeing his own hand and nothing else,[3]
where by 'seeing nothing else' he presumably means to
imply both that the subject is seeing no other physical
object and also that he is seeing, in a different sense of
'see', no other element of a direct visual field than what
is involved in his seeing his hand.

[1] *Contemporary British Philosophy*, Second Series, p. 218.
[2] 'Moore's Theory of Sense-Data', *The Philosophy of G. E. Moore*,
pp. 203-221.
[3] 'A Reply to My Critics', *The Philosophy of G. E. Moore*,
pp. 629-631.

Now if the problem were merely that of distinguishing a visual sense-datum of a person's hand from other visual sense-data, it would be perfectly correct to say that the sense-datum could be picked out from the subject's direct visual field, and to add the proviso that it could not be so picked out if the subject who was supposed to be in a position to distinguish it was seeing nothing besides his own right hand. But surely what Moore was trying to provide in the passage quoted was a means of identifying sense-data in general, and not merely of distinguishing one sense-datum from another. He was addressing himself to people who were assumed to understand what was meant by 'seeing a physical object' but not to understand what was meant by 'seeing a sense-datum'; and the point of his example was to show how seeing a sense-datum of a certain sort was involved in the familiar situation of seeing one's own right hand. But if this is so, the description of a process which consists in concentrating upon one element of a direct visual field is not very helpful ; for if the person to whom one is trying to teach the meaning of the word 'sense-datum' does not understand what is meant by 'a direct visual field' he will not be any the wiser ; and if he does understand this, it is sufficient to tell him that a visual sense-datum is a constituent of a direct visual field, without introducing the complication of a selective process which turns out to be a process of discriminating between sense-data. And while it is true, analytically, that a person who is seeing his own right hand and nothing else cannot then 'pick out' a sense-datum which is related to the hand in the requisite way, if picking out such a sense-datum implies distinguishing it from other visual sense-data, which are simultaneously presented but not similarly related to

F

the hand, I can see no reason for holding that someone who was seeing his own right hand and nothing else would be unable even to identify a single sense-datum of the sort to which Moore was referring. For if this person is seeing his right hand there is presumably at least one object that he is directly seeing, in Moore's sense of 'directly see', and if he understands what is meant by 'directly seeing' then he should be able to identify at least one sense-datum as the object that he is directly seeing, or as the constituent of his direct visual field; and the question whether there are also other objects that he is directly seeing, so that he is able simultaneously to recognize other sense-data, appears irrelevant. It seems to me indeed that the use in this context of the expression 'pick out' may have misled Moore and may easily mislead others. For it suggests that what we are concerned with is an operation analogous to that of distinguishing one physical object from another, or one sense-datum from another, as it might be selecting a book from a shelf or discovering in a tune the sound of a particular note. Now in cases of this sort, when the person to whom one is giving directions does not know what to look for, one can enlighten him by giving him a description in terms of physical or sensory characteristics, thereby enabling him to differentiate the object in question from other physical objects, or from other sense-data. But a description of this kind would be of no use to the person who is envisaged in Moore's example. For his position is not that he does not know what special sort of sense-datum he is required to discover, but that he does not know what sense-data are in general; so that his natural response to the kind of direction for finding a sense-datum that Moore gives in his 'Defence of Common

Sense' would be to look for some other physical object that was related to his hand in the peculiar way that Moore describes, and on failing to discover one, to doubt the existence of the sense-datum. And this is the line of attack that Mr. Bouwsma, for example, pursues. The problem is indeed complicated for Moore by the fact that he is not prepared to say that the sense-datum is not at any rate part of a physical object, since he holds that, in the example in question, it may turn out to be identical with part of the surface of the hand. At the same time he also holds that it may very well not be identical with any part of the surface of the hand, and consequently not be even part of any physical object. But if the sense-datum is not necessarily a physical object or part of one, the person who is supposed to 'pick it out' will be likely to require some further indication of the kind of object that it is, and one way of giving him this indication is to show him how certain expressions are being used. And so we return to the question of the meaning that Moore is attaching in this context to such expressions as 'directly see'.

The only explanation that Moore himself gives is that he takes the sense of the word 'see' in which one can properly speak of seeing a sense-datum, according to his usage, to be the same as that in which one speaks of seeing an after-image with closed eyes, or of Macbeth's having seen his visionary dagger.[1] Now this establishes the point that it is permissible to say of something which is not a real physical object, or part of a real physical object, that it is directly seen; and since it is an empirical fact that people do sometimes have visual after-images, and that they do have visual hallucinations, in the sense in which Macbeth's

[1] *The Philosophy of G. E. Moore*, pp. 629-630.

perception of the dagger may be described as a visual
hallucination, we may infer that there are visual sense-
data, in Moore's sense of the term, which are not even
parts of any real physical objects. We are not, however,
entitled to infer that this is true of all visual sense-data.
For Moore holds that 'the sense of "see" in which you
see an after-image with closed eyes', though certainly
not identical with the sense in which you see your hand,
may possibly be identical with the 'sense in which you
see that part of its surface which is turned towards
you',[1] and if it is so identical, it follows that some visual
sense-data are, in this usage, literally parts of physical
objects, though others are not. That Moore himself is
disposed to accept this conclusion is shown by his
saying that he is 'strongly inclined to agree that we do
constantly *see directly* parts of the surfaces of physical
objects'.[2] On the other hand he is also inclined to
believe that no part of the surface of a physical object is
ever directly seen, and this because of the familiar fact
that the appearances of physical objects vary in different
conditions. For he allows that in every instance of this
kind there are good, though not, he adds, conclusive
reasons for supposing that the directly seen object really
has the different quality that the surface of the physical
object merely seems to have;[3] and since in every case
in which one might be tempted to identify the sense-
datum, which by definition was being directly seen,
with part of the surface of a physical object, it is true
that the surface of the physical object might have looked
different without really being so, the assumption that
the sense-datum would then really have been different
entails the conclusion that the sense-datum and the

---

[1] *The Philosophy of G. E. Moore*, p. 632.
[2] *Ibid*. pp. 649-650.   [3] *Ibid*. p. 642.

part of the physical surface in question are not, after all, identical. Similarly, in the domain of sounds, Moore thinks that there are good, though not conclusive, reasons for supposing that sounds which are directly heard really have the qualities that the corresponding physical sounds in some cases merely seem to have, and so is inclined to draw the inference that auditory sense-data, which are by definition directly heard, are not ever identical with physical sounds, though he also says that it is not obvious to him that there is any contradiction in asserting that they sometimes are.[1]

It would seem then that the possibility of identifying objects which are directly apprehended with the relevant physical objects, or with parts of the relevant physical objects, depends upon the assumption that the objects which are directly apprehended, or in other words the sense-data, may themselves appear to have qualities that they do not really have; and this is an assumption which many philosophers have regarded as self-contradictory. Moore, however, is not convinced that this is so, any more than he is convinced that it is impossible, as some philosophers have maintained, for what he would call sense-data to exist without being perceived. Since it is undoubtedly possible, by definition, for physical objects to exist without being perceived, it would follow here again, if these philosophers were right, that no sense-datum was ever identical with a physical object, or with part of the surface of a physical object; but while Moore is disposed to agree with these philosophers, he is not wholly persuaded. Thus he says: 'Although I am still inclined to think that no after-image (and, therefore, also no 'sense-datum') can possibly exist except while

[1] *Ibid.* pp. 641-643.

it is being directly apprehended — and, more than this, none that I directly apprehend can possibly exist except while I am directly apprehending it — I cannot see *why* there should be a contradiction in supposing the opposite, I cannot see *where* the contradiction lies'.[1] His use in this passage of the phrase 'and, therefore, also no sense-datum' suggests that he is taking this to be a matter in which sense-data do not differ from one another, so that if it were proved that sense-data of one type could not exist except while they were being directly apprehended, it could legitimately be assumed that all sense-data were in the same case. It is doubtful, however, if he does mean this, since he says in one place that a toothache, which he has given as an instance of a sense-datum, 'certainly cannot exist without being felt',[2] and yet does not infer the corresponding propositions with regard to sense-data of other types. Perhaps, therefore, his view is that while it is certain that some sense-data cannot exist without being directly apprehended, it may be the case that others can, just as his view is that while it is certain that some visual sense-data are not parts of the surfaces of physical objects, it may be the case that others are.

2. How are the Problems which Moore raises to be resolved?

Passing now to criticism of Moore's position, we may begin by remarking that these propositions about sense-data, which are the subject of his hesitations, are not such as can be put to an empirical test. At first sight, indeed, it might appear that a philosopher who asserted that he directly saw the surface of his hand, or

---

[1] *The Philosophy of G. E. Moore*, p. 660.   [2] *Ibid.* p. 653.

that a particular after-image continued to exist when
he had ceased to see it, was making an empirical claim
which an appeal to experience could substantiate or
confute. But to assume this would be to misconceive
the point at issue. For while the philosopher may be
making what is literally an empirical statement, the
empirical truth of this statement is not what he is
concerned to establish. It may indeed be an empirical
fact that he is seeing the surface of his hand; and if
it is the case that the surface of his hand is the sort of
object that can be directly seen, that he is directly
seeing it may also be an empirical fact. But what he
means to affirm in making such a statement is the logical
possibility of directly seeing the surfaces of physical
objects, and this is not to be determined empirically,
any more than it is possible to settle by experiment
whether or not sense-data can exist while they are not
being apprehended. And a proof of this is that another
philosopher may disagree with him about this question
without any of the observable facts being in dispute
between them. It follows, what Moore himself
admits,[1] that no acquisition of further empirical
evidence will enable us to discover whether the surfaces
of physical objects can be directly seen. For if, to take
one alternative, the proposition that no part of the
surface of any physical object ever is directly seen is
true at all, it is true analytically. If it is true, its truth
must be a matter not of empirical circumstance but of
logical necessity, depending upon what is meant by
'being part of the surface of a physical object' and by
'being directly seen'. And the same applies to the
other questions that Moore raises, such as the question
whether sense-data can exist while they are not being

[1] *Ibid.* p. 637.

directly apprehended, or whether they can appear to have qualities that they do not really have.

It would seem then that the way to settle these questions is to reflect upon the actual usage of the various expressions involved. But here we meet with the difficulty that there appears to be no established usage of such expressions as 'directly see' that is relevant to the issue. If such expressions are ever used outside of philosophical discussions, I suppose that they would appear in contexts where the speaker wished to contrast 'direct' with 'indirect' perception. Thus he might choose to refer to an object, which was seen reflected in a mirror, as being indirectly seen, or to a sound, which was heard in echo, as being indirectly heard, and he might then use the word 'directly' to mean 'not indirectly', in this sense; and this, I think, is the way in which most people would be inclined to interpret these expressions, if they were presented with them without further explanation. It is, however, clearly not the way in which Moore is interpreting them; for if it were, he would not find any occasion to doubt that the surfaces of physical objects were directly seen, or that physical sounds were directly heard. Neither do I think that there is a recognized philosophical usage which Moore can here be assumed to be following. No doubt other philosophers have used the word 'sense-datum' in ways that correspond more or less closely with the way in which Moore is intending to use it; and some of them have also used words like 'acquaintance' or 'sensing' or 'direct awareness' in ways that may in some measure correspond with the way in which he appears to be using 'direct apprehension'; but there is no reason to suppose that Moore would consider such precedents as binding upon himself, or that he conceives his problem as being that of explicating the meanings which other philosophers have attached to their words. Thus the fact that Professor Price, for example, has taken the view that sense-data, regarded as the objects of acquaintance, cannot be identical with parts of the surfaces of physical objects, or that Professor Broad has been inclined to hold that 'sensa' can continue to exist while they are not being sensed, cannot be accepted as a sufficient ground for inferring that similar conclusions apply to the sense-data which are directly apprehended, according to Moore's usage of these terms. But if the questions which Moore raises are not to be settled either by the method of empirical verification, or by the analysis of any standard usage of words, whether common or philosophical, what possible means have we of deciding them?

I think that the answer to this is that we have no means of deciding them; and the reason why we have no means of deciding them is that Moore has failed to give us the information which alone could make such a decision possible. For the answers to such questions as whether sense-data can exist while no one is directly apprehending them, or whether the surfaces of physical objects can be directly seen, depend, as we have already remarked, upon the meanings that are attached to the technical terms involved; and although Moore has given some indication of the meaning that he is attaching to such expressions as 'directly see', he has not given a sufficient indication to enable anyone to say how these problems about sense-data are to be resolved in accordance with his usage. In short, his usage is incompletely specified; and the proof that it is so is precisely that these problems are left unresolved.

Accordingly, I agree with Mr. Bouwsma that for someone who finds himself in a state of doubt as to whether
a part of the surface of his hand, which he is seeing, is
or is not to be accounted a visual sense-datum, in
Moore's sense of the term, there is nothing for it but
to go on doubting.[1] To this Moore indeed has replied
that there is another alternative, namely, to go on
thinking about it.[2]   But to what is this thinking
supposed to be directed ? Not to any fact of experience,
for this is admittedly not an empirical question ; and
not to the implications of any recognized verbal usage,
for there is none that is relevant.[3]   But what else

[1] *The Philosophy of G. E. Moore*, p. 207.
[2] *Ibid*. p. 638.
[3] In an addendum to the reply to his critics which appears in the
second edition of *The Philosophy of G. E. Moore*, Professor Moore
challenges this statement. He agrees that the questions which he
raises about sense-data cannot be settled by the method of empirical
verification, but he thinks that I have 'gone hopelessly wrong' in
supposing that the answer 'cannot be discovered by the analysis of
any standard usage' (*loc. cit*. p. 680). He admits that there is no
standard usage of such philosophical terms as 'sense-datum', 'directly
apprehend', or 'directly see', but denies that this proves my point :
for he thinks that such a question as whether the surfaces of physical
objects are directly seen can be reformulated in a way which does not
bring in any of these technical expressions, and he thinks that 'the
answer to it does depend upon the analysis of expressions which
undoubtedly have a standard usage in ordinary life'. 'The expressions
I mean', he continues, 'are those which consist in saying such words
as "This is a penny" or "That is a penny", *together with* some
standard gesture which seems to explain what object we are referring
to by the words "this" and "that" : and if we could only discover
the right analysis of what is meant by such expressions, my question
would be answered' (*loc. cit*. p. 680). Moore's reason for thinking
this is that he holds that when expressions like 'this is a penny' are
used in this way there is one and only one object to which the demonstrative refers, an object which he describes by saying that in every
case of visual perception in which certain familiar conditions, which
he lists, are satisfied, it is 'an object which it is tempting to suppose
to be identical with *the* part, which (the percipient) is seeing of the
physical object's surface but with regard to which, on the other hand,
there are strong reasons for supposing that it cannot be identical with
the part which he is seeing, of the physical object's surface' (*loc. cit*.
p. 679). Moore regards it as certain that this is the object about

remains ? Nothing, I think, so long as it is assumed that the truth or falsehood of the proposition, which is supposed to be doubted, is already there to be discovered. The position is different, however, if the problem is regarded, as I believe it should be, not as that of assessing the validity of a proposition on the evidence already available, but rather as that of manufacturing the evidence. More concretely, I am suggesting that what we must think about, in order to resolve such doubts as Mr. Bouwsma raises, is not the actual truth or falsehood of the propositions in question (for this is not determinable) but the advisability of making

which we are saying something when we use expressions like 'this is a penny' in the way that he describes. The question which puzzles him is what it is that we are saying about it, and in particular whether we are saying of it that it is part of the surface of a penny: and it is this question that reflection on the standard usage of expressions like 'this is a penny', when uttered with the appropriate standard gestures, is supposed to enable us to decide.

Now I admit that if the analysis of what is meant by these ordinary expressions did show that the demonstratives referred to the objects which Moore calls sense-data, it would be reasonable to assume that the answer to questions about the relationship of such sense-data to physical objects depended only upon standard usage. But my difficulty is that I cannot see any warrant in the ordinary usage of expressions like 'this is a penny' for holding that the demonstrative refers to such an object as Moore describes. In fact, I do not think that when I am looking at a penny there normally is any object which I am tempted to identify with *the* part, which I am seeing, of the penny's surface but with regard to which there are strong reasons for supposing that it cannot be so identified. In the case where I really am looking at a penny and say, with the appropriate gesture, 'this is a penny', I think that the correct answer to the question 'What does the word "this" denote?' is just 'the penny'. Not 'the surface of the penny' or 'part of the surface of the penny'. These would be the correct answers if I had said 'this is the surface of a penny' or 'this is part of the surface of a penny', but neither of these sentences would, in this context, normally be understood to mean exactly what is meant by 'this is a penny'. In the case where I mistake some other object for a penny and say 'this is a penny', I think that the correct answer to the question 'What does the word "this" denote?' is that it denotes whatever object it is that I am mistaking for a penny. And in the case where I am undergoing a complete hallucination and say, with a gesture that would be appropriate if I really were looking at a physical them true or false. Thus, when Moore says that he is inclined, on the one hand to hold that some visual sense-data are identical with parts of the surfaces of physical objects, and on the other hand to accept propositions about sense-data from which it would follow that none of them could be thus identified, the only way out of the impasse in which he otherwise leaves us is to assume that what he is really doing, whether he admits it or not, is hesitating over the choice of alternative verbal conventions. For whereas, in the case of physical objects, such questions as whether they can appear to have characteristics that they do not really have, or can continue to exist while no one is perceiving them, can be settled by reference to the implications of our ordinary usage of words, this is not true of sense-data. In the case of sense-data the

object, 'this is a penny', I think that the question 'What does the word "this" denote?' can properly be answered by saying that it does not denote anything at all.

It seems clear, however, that the meaning of the words 'this is a penny' is the same in all three cases, although it is only in the first case that they are used to make a true statement : and this may at first sight seem hard to reconcile with the view that the word 'this' denotes a different object in the first two cases and none whatsoever in the third. But what is shown, I think, is just that it is a mistake to identify the meaning even of a demonstrative with its denotation. We can explain how words like 'this' are used in these contexts without making the assumption that there are any objects which they are used to stand for. If, on the other hand, we are going to insist upon the demonstratives having a denotation and, what is more, the same denotation whenever they are used with the same meaning, we have to provide one for them : and this, I still think, is what Moore is doing when he brings in sense-data. It is, in my opinion, a perfectly legitimate procedure ; but my criticism still remains that if he leaves us in doubt as to whether a sense-datum can ever be identical with the surface of a physical object it is because he has not given us a sufficient indication of the way in which he intends the term 'sense-datum' to be understood. I do, however, go on to argue that if he makes certain stipulations about sense-data, which I think that he does, he cannot consistently allow that they are ever identical with the surfaces of physical objects.

answer to such questions is not prescribed by any antecedent usage. On the contrary, we are dealing here with expressions whose usage has itself to be prescribed. It is accordingly for us to decide how these questions are to be answered; and the way in which we decide to answer them will help to determine what the relevant expressions are to mean.

3. On the Possibility of treating Physical Entities as Sense-data

Suppose now that we accept Moore's definition of sense-data as the objects of direct apprehension, and that we begin by defining direct apprehension in such a way that the propositional function 'x is seen', where x may be a physical entity, is made to entail the propositional function 'there is some object y which is directly seen', and that the corresponding entailments are understood to apply to the other varieties of sense-experience. And suppose further that we admit the possibility that y may be identical with x, where x is a physical entity, or, in other words, that we allow, as Moore is inclined to do, that physical entities can be directly apprehended. Then what we are doing is deciding to attach a meaning to such sentences as 'I am directly seeing part of the surface of my right hand' or 'I am directly hearing the (physical) sound of a bell'; and since what is directly seen, or heard, or otherwise directly apprehended, is by definition a sense-datum, the propositions which these sentences are used to express could also, according to this ruling, be expressed by saying 'a visual sense-datum, which I am directly seeing, is identical with part of the surface of my right hand' or 'an auditory sense-datum, which I am directly hearing, is identical with the (physical) sound of a bell'. And in this case we must also make it legitimate to say of a sense-datum such things as that 'it looks purple but is really red', or that 'it sounds fainter than it really is'. For while it is very often true of physical entities, in a perceptual situation, that they do not, in a given respect, appear other than they are, nevertheless, it always makes sense to say of them that they do; so that if we are to hold that sense-data are capable of being identical with physical entities we are obliged to allow that it is also meaningful to say this of sense-data.

Provided that one rejects the ruling that sense-data cannot appear to have qualities that they do not really have, the assumption that some sense-data may be identical with physical entities need not be inconsistent with the possibility of qualitative perceptual illusions. But what of the possibility of existential illusions? How are we expected to deal with such cases as Macbeth's perception of the dagger, where the delusion consisted, not in investing a real physical dagger with some quality or qualities that it did not really possess, but in imagining that a physical dagger was really there at all? In the ordinary way, we might describe this situation either by saying that Macbeth saw a dagger which did not exist, or by saying that he imagined he saw a dagger, but did not really see it. If we say that he saw the dagger, then we are using the word 'see' in such a way that from the propositional function 'x is seen' it does not follow that 'x exists'. If, on the other hand, we use the word 'see' in such a way that 'x is seen' does entail 'x exists', we must say not that Macbeth saw the dagger, but that he imagined that he saw it; and both usages are legitimate. But now the question arises which of them we are to adopt in the case of direct apprehension. Are we to say that 'x is directly seen (or otherwise directly apprehended)' does, or that it does not, entail 'x exists'?

Moore himself is not altogether explicit on this point, but I think it is fairly clear that he does not wish to allow the possibility of directly apprehending what does not exist. Thus, in the case of Macbeth's vision, I think he would say that there existed a sense-datum which Macbeth was directly seeing, though this sense-datum was not identical with part of the surface of a real physical dagger, or presumably with any other physical entity. And, in general, I think he would hold that to say of anything that it was directly seen, or otherwise directly apprehended, would entail saying that it existed, even if it did not entail saying that it had whatever qualities it appeared to have. But, if this is so, he is mistaken in supposing that he can consistently allow the possibility of identifying any sense-data with physical entities. For with regard to any physical entity it always makes sense to say of it that it is seen, or otherwise perceived, in a sense of the word 'see' (or the word which stands for whatever other mode of perceiving is in question) from which it does not follow that it exists. And though it may be empirically false, it is never self-contradictory to say of a physical entity both that it is seen, or otherwise perceived, in this sense, and that it does not exist.[1] But if it be assumed

---

[1] This statement has been challenged by Mr. C. Lewy in a note, bearing the same title as my paper, which he published in *Mind*, vol. lv, no. 218. Mr. Lewy denies that it makes sense to say of a physical entity that it is seen but does not exist, on the ground that if what is seen does not exist it is not a physical entity. He admits that it is legitimate to describe Macbeth's experience by saying that he saw a dagger which did not exist, but denies that this proves my point, his argument being that the words 'a dagger' may be taken to

that sense-data cannot be apprehended otherwise than directly, and that part of what is meant by saying of something that it is directly apprehended is that it exists, then there is no sense in which it can significantly be said of a sense-datum that it is 'perceived' but does not exist. And from this it follows that no sense-datum can possibly be identical with any physical entity. For if x and y are identical it must be the case that everything that can significantly be said of x can

refer, not to a physical, but a sensory dagger. 'But', he continues, 'if we want to make it clear that we *are* talking of a physical entity and substitute for the variable (in the function "x is seen") the phrase a "physical dagger", it is surely obvious that the result—"Macbeth saw a physical dagger but no physical dagger existed"—is a contradiction' (*loc. cit.* p. 169). In saying this Mr. Lewy takes it for granted that the word 'physical' has in this case the force of the word 'real' and it is not so obvious to me, as he says it is to him, that he is right. I do not think that it need be an abuse of English to interpret the sentence which he quotes in such a way that it does not yield a contradiction. But even if Mr. Lewy be right on this question of usage, he is certainly wrong in supposing that the words 'a dagger' when they replace the variable in the function 'x was seen but did not exist' may be taken to refer to a sensory dagger, if he means by a sensory dagger what I am supposing Moore would call a sense-datum. For on my interpretation of Moore's usage, which Mr. Lewy does not here dispute, it would be a contradiction to say of a sense-datum that it was seen but did not exist. And this being so, my argument still stands. For while in a case where a physical entity is said to be perceived it is possible to describe the physical entity in a way which implies that it exists, it is also possible to describe it in a way which leaves the question of its existence open: one may use an expression, like the expression 'a dagger' in the example given, which designates what, if it exists, is a physical entity without itself carrying the implication that what it designates exists. Now an expression of this sort can legitimately be substituted for the variable 'x is seen', in a sense of 'seen' which is such that from 'x is seen' it does not follow that x exists. But if I have understood Moore correctly, the same will not be true of any expression which stands for what he would describe as a sense-datum.

Professor Moore himself in his addendum to the reply to his critics uses much the same argument as Mr. Lewy. Considering my example of Macbeth, he admits that 'two apparently contradictory statements can, in such cases, both be true, namely, in our case both (1) he was seeing a dagger and (2) he was not seeing a dagger' (*loc. cit.* p. 685). And he allows this to be a proof that '*this whole phrase* also significantly be said of y; but whereas it is always significant to say of a physical entity that it is seen, or otherwise perceived, in a sense which does not necessarily involve its existing, and that it does not exist, it is not, according to the assumptions we are making, ever significant to say this of a sense-datum.

To this it may perhaps be objected that a person may see, or otherwise perceive, a physical entity and know for certain that it exists; and that in this event

"he was seeing a dagger" must be used in a different sense in (1) from that in which it is being used in (2)'. But then he goes on to argue that it by no means follows that it is the word 'seen' that is being used in a different sense in either case. What I have culpably overlooked is the possibility that it is the sense of the word 'dagger' that is different; and Moore thinks that this oversight may in part account for my making the 'fallacious inference' that the fact that Macbeth did see a dagger entails that he saw a physical entity. Moore's proof that this inference is fallacious is that to the question whether 'Shakespeare is representing Macbeth as seeing a physical entity, when he represents him as having a visual hallucination of a dagger', the correct answer is obviously: No. But what is it, I ask, that Shakespeare represents Macbeth as thinking that he saw, or wondering whether he saw, if not a physical dagger? There is no question of Macbeth's asking whether it was a sensory dagger that he saw before him. And if, as Moore admits, it is legitimate to describe Macbeth's experience by saying that 'he really did see a dagger, but it wasn't a real dagger', surely what is here said to be unreal is not a sensory but a physical dagger. To speak of someone's seeing an unreal, or non-existent, sensory dagger would, on Moore's own showing, be a contradiction in terms. Admittedly 'a dagger which does not exist' is not a physical but at best a sensory dagger. If in the sentence 'he was seeing a dagger' we make the words 'a dagger' do duty for the phrase 'a dagger which did not exist', or, as Moore prefers to put it, 'a dagger which was not a real dagger', they are being used in a different sense from that in which they are used when it is said that Macbeth did not see a dagger but only thought he saw one. But it does not follow that the words 'a dagger', as they are used *within* the phrase, and not as a substitute for it, are being used in a special sense. On the contrary it is only if they are taken, in the normal way, as referring to a physical entity that the phrase has any meaning in this context, and this, I think, is just what my argument requires.

What it also requires is that the sense in which I use the word 'exist' when I say of Macbeth that he saw a dagger which did not exist should be the same as that in which Moore uses it when he says

G

it may still be justifiable to identify with this physical entity, which he knows to exist, the sense-datum which he is directly apprehending. But even if the premiss of this argument be granted, the conclusion does not hold good. For, to return to Moore's example, it is always legitimate, in describing such a situation as that of a man's perceiving his own right hand, to use the word 'see' in such a way that to say of something

that 'x exists' is entailed by 'x is directly apprehended'. I did, in fact, assume that it was, and Moore's final argument against me is that this assumption is quite certainly false. For he thinks that by 'a dagger which did not exist' I must mean 'a dagger which was not a physical entity', and it is obvious that when he himself says that 'x is directly apprehended' entails 'x exists' he does not mean by 'x exists' 'x is a physical entity'. Now I agree that it is proper to use the expression 'a dagger which was not a physical entity' to mean what I meant by 'a dagger which did not exist': but it does not follow that I was using the words 'did not exist' to mean 'was not a physical entity'. To say that Macbeth saw a non-existent physical dagger is, I still think, a legitimate way of saying that what he saw was not a physical dagger at all; I do not, therefore, take it to be a way of saying that what he saw both was and was not a physical dagger. But this, it seems to me, is what I should be saying if I were simply using the words 'did not exist' to mean 'was not a physical entity'. It is rather the fact that I was using the word 'dagger' to refer to a physical entity that makes the substitution of these phrases possible. Another example may help to make this clearer. Having said, rightly or wrongly, that Sir Galahad never existed, I may re-express my proposition by saying that Sir Galahad was not a real person. It does not follow that I am in this case using the words 'never existed' to mean 'was not a real person'. Surely when I say that Sir Galahad did not exist I am using the word 'exist' in exactly the same sense as I use it when I say that Macbeth saw a dagger which did not exist; the reason why I can in the one case substitute 'was not a physical entity' for 'did not exist' and in the other 'was not a real person' is just that what I am denying the existence of is in the one case a physical object and in the other a person. The difference lies in the use of the words 'a dagger' and 'Sir Galahad' and not in the use of the word 'exist'. Neither can I see any reason to believe that the way in which the word 'exist' is used in these examples is any different from the way in which Moore uses it when he says that 'x is directly apprehended' entails 'x exists'. I do not think, therefore, that he has made good his claim to have discovered in this point about the use of the word 'exists' 'a conclusive reason' for rejecting my argument.

that it is seen does not entail saying either that it exists or, of course, that it does not exist; and if the word 'see' is used in this sense, then it is not self-contradictory to say that the part of the surface of his right hand which the person in question is seeing does not exist. If it be assumed that he knows for certain that it does exist, then it follows that the proposition which states that he sees it but that it does not exist is empirically false, but it does not follow that it is self-contradictory; for the question whether it is self-contradictory depends solely upon the meaning of the proposition, and this is not affected by the empirical fact that someone knows it to be true or to be false. There is, perhaps, a danger here of confusing a proposition of the form 'It is self-contradictory that "A knows p and p is false"', which is necessarily true, with a proposition of the form '"A knows p" and it is self-contradictory that p is false', which is not true at all in the instance that we have been considering. But, on the assumptions we are now making, it is always self-contradictory to say of a sense-datum that it is seen, or otherwise apprehended, in the sense of words like 'see' which alone is applicable to sense-data, but that it does not exist. And from this it follows, as has already been shown, that sense-data and physical entities cannot in any instance be identical.

If this argument is correct, and we still adhere to the definition of sense-data as objects of direct apprehension, then the only way in which we can maintain the possibility of taking any physical entity to be a sense-datum is by resolving so to use the words which stand for the various modes of direct apprehension that to say of something that it is directly apprehended does not entail saying either that it has whatever characteristics it appears to have or that it exists. But while this is a feasible course, it does not meet the purpose which philosophers who have used the term 'sense-datum', or some equivalent term, have commonly intended it to fulfil. It is true indeed that there is an ambiguity in our ordinary use of perceptual words, in that we speak indifferently of 'seeing' a hand and 'seeing' a part of its surface, or of 'hearing' a clock and 'hearing' its tick, and there may therefore be some advantage in finding an expression to replace the word 'see' in the sense in which one is obliged to say that one sees, not a whole hand, but only a part of its surface, or to replace the word 'hear' in the sense in which one is obliged to say that one hears the ticking rather than the clock; and, having done this, one may then be inclined to introduce some general term as a means of referring indefinitely to what is seen, or heard, or otherwise apprehended in this sense. But the choice of the actual word 'sense-datum' does not seem happy for this purpose, nor that of expressions like 'directly see' if we are going also to speak of directly seeing sense-data. For one of the motives that have led philosophers to introduce the terminology of sense-data has been their desire to be able to say, in such cases as that of Macbeth's vision, that something, which existed, was being seen, even though it was not a real physical object; and one advantage of this procedure has been that it serves to clarify the meaning of statements about physical objects by relating them to statements of a different logical form. But this desire is not satisfied, nor the advantage secured, by a procedure which makes the class of sense-data overlap with that of physical entities, and allows the apprehension of sense-data to be itself both qualitatively and existentially delusive.

Another course, which is the one that I have rightly or wrongly been attributing to Moore, is to define 'direct apprehension' in such a way that to say of something that it is directly apprehended entails saying that it exists, but does not entail saying that it has whatever characteristics it appears to have. Now if the word 'sense-datum' is used for what is directly apprehended, in this sense, and cannot be apprehended otherwise than directly, this procedure does have the effect, as I have tried to show, of separating sense-data from physical entities; but it may, I think, fairly be objected to it that it does not do so very clearly. Moreover, if one is going to deal with cases of existential illusion by saying that a sense-datum, which the observer is directly apprehending, really does exist, even though the physical object, which he may imagine he is perceiving, does not, there seems to be no valid ground for refusing to deal with cases of qualitative illusion in a similar way. For surely we have as good a motive for saying that something, a sense-datum, which Lady Macbeth was directly seeing, really was maculated, though the hand which appeared to her to be so was not, as we have for saying, in the case of Macbeth's hallucinatory perception of the dagger, that something, a sense-datum, which he was directly seeing, really did exist?

It seems then that, if we are going to use the terminology of sense-data, our best course is to exclude the possibility of their being either qualitatively or existentially delusive by making 'x is directly apprehended' entail 'x has whatever characteristics it appears to have' as well as 'x exists'. And in order to minimize the danger of confusing sense-data, in this usage, with physical entities, I think it is also advisable to make 'x exists' entail 'x is directly apprehended', where x is a sense-datum, and, more specifically, to make the existence of a sense-datum logically dependent upon its being directly apprehended on a particular occasion. There is no question here of *proving* that it is self-contradictory to say that a sense-datum exists while it is not being apprehended, for there is no established usage to provide the material for any proof. It becomes self-contradictory only if we choose to make it so. Nor, in thus making *esse est percipi* true of sense-data, are we legislating about the character of empirical facts. It is simply a matter of deciding that the expression 'x exists', where x is a sense-datum, is to be understood both to be entailed by and to entail 'x is directly apprehended'. Neither can there be any doubt that sense-data do, in fact, exist in this sense, since we have so defined our terms that it must be true that something is being directly apprehended in every case in which it is true that anything is being in any manner perceived.

4. CAN SENSE-DATA HAVE CHARACTERISTICS THAT THEY DO NOT APPEAR TO HAVE?

A question which may now be raised is whether, in addition to saying that sense-data cannot appear to have characteristics that they do not really have, we should also make it a rule that they cannot really have characteristics that they do not appear to have. By resolving that 'x exists', where x is a sense-datum, is to be understood as entailing 'x is directly apprehended', we do indeed make it impossible for a sense-field to have constituents which are not apprehended at all, but it does not follow that these constituents may not, individually or collectively, have some features that the owner of the sense-field in question does not succeed in detecting. What is excluded by our definitions is that he should notice any features that are not really present, but not, so far, that he should fail to notice some of those that are. We have, therefore, still to decide whether or not we are going to attach a meaning to statements which imply, for example, that sense-data 'may be much more differentiated than we think them to be' [1] or that 'two sense-data may be really different when we cannot perceive any difference between them',[2] or that a sense-field may really contain a definite number of constituents of a certain kind without their being apprehended otherwise than as merely numerous.

In a previous discussion of this question,[3] I argued that to allow such statements to be meaningful would involve, at least in some cases, the use of a physiological criterion to determine the real characteristics of sense-data, and I maintained that this should be avoided if possible, both because such a criterion would be difficult to apply, and because the utility of the sense-datum terminology, as a tool for the analysis of propositions about physical objects, would be considerably diminished if the 'reality' of sense-data was itself defined in physical terms. Accordingly, I proposed that in the domain of sense-data whatever appeared, and only what appeared, should be taken as real, and I tried to show that this convention was not inadequate to the description of the empirical facts. Thus, the fact that the use of a microscope, for example, might

---

[1] Professor C. D. Broad, *Scientific Thought*, p. 244.
[2] Bertrand Russell, *Our Knowledge of the External World*, p. 141.
[3] *The Foundations of Empirical Knowledge*, pp. 116-135.

reveal details in an object that were previously un-
detected did not, according to my argument, oblige us
to allow that some sense-data were more differentiated
than they originally appeared to be, since the situation
could equally well be described by saying that one set of
sense-data was replaced by another; nor, in my opinion,
did the fact that two sense-data might each be indistinguishable from a third, without being indistinguishable
from one another, make it necessary to admit that sense-
data must sometimes really differ in ways that were
not apparent, since this conclusion depended upon
the assumption that the relation of exact resemblance
was transitive in its application to sense-data, as well
as in its application to physical objects, and this
assumption could reasonably be denied. And in a case
such as that of a person's 'seeing stars', where a
number of sense-data were apprehended without being
apprehended as a definite number, I argued that it
could legitimately be held that, while the sense-data
in question really were numerous, no definite number
of them existed. I admitted that it would be self-
contradictory to say of a group of physical objects that
it was numerous without consisting of any definite
number, but I saw no reason to suppose that the same
must be true also of sense-data.

To this last point exception has been taken by
Professor Price,[1] and also by Mr. Chisholm,[2] on the
ground that it commits us to saying that 'a sense-datum
can have a determinable characteristic, without having
any of the determinate characteristics which fall under
that determinable', which, according to Mr. Chisholm,

[1] H. H. Price, Review of 'The Foundations of Empirical Knowledge', *Mind*, N.S. 50, pp. 280-293.
[2] R. Chisholm, 'The Problem of the Speckled Hen', *Mind*, N.S.
51, pp. 368-373.

is like saying that an event will occur in a given year but not in any of the particular months of which the year is composed. But this is to overlook the fact that when such an epithet as 'numerous' is applied to sense-data, it need not have the same meaning as it has when it is applied to physical objects. Thus, to take Price's example of a striped tiger, it is true that the tiger cannot have a number of 'physically-dark stripes on the left-hand side of its body'[1] without having some definite number, since to say that it had many such stripes, but no definite number of them, would be self-contradictory. But it does not follow that it is self-contradictory to say of the visual sense-field, which corresponds to the physical expanse of the tiger, that it contains a number of stripes without containing any definite number. For the characteristics which are supposed to be ascribed to this sense-field are not necessarily those that the tiger really has, but only those that it appears to have, so that the model on which we have to base our usage of the expression 'being numerous', in this context, is not the physical characteristic of being numerous but the physical characteristic of looking numerous; and, as Price admits, to say that the stripes on the tiger look numerous does not entail saying that they look to be of any definite number. Thus, in saying that the sense-field in question contains a number of stripes, we need be saying no more than that it has the *Gestalt* quality of being striated; and, while the presence of this quality is compatible with there being some definite number of stripes, it does not logically necessitate it. In the same way, as Price remarks, a sense-datum, let us say, of a flower, 'might be blue without having any definite

[1] *Mind*, N.S. 50, p. 285.

shade of blue', or it 'might have a roundish shape, but not any definite *sort* of roundish shape'; [1] for if it be granted that 'looking blue' does not entail 'looking any definite shade of blue', and that 'looking a roundish shape' does not entail 'looking any definite sort of roundish shape', the same reasoning will apply as in the case of the number of the sense-data. And if it be objected that the very meaning of the word 'determinable' is such that it is logically impossible for anything, whether physical object or sense-datum, to have a determinable characteristic without having some determinate characteristic which falls under the determinable, the answer is that, in that case, words like 'blue' and 'roundish' are not, in this usage, the names of determinable characteristics, but of qualities which are simple in the sense of not being analysable into a disjunction of others, just as a word like 'striated', when applied to a sense-field, may be used as the name of a *Gestalt* quality, which is not analysable in terms of a numerical disjunction of stripes.

But 'suppose', continues Price, that 'I do start to count the stripes in my sense-datum of the tiger. A very singular process must then occur, which is certainly not change, nor even exactly creation. At first there is no determinate number of stripes at all — merely "many". Then there are more than one, but no determinate number more; then more than two, more than three, etc., but no definite number more; until at last when I have finished (but not before) there are exactly twenty-three. What is this process, by which an entity passes from having "many" parts but no definite number of parts, to having exactly twenty-three?' [2] He remarks, correctly, that I should answer

[1] *Mind*, N.S. 50, p. 286.　　　　[2] *Ibid*. pp. 286-287.

this by denying that there was any such process, on the ground that 'when I count the stripes, what I am aware of is a series of sense-data, not just an individual one'. But to this he objects that 'it is an exceedingly queer sort of series', the members of which are ordered by 'the degree to which numerical definiteness has spread itself over each of them'.[1] Similarly, in the case where, as he puts it, the result of attending to a sense-datum is that 'it *acquires* a more and more definite colour, though it had none at first', he asks 'What sort of a becoming is this?' 'Or if', he continues, 'you prefer to call it a series, what sort of a series is it, in which the members stand progressively lower and lower in the determinable-determinate scale'?[2]

I confess that I do not see the difficulty here. I do not find anything excessively strange in the idea of the occurrence, within a given sense-history, of a series of sense-fields, which differ from one another in quality in a way which may be represented as a progression in numerical definiteness. Thus, to revert to Price's example, we may suppose that the first term of the series is striated in a way that does not involve there being any definite number of stripes, that the last term is not striated in this way, but does contain a definite number of stripes, and that the intermediate terms include in their composition a part which is striated in the manner of the first term, and a part which contains a definite number of stripes, this number being in each case one greater than the definite number of stripes which existed in the immediate temporal predecessor of the sense-field in question. No doubt such a series is 'more easily conceived than described', but that in itself is not an objection to the possibility of its

[1] *Ibid.* p. 287.   [2] *Ibid.* p. 287.

occurrence. Neither do I find it paradoxical that a sense-datum which is 'merely bluish' in colour should be replaced in a subsequent sense-field by one that is sky-blue. Moreover, even if one adopts a way of speaking which I should prefer to avoid, and treats the emergence of the definite number, or the more specific colour, as a process occurring within a single sense-field, I cannot see why it should not be regarded as a process of change. Admittedly, the physical character-istics, which 'correspond' to the sensory characteristics in question, are assumed to be unchanging; it is assumed that the tiger has twenty-three stripes all along, and that the colour of the flower is consistently sky-blue. But it does not follow from this that the sensory characteristics themselves do not change. Neither does Price, so far as I can see, put forward any argument to support his view that 'the process by which an entity passes from having "many" parts to having exactly twenty-three' is 'certainly not a process of change'. I suspect that the reason he would give is that the process would have to be regarded as being due to an effort of attention on the part of the observer, and that such an effort of attention cannot in itself alter the real character of what is observed. But even if this were true of the observation of physical entities, it again would not follow that it was true of the observation of sense-data. It is indeed common ground that the character of a sense-field may be determined by psychological, as well as by physiological, factors; and I do not see why attention should not in some cases be reckoned among them. But, even if there is a difficulty here, we may in any case avoid it by represent-ing the process as a matter of the successive replacement of one sense-field by another.

The point, which Mr. Chisholm raises, that one may even so miscount the stripes, or whatever other set of sense-data is in question,[1] does not, I think, affect the argument. If the sense-data that one is supposed to be counting are too scattered or too numerous to fall within a single sense-field, then indeed one may come to miscount them through an error of memory; but the possibility of such an error of memory is in no way incompatible with the rule that the sense-data are in every respect what they appear to be. It may be, however, as in the example given by Price, that the process of counting terminates in the occurrence of a sense-field which contains the de-numerated set of sense-data entirely in itself. In that case, the question arises whether the observer, in assigning a number to the sense-data, is or is not intending to make a reference to anything outside the content of his present experience. If, as Mr. Chisholm suggests,[2] he is judging that this particular set of sense-data exactly resembles certain other sets in its appearance of numerousness, then, on the assumption that these other sets of sense-data are not actually present to his observation, his judgement may conceivably be erroneous. For the fact that no direct comparison can be made leaves a certain room for doubt; it admits the possibility that if the direct comparison had been feasible, the requisite resemblance would have been found not to obtain. To concede this is not, however, to allow that a sense-field may really have characteristics that it does not appear to have, for the property of resembling, or failing to resemble, other sense-fields, which are not sensibly contemporaneous with it, is at least partly extrinsic to the given sense-field, and is

[1] *Mind*, N.S. 51, p. 370.   [2] *Ibid.* pp. 371-373.

therefore not a characteristic of it, in the sense in which the word 'characteristic' is here being used. On the other hand, if, in assigning a number to the sense-data, the observer intends merely to name a certain feature of his present sense-field, then I think it would be incorrect to say that he might be mistaken about the number, except in a verbal sense. He can be mistaken in a verbal sense, inasmuch as he may misdescribe the number by giving it a name which is not its correct name in the language that he purports to be using. But he cannot be factually mistaken, since the possibility of his being factually mistaken requires that he be making some claim upon the facts which is subject to the test of further experience. And this, by hypothesis, he does not do.

5. PROFESSOR PRICE'S DISTINCTION BETWEEN 'LOOKING' AND 'SEEMING'

Disagreeing, as he does, with my proposal to limit what is sensed to what is noticed, Price remarks that I may, in this instance, have been misled by an ambiguity in the use of the word 'appear'. His point is that 'appearing' may mean either 'seeming', which, according to him, 'has reference to judgements or assertions, usually of a spontaneous and unconsidered kind', or 'looking', which 'has reference to sensation'.[1] Thus, he agrees that it is nonsensical to say 'the flower appeared sky-blue but I did not notice that it did', if 'appeared' is being used to mean 'seemed', but he does not think that a statement of this kind is nonsensical if 'appeared' is being used to mean 'looked'. For he maintains that 'it is perfectly good sense to say "it did

[1] *Mind*, N.S. 50, p. 288.

in fact *look* sky-blue, but I only noticed that it was bluish "'"; and from this he infers that it is also good sense to say 'the sense-datum *was* in fact sky-blue, but I only noticed that it was bluish'. The fact that I am unwilling to accept this conclusion suggests to him that I may have confused 'looking' with 'seeming', and so have fallen unconsciously into 'the mistake of the idealists who maintained that all cognition is judging, and denied the existence of acquaintance'.[1]

Now it may be doubted whether the accounts of 'looking' and 'seeming', which Price has given here, are strictly in accordance with ordinary usage; but even if he could be shown to be mistaken on this verbal point, it would not be fatal to his argument. For if it be admitted that an object may appear to someone to have a certain characteristic, in a sense of 'appear' which does not entail that any judgement about it is being made by the person to whom the appearance occurs, then the question whether the word 'look', as opposed to 'seem', can most properly be substituted for the word 'appear', in this sense, is not of any great importance. We can, if necessary, say that 'look' is here being given a technical meaning, which is characterized by the fact that a proposition such as 'the flower looks sky-blue' does not entail any proposition to the effect that someone judges that the flower looks sky-blue. Then if, as Price supposes, it is this meaning of 'look' that is in question when the rule is made that the characteristics that certain sense-data really have are to be those that the corresponding physical objects look to have, it will follow that to say that the relevant sense-datum of the flower really is sky-blue does not entail saying that anybody judges that it is. And from

[1] *Ibid.* p. 289.

this it is a reasonable step to derive the general principle
that 'being acquainted with', or 'sensing', or 'directly
apprehending' a sense-datum as having a certain
characteristic, or as being of a certain sort, does not
entail judging that it has the characteristic, or that it
is of the sort, in question. It is indeed open to anyone
to define 'acquaintance', or whatever equivalent term
is chosen, in such a way that being acquainted with a
sense-datum does entail making a judgement about it,
but I take it that Price would maintain that for someone
to be acquainted with a sense-datum in this way it was
logically necessary that he should also be acquainted
with it in a more primitive sense of 'acquaintance'
which did not entail judgement; and the mistake which
he would then attribute to the idealists would be not
that of defining 'acquaintance' in a different manner,
which they are free to do if they please, but that of
denying, or at any rate ignoring, the fact that if they do
so define it, the other sense of 'acquaintance' is still
logically presupposed.

The argument which Price uses in his work on
'Perception',[1] to support this view, is that in order
for a judgement to be made about something it is
necessary that the object in question should *already*
be 'given'. On the face of it, this argument is plausible, but it does not seem to me to be conclusive,
since it is open to the idealists to reply that the
making of the judgement is a necessary part of what
constitutes the object's being given. Nor would they
have to meet the objection that such a judgement might
be mistaken, since Price himself concedes that judgements which are purely descriptive of the given are
indubitable. Nevertheless, I think that Price is right

[1] H. H. Price, *Perception*, ch. 1.

on this issue, if only for the reason that beings which have not acquired the use of language may still be supposed capable of apprehending sense-data, whereas I assume that the making of a judgement, since it involves the entertainment, if not necessarily the expression, of a proposition, does presuppose the use of language. Thus, I think it improbable that animals, or very young children, have the ability to make judgements, but I should not for that reason deny that they were capable of being acquainted with sense-data. Accordingly, I find it necessary to admit a sense of acquaintance with, or direct apprehension of, sense-data that does not entail the making of any judgement about them, and I am prepared to agree with Price that anyone who does make a judgement about a present sense-datum is also acquainted with it in this sense. For there does not seem to be any good reason to believe that the acquisition and exercise of the power to make judgements about sense-data essentially alters the nature of one's direct apprehension of them.

Reverting now to Price's example, we may admit that if the word 'look' is understood as he proposes, it is possible for the flower to have looked sky-blue to me without my having judged that this was so. It does not follow, however, that the flower could have looked sky-blue to me without my having noticed that it did, if 'my having noticed that it did' is taken to imply no more than my having been aware of the flower as looking sky-blue. Price's actual claim that it makes good sense to say 'it did in fact look sky-blue, but I only noticed that it was bluish' is misleading in this context, since the statement that 'it did in fact look sky-blue' could be interpreted as meaning that it would have looked sky-blue to someone who was in the

H

situation of a 'standard' observer, and, on the assumption that I was not myself in the situation of a standard observer, this is indeed consistent with my having noticed only that it was bluish. It is clear, however, that what Price intended to claim was that it made good sense to say 'the flower did in fact look sky-blue to me, but I only noticed that it was bluish'; and with this I disagree. I do not deny, indeed, that there may be some legitimate uses of the words 'look' and 'notice' that would make this sentence meaningful, but these uses would not, in my opinion, be such as to justify our taking the further step of attaching meaning to the statement that 'my sense-datum of the flower really was sky-blue, but I noticed only that it was bluish'; and it is the propriety of this further step that is the main point at issue. My principal objection to Price's view is that it makes it impossible to take what the observer is aware of as an adequate criterion of the characteristics that the physical object appears to have, or the sense-datum really has, and I do not see what alternative criterion is available. I cannot, for example, think of any criterion the use of which would make it intelligible to say of an after-image, which was consciously seen only as bluish, that it was really sky-blue, and I cannot see any ground for drawing a distinction in this respect between an after-image and a visual sense-datum which happens to 'correspond' to a physical object.

The upshot of this discussion is that I do not think that Price has produced any wholly convincing argument against my view that the sensory characteristics that sense-data really have should be regarded as co-extensive with those that they appear to have. And with regard to the meaning of the word 'appear'

in this context, I think that I am using it in such a
way that to say of a sense-datum that it appears to
someone to have a certain characteristic is equivalent
to saying that this person is aware of it, or directly
apprehends it, as having this characteristic, in a sense
of 'being aware of' or 'directly apprehending' which
does not entail either any proposition about a physical
fact, or any proposition to the effect that the person in
question is making any judgement about the sense-
datum.   It is indeed a weakness in my position, no less
than in Moore's, that I am unable to say anything
more positive about the nature of this 'awareness' or
'direct apprehension': but, although I am anxious to
believe that some further analysis of it can be given, I
confess that I do not at present see on what lines it is
to be developed.

6. The Priority of the Sense-datum Language

There remains one further point upon which I
wish, very briefly, to express my agreement with Price.
In arguing that the solution of the current philosophical
problems about sense-data depended, not upon our
discovering the properties of a strange sort of object,
but rather upon our establishing the use of a new set of
technical terms, I implied, or seemed to imply, that
the terminology of sense-data, though philosophically
convenient, did not enable us to express any propositions about our perceptual experience that we were
not already able to express in the language of common
sense, by referring to physical objects.[1]   At the same
time, I also argued that the possibility of applying
the 'physical-object language' depended upon the

[1] In the *Foundations of Empirical Knowledge*, Parts I and II.

constancy of certain relations between sense-data, which might conceivably not have obtained.[1] That is to say, I held it to be a contingent fact that the structure of our sensory experience was such as to make it possible to 'construct' out of it the world of material things; and with this Price says that he agrees. Thus, as he remarks, 'our visual and tactual data might have an eurhythmic rather than a thing-like order, arranging themselves as it were in visible or tangible tunes'.[2] But from this it follows, as he points out, that the 'sense-datum language' is, in a certain sense, more comprehensive than the 'physical-object language'. For whereas in every case in which it is possible to apply the physical-object language, it is also possible, at least in principle, to apply the sense-datum language, one can conceive an order of experience to which the sense-datum language would have application, but the physical-object language would not. Thus, while it is convenient, for purposes of exposition, to introduce people to the sense-datum terminology by setting forth sentences which refer to sense-data as translations of sentences which refer to physical objects, it would be a mistake to conclude from this that the sense-datum language was nothing more than a technical substitute for the other. There is, on the contrary, an asymmetry between the two languages which may be described by saying that the sense-datum language is logically prior; and this is shown by the fact that, while referring to sense-data is not necessarily a way of referring to physical objects, referring to physical objects is necessarily a way of referring to sense-data.

---

[1] *Foundations of Empirical Knowledge*, pp. 243-263.
[2] *Mind*, N.S. 50, p. 291.

5

BASIC PROPOSITIONS

PHILOSOPHERS who concern themselves with the theory of knowledge are apt to be haunted by an ideal of certainty. Seeking a refuge from Descartes' malicious demon, they look for a proposition, or class of propositions, of whose truth they can be absolutely sure. They think that once they have found this basis they can go on to justify at least some of their beliefs, but that without it there can be no defence against scepticism. Unless something is certain, we are told nothing can be even probable.

The discussion of this problem is not usually confined to the case of empirical propositions. For what is required is certainty about matters of fact, in Hume's sense of the term; and while it is generally agreed that *a priori* propositions can be certain, it is also held that they do not afford us knowledge about matters of fact. But even the claim that *a priori* propositions are certain is not without its difficulties. For surely it is possible to doubt them. People do make mistakes in mathematics and in logic; they miscalculate, they draw invalid inferences, they construct abstract systems which turn out to be self-contradictory. And I suppose that someone who had discovered that he was addicted to such errors might come to doubt the validity of any *a priori* statement that he made. Admittedly, his only ground for supposing

that a particular answer was wrong would be that it
failed to tally with some other answer which he took to
be right; nevertheless the assumption that he was
justified in so taking it would be one that he could still
go on to question. Recognizing that some answers must
be right, he would remain eternally in doubt as to which
they were. 'Perhaps', he would say to himself, 'the procedures that I am trying to carry out are not the correct
procedures; or, even if they are correct, perhaps I am
not applying them properly in this particular case.'

But all that this shows, it may be said, is that we
must distinguish the propositions of mathematics and
logic as such from empirical propositions about the
behaviour of persons who do mathematics or logic.
That someone is carrying out the right procedure, or
that someone is carrying out a certain procedure
rightly, is an empirical proposition which can indeed
be doubted. But the result at which he arrives, the
a priori proposition of logic or mathematics itself, is
either certainly true or certainly false; it is certainly
true, if it is true at all. But what is meant here by
saying of such a proposition that it is certain? Simply
that it is *a priori*. To say that the proposition is certainly true, or that it is necessary, or that it is true
a priori, is, in this case, just to say the same thing in
three different ways. But what then is the point of
saying that *a priori* propositions are certain if it is to
say no more than that *a priori* propositions are *a priori*?
The answer is that people wish to pass from '*p* is
certainly true', in this sense, to '*p* can be known for
certain to be true'. They make the tacit assumption
that the truth of an *a priori* proposition can be 'clearly
and distinctly perceived'. But if their ground for
saying that such a proposition can be known for certain

is simply that it is certain in the sense of being *a priori*, then their use of the word 'certain' gains them nothing. They are still saying no more than that an *a priori* proposition is an *a priori* proposition. And if by saying that such propositions can be known for certain they mean that they sometimes are known for certain, then their conclusion does not follow from their premiss. For in any case in which such knowledge is claimed, there is room for the empirical doubt; perhaps this is not the correct procedure, or perhaps it has not been applied correctly in this instance. Thus, while there is a sense in which *a priori* propositions are unassailable, to explain which would be to explain what was meant by calling them *a priori*, there is also a sense in which they are not. They are not unassailable, inasmuch as it can always be asked of any 'clear and distinct perception', in Descartes' sense of the term, whether it really is clear and distinct. Of course, such a question easily becomes futile. If I doubt whether I have done a sum correctly, what can I do except look up the rules as set out in the textbooks, check my result with those of other people, go over the sum again? And then it remains possible that I have misread the textbooks, that other people are deceiving me, that if I went over the sum yet again I should get a different answer. Now clearly this process can go on for ever, and just for that reason there is no point to it. If nothing is going to satisfy me, then nothing is going to satisfy me. And if nothing counts as satisfying me, then it is necessarily true that I cannot be satisfied. And if it is necessarily true, it is nothing to worry about. The worrying may, in fact, continue, but at this point the state of doubt has become neurotic. It is never settled because it is not allowed to be.

For the most part, however, philosophers are not troubled in this way about *a priori* propositions. They are content to say that these propositions are certain, and they do not regard it as an objection to this way of speaking that people often reason incorrectly or that they get their calculations wrong. On the other hand, they are very often troubled about empirical propositions, just because they are not *a priori*. For, following the same line as before, they argue that since these propositions are not necessary, they are not certain; and that since they are not certain they cannot be known for certain to be true. But, reasoning in this way, they find themselves exposed to the taunts of the G. E. Moore school. 'Of course empirical propositions are not certain in the way that *a priori* propositions are. Of course they can be denied without self-contradiction. If this were not so, they would not be empirical propositions. But it does not follow from this that they cannot properly be said to be certain in any sense at all. It does not follow that they cannot be known for certain to be true. Do you mean to tell me', says Professor Moore, 'that you do not know that you are awake and that you are reading this? Do you mean to tell me that I do not know that I have a pen in my hand? How improper it would be, what a misuse of English, to say that it was not certain that I had a sheet of paper in front of me, but only highly probable. How absurd it would be to say: "Perhaps this is not a pen. I believe that it is but I do not know it".'

Now clearly Professor Moore and his friends are right. It is good English to use the words 'know' and 'certain' in the way that they encourage us to use them. If someone wants to know what day of the week it is and, when I tell him it is Monday, asks me whether

this is certain, then an answer like 'Yes, quite certain ;
I have just seen it in the newspaper, and anyhow I
remember that yesterday was a Sunday' is a correct
answer. To answer, 'Well, I seem to remember that
yesterday was a Sunday, and I believe that this is
to-day's newspaper, and I seem to see "Monday"
written on it ; but I may be wrong about the newspaper,
and anyhow both memory and perception are fallible.
Therefore I cannot be certain that it is Monday but
I think it very probable' — to give an answer of this
sort would be tiresome, and not only tiresome but
misleading. It would be misleading because, in the
ordinary way, we say that something is not certain, but
at best highly probable, only in cases where we have
some special reason for doubting, some reason which
applies particularly to the case in question. Thus, in
the example that I have just given, I might be justified
in saying that I did not know that it was Monday if
my memory were frequently at fault in matters of this
kind, or I had glanced at the newspaper only carelessly,
or the newspaper could not be relied on to print the
right date. But if my reason for saying that it is not
certain is merely the general reason that all empirical
beliefs are fallible, then it is not consonant with ordinary
usage to say that it is only probable. It is correct to say
that it is certain. It is correct for me to say that I know.

All the same, this does not take us very far. It is all
very well for Moore to prove the existence of external
objects by holding up his hands and saying that he
knows that they exist ; [1] the philosopher who sees this
as a problem is unlikely to be satisfied. He will want to
say that Moore does not really know that these physical

[1] *Proof of an External World* (British Academy Annual Philosophical Lecture, 1939).

objects exist, that he cannot know it. At the very least he will want to raise the question, 'How does he know it?' Now it may be argued that this is not a sensible question. But one is not going to stop people from asking it merely by giving them an English lesson, any more than one is going to make people feel comfortable about induction merely by arguing that it is correct for a schoolmaster to say that he knows the truth of Archimedes' law, that he would be misleading his pupils if he said that he did not know it to be true but only thought it probable. Even if this is so, it is beside the point.

But in that case what is the point? Why are people not satisfied with Moore's sort of answer? Presumably the reason is that they feel that it does not meet the question which they are trying to ask. After all, it is to be supposed that the philosopher who says that Moore does not really know, that he cannot really know, what he says he knows is as well acquainted with the English language as Moore. He is not making a philological blunder, nor is he casting doubts upon Moore's honesty. If he says that Moore does not know for certain the truth of such a proposition as 'this is a human hand', it is because he thinks that nobody can know for certain that such a proposition is true, that it is not the sort of proposition that can be so known. But this means that he has decided to use the word 'know' in an unconventional way. He is making it inapplicable to a set of propositions to which it does apply in ordinary usage. And this, we may assume, is not a mere piece of eccentricity on his part. He has some reason for his procedure. Let us consider what it might be.

I can think of two reasons for taking such a course, both of which are good reasons in the sense that they call attention to valid points of logic. In the first place, it may be suspected that someone who claims to know, without giving any proof, that such and such is the case, is relying on an act of intuition; and then the rejection of the claim proceeds from the denial that any act of intuition can constitute knowledge. The logical point is that from the fact that someone is convinced that a proposition is true it never follows that it is true. That A believes p may be a good reason for accepting p, if A is a reliable person; but it is in no case a conclusive reason. It is never self-contradictory to say both that A believes p and that p is false. It is indeed self-contradictory to say that A knows p and that p is false, but the explanation of this is just that part of what is meant by saying that A knows that p, as opposed to merely believing it, is that p is true. If p turns out not to be true, then it follows that it was not known, though it does not follow that it was not believed. Now one way of bringing out this distinction is to say that knowledge guarantees the truth, or reality, of its object, whereas belief does not; and this can be allowed to pass so long as it is nothing more than a picturesque way of expressing the linguistic fact that it is self-contradictory to speak of knowing something which is not the case, but not self-contradictory to speak of believing what is not the case. But what such formulations are all too often taken to imply is that the property of guaranteeing the truth or reality of its object belongs to knowledge as a special kind of mental activity; from which it is concluded that the truth, or reality, of the supposed 'object of knowledge' can be inferred simply from the occurrence of the act of knowing, considered in itself. And this is a serious mistake. For knowledge, in the sense which is here alone in question, is always

knowledge that something or other is so. In order
that it should be knowledge, it is necessary that the
symbols which express what is known should state
something true ; and whether this is so depends upon
the existence or non-existence of the situation to which
the symbols refer. It is not to be decided merely by
examining the 'state of apprehension' of the knower.
My own view is that it is extremely misleading to speak
of 'acts of knowing' at all. But even if we allow that
something is described by this expression, it can never
follow from the occurrence of such an act, considered
in itself, that anything is known.

Thus, if Moore's ground for saying 'I know that this
is a human hand' were merely that he apprehended
that it was so, it would not be conclusive ; and it may
be because some people have thought he was maintaining that it was conclusive that they have wished to
reject his claim. But, in fact, one's reason for making
an assertion like 'This is a human hand' is never just
that one is convinced of it. It is rather that one is
having certain visual or tactual experiences. And this
brings us to the second of my reasons why people may
be dissatisfied with the 'What I know, I know' tech-
nique. It is that in the case of propositions like 'This
is a chair', 'This is a human hand', 'There is more than
one picture in the room' — all of which I should say
that I now knew — it is not absurd for someone to ask
me 'How do you know?' And the answers he will get
are 'Because I can see it', 'Because I can touch it',
'Because I have counted them', 'Because I remember
seeing it', and so on. In short, a proposition like
'I know this is a chair' cannot be true unless some
propositions of the form 'I am seeing . . .', 'I am
touching . . .', 'I remember . . .' are true. On the

other hand, a proposition of this type can be true in cases where the corresponding proposition at the 'I-know-this-is-a-chair' level is false. Next, let us give the name 'sense-datum statement' to a description of what is seen, touched, or otherwise perceived, in a sense of words like 'see' and 'touch' which does not carry the implication that what is so perceived is a physical object. Then, no statement like 'This is a chair' can be true unless some sense-datum statement is true; but once again the converse does not hold. And this, I think, explains why some philosophers have wished to deny that any proposition which asserts the presence of a physical object can be known for certain to be true. The point that they are thereby making is that such a proposition does not follow from any one sense-datum statement; it is based upon the fact that somebody is having some sensory experience, but the description of the experience in question does not logically entail it.

This gives us the clue also to what is meant by those who say that propositions about physical objects can never be certain. They are not denying that there is a good and familiar sense of the word 'certain' in which it can apply to such propositions, nor that it is good usage to say that one knows them to be true. What they are maintaining is simply that they do not follow from any finite set of sense-datum statements. The suggestion is that however strong the evidence in their favour may be it is never altogether sufficient; it is always consistent with their being false. Now this, indeed, may be disputed.[1] It might be argued that we

---

[1] Cp. C. Lewy, 'On the Relation of Some Empirical Propositions to Their Evidence', *Mind*, vol. liii (1944), 289, and 'Entailment and Empirical Propositions', *Mind*, vol. lv (1946), 74; also A. H. Basson, 'The Existence of Material Objects', *Mind*, vol. lv (1946), 308, and my own paper, 'Phenomenalism', pp. 135-137.

should in fact take a finite quantity of sensory evidence to be sufficient; and that if subsequent evidence proved unfavourable we should account for it in some other way than by saying that what we took to be a physical object never really was one; we might prefer to distrust our present experience, or to save the appearances by introducing some new physical hypothesis. The difficulty is that there is no established rule to meet such cases. A procedure has to be laid down; and this, I think, is what is being done by those who deny that any proposition about a physical object can be certain. They are expressing a resolve to treat all such propositions as hypotheses, which are liable to revision in the light of further experience.

Now we may or may not agree with this proposal. But even if we reject it in favour of allowing the existence of a physical object to be conclusively established by a finite number of sensory experiences, we shall still have to recognize that no description of any one such experience entails the descriptions of the others. So that, if the test which a proposition has to satisfy in order to be certain is that it should follow from the description of a particular experience, we shall still reach the conclusion that all propositions about physical objects are uncertain. But all that this then comes to is that a proposition about a physical object is something more than a description of some particular experience. To say that it is therefore uncertain is to imply that of all empirical statements only those that refer exclusively to some immediate, present, experience are to be regarded as certain. Now this, again, is not an account of ordinary usage. It is a philosopher's recommendation. The question which concerns us is why anyone should wish to make it.

The answer is that 'certainty' is reserved for statements of this kind because it is thought that they alone can not be challenged. If I make a statement of the form 'I perceive . . .' or 'I know . . .' or 'I remember . . .', the truth of my statement can be questioned. It may turn out that I was having an hallucination, or that what I claimed to know was false, or that my memory was betraying me. But suppose that I am more cautious. Suppose that I merely say 'It looks to me . . .', 'I have a feeling that . . .', 'I seem to remember. . . .' How can these statements be challenged? In what way could one set about refuting them? Of course, someone who says 'I feel a headache' or 'There is a red patch in the centre of my visual field' may be lying. But surely, it is argued, he must know whether he is lying or not. He can deceive others about what he sees or feels. But if his statement refers only to the content of his present experience, how can he possibly be mistaken? How can he even be in doubt as to whether it is true?

Let us look into this. Is it impossible that someone should wonder whether he was in pain? Certainly it would be a queer sort of doubt. Suppose that someone were to tell me 'You think you are in pain but you really aren't'. What should I understand him to be saying? Perhaps that nothing was wrong with me physically, that it was all my imagination, or, in other words, that the cause of my pain was psychological; and this might very well be true. But it would not follow that I was not feeling pain. To suggest to me that I do not feel it may be a way of making the pain stop; but that is a different matter. It does not alter the fact that when I feel the pain, I feel the pain. This is, indeed, an analytic truth.

But this, it may be objected, is not the point at issue. The question is 'What am I feeling?' Might I not think that it was pain when it was really something else? Might I not think that such and such a coloured patch was magenta when it was really scarlet? Might I not think that such and such a note was E sharp when it was really E natural? Surely one can misdescribe one's experience. And if one can misdescribe it, can one ever be certain that one is describing it correctly? Admittedly, I see what I see, feel what I feel, experience what I experience. That is a tautology. But, so it may be argued, it does not follow that I know what I am seeing, or that I know what I am feeling. For my knowing what I am seeing entails that some set of symbols, which I use to describe what I am seeing, does describe it correctly; and this may not be so.

But what is 'misdescribing' in this case? What is the test by which it is determined that the coloured patch which I have called 'magenta' is really scarlet. Is it a physical test? In that case I can very well be making a mistake, and a factual mistake. Is it what other people would say? Here again I can easily make a factual mistake. But suppose I intend merely to name what I am seeing. Can I be mistaken then? Plainly the answer is that I can not, if I am only naming. But if that is all that I am doing, then I am not saying anything at all. I can be neither wrong nor right. But directly I go beyond naming and try to describe something, then, it may be argued, I run the risk of being mistaken even about the character of my own immediate experience. For to describe anything is to relate it to something else, not necessarily to anything in the future, or to anything that other people experience, but at least to something that one has oneself experienced in the past. And the attributed relation may not, in fact, obtain.

Now this is a very common view, but I am persuaded that it is mistaken. No doubt, if I have learned to use a sensory predicate correctly in the first place, it will in fact be true that any object to which I properly apply it on any occasion other than the first will resemble some object to which I have properly applied it in the past. But it does not follow that in using the predicate I am making any reference to the past. Many philosophers have thought that it did follow, because they have assumed that an ostensive word was defined in terms of the resemblance of the objects which it denoted to some standard object. Thus, allowing, what is undoubtedly true, that I learned the use of the English word 'green' by being shown certain objects which resembled each other in respect of being green, it is suggested that what I now assert when I say, for example, that the blotting paper in front of me is green is that it resembles these objects in the way that they resembled one another. But this suggestion is false; and to see that it is false we have only to reflect that from the statement that this piece of blotting paper is green it cannot be deduced that anything else exists at all. No doubt, what justifies me in calling it green, as opposed, say, to blue, is the fact that it resembles one set of objects rather than another; but this does not mean that in calling it green I am saying that it resembles any other objects. There are two propositions here which we must be careful not to confuse. One is that if a and b are both green they resemble one another in colour more than either of them resembles in colour anything outside the class of green things; and the other is that if a is green there is at least one other

I

thing b which it resembles in colour more than it resembles in colour anything outside the class of green things. The first of these two propositions is analytic, it exemplifies the grammar of colour classification ; but the second is empirical. That there is such another thing b is at best a matter of fact which has to be established independently. It does not follow from the fact that a is green.

This shows, incidentally, how little is accomplished by talking about classes in preference to talking about predicates. For suppose that for 'a is green' we substitute 'a belongs to the class of green things'. Then how is the expression 'belongs to the class of green things' to be interpreted ? If it is merely a way of saying 'is a green thing' there is no point in the substitution. If it is taken as equivalent to 'is one of the things that are green', it is a mistranslation, since from the fact that a is green it does not follow that there are any other green things. If it is taken as equivalent to 'resembles other things in being green', it is again a mistranslation for the same reason as before. There remains the possibility that the class is to be defined by enumeration. But then we have the strange consequence that all ascriptions of class membership become either analytic or self-contradictory : analytic, in our example, if a, in fact, is green, since 'a is green' will then mean 'a is either a or b or c or d . . .', where the alternatives comprise the list of green things ; and self-contradictory if it is not, since 'a is green' will then mean 'a is either b or c or d . . .', where it is understood that b, c, d . . . are other than a. Another strange consequence will be that 'a is green' does not formally contradict 'a is not green' ; for if, in fact, a is not green, then 'a is not green' will mean 'a is not either b or c or *d* . . .', and if in fact *a* is green, then '*a* is green' will mean '*a* is either *a* or *b* or *c* or *d* . . .'; and these two propositions, so far from being incompatible, are both necessarily true. The explanation of this is that when it is interpreted in this way the meaning of the word 'green' varies according to its denotation. So that the result of turning predicates into classes and treating these classes extensionally is that one cannot tell what a sentence means until one knows whether it is true. Now I agree that to know what a sentence means is to know what would make it true. But it would ordinarily be held, and I think with reason, that one could not tell whether it was in fact true unless one already knew what it meant. For otherwise what would it be that one was verifying?

However this may be, the fact remains that the ascription to one member of a class of the predicate by which the class is defined does not imply that the class has any other members. And from this it follows that if I use a sensory predicate to describe what I am now experiencing I need not be making any claim about a situation other than the one before me. Accordingly, no appeal to such other situations can show that I am mistaken. They are not relevant, since my statement makes no reference to them. But then am I saying anything even about this situation? We seem here to have fallen into a dilemma. Either I just name the situation, in which case I am not making any statement about it, and no question of truth or falsehood, knowledge or ignorance, certainty or uncertainty, arises; or I describe it. And how can I describe it except by relating it to something else?

The answer is, I suggest, that I do describe it, not by relating it to anything else, but by indicating that a certain word applies to it in virtue of a meaning rule of the language. I may be in doubt as to its description in the sense that I may hesitate over what word to apply to it, and I may be mistaken about it in the sense that I may describe it incorrectly, the standard of correctness being furnished by my own verbal habits, or by the verbal habits of others who use the same language. Let me try to explain this further.

It would now be generally conceded that a descriptive language, as opposed to a merely formal language, is not sufficiently characterized by its formation and transformation rules. The formation rules prescribe what combinations of signs are to constitute proper sentences of the language; and the transformation rules prescribe what sentences are validly derivable from one another. But if we are to use and understand a language descriptively, we require also rules which correlate certain signs in the language with actual situations; and it is these that I am calling meaning rules. Thus it is a meaning rule of English that anyone who observes something green will be describing it correctly if he says that it is green; or that anyone who feels pain will be describing what he feels correctly if he says that he feels pain. These examples sound trivial, because the statement of these rules is not informative, except where it is a question of translation from one language into another. The rules are learned ostensively. The verbal statement of them is normally superfluous. For that reason it may even be misleading to call them 'rules' at all. But, whatever they may be called, unless one knows how to employ them, one does not understand the language. Thus, I understand the use of a word if I know in what situations to apply it. For this it is essential that I should be able to recognize the situations when I come upon them; but in order to effect this recognition it is not necessary that I should consciously compare these situations with memories of their predecessors. Neither is it necessary, as some philosophers have mistakenly supposed, that I should have a previous image with which the situation is found to agree. For if I can recognize the image, then I can recognize the situation without the image; and if I cannot recognize the image, then it does not help me to identify the situation. In either case its presence is superfluous. Whether I recognize the situation or not is to be decided by my behaviour; and one of the criteria is my being disposed to use the appropriate words.

Thus, the sense in which statements like 'This is green', 'I feel a headache', 'I seem to remember . . .' can be said to be indubitable is that, when they are understood to refer only to some immediate experience, their truth or falsehood is conclusively determined by a meaning rule of the language in which they are expressed. To deny them in the situations to which they refer is to misapply the language. And it is in this sense also that one can know for certain that they are true. But it is to be remarked that this is rather a case of knowing how than of knowing that. If I have an experience, say an experience of pain, it does not follow that I know what experience I am having. It is perfectly possible for me to have the experience without knowing anything at all. My knowing what experience it is is my being able to identify it as falling under a particular meaning rule. It is therefore not a matter of my knowing or ignoring some empirical fact but of my knowing or not knowing how to use my language. I have certain knowledge in the sense that the truth of what I say is not open to question, on the assumption that I am using my words correctly; but this is an assumption which remains open to doubt. And here the doubt is not like the ordinary empirical doubt, which turns upon the accuracy of some extrapolation, but like the logical doubt which we considered at the outset. It is to be settled by looking up the rules. But this again lets in the empirical doubt as to whether one has actually carried out the correct procedure. I am told that 'magenta' is the correct name for this colour, and I find this confirmed by the colour atlas. But perhaps my informant is deceiving me, or perhaps I misheard him, or perhaps this colour atlas is untrustworthy, or perhaps my eyes are playing me false. There are ways in which these suppositions can be tested, but the results of such tests can be questioned in their turn. So that here again the doubt may become neurotic and interminable. In this sense, therefore, nothing need be certain. Only, if nothing is allowed to be certain, the word 'certain' ceases to have any use.

It is sometimes made an objection to the choice of sensory predicates as basic that sense-experience is private. For it is argued that the fact that I have the sensations that I do is not of any great significance, since I cannot communicate them to anybody else. But the answer to this is that I can and do communicate them, inasmuch as my coming out with such and such a statement on such and such an occasion will count for another person as evidence in favour of the proposition that I am having such and such a sensation, and of any other proposition for which this proposition counts as evidence. His assumption is that I am using the language correctly; and this he can test by his own

observations of my behaviour and of my environment.
The meaning rules are impersonal in the sense that they
do no more than prescribe what words are to be used
in what situations. That some other person is in such
and such a situation is an empirical hypothesis which I
test by making observations, the proper description of
which will in its turn depend upon a further meaning
rule. The making of an observation is, of course, a
private experience. But this is not to say that my
description of it cannot be understood by anybody else.

It is, however, to be noted that while it is necessary
that a descriptive language should contain meaning
rules, it is not necessary that it should contain any
sentences which express basic propositions, if a basic
proposition is defined as one whose truth or falsehood
is conclusively established, in a given situation, by a
meaning rule of the language. It might be that the
rules were such that every correct description of an
empirical situation involved some reference beyond it;
and in that case, while the use of the sentence which
was dictated by the relevant meaning rule would be
justified in the given situation, its truth would not be
conclusively established. Suppose, for example, that
our language contained no purely sensory predicates,
so that the lowest level sentence that one could express
in it was a sentence which ascribed some property to a
physical object. Such a language could perfectly well
be understood and consistently applied. Words like
'table' would be introduced, as indeed they normally
are introduced, by meaning rules; and understanding
these words would again be a matter of knowing in
what situations to apply them. The difference would
be that from the fact that it was correct to use a given
sentence in a given situation it would not follow that

what the sentence expressed was true. That the use of the sentence was prescribed in these circumstances by a meaning rule would establish that what the sentence stated was probable but not that it was certain.

Thus, if my reasoning is sound, it is at least misleading to say that unless something is certain nothing can be even probable. What is true is that no proposition can ever be discovered to be even probable unless someone has some experience. But to say that someone has some experience is not, in any ordinary sense, to say that anything is certain. Whether anything is certain or not, in the sense which is here in question, will depend upon the meaning rules of the language; whether they are such as guarantee the truth or falsehood of a given statement in the appropriate situation, or merely justify its use. In neither case, as we have seen, is doubt excluded; but at the point where such doubt becomes perpetual, it ceases to be of any theoretical importance.

6

PHENOMENALISM

I

I SHALL be concerned in this paper with phenomenalism as a theory of perception. In the form in which it is
usually held nowadays, it is the theory that physical
objects are logical constructions out of sense-data.
Assuming that we understand what is meant by a
physical object, in the sense in which chairs and tables
and match-boxes are physical objects, we are left with
the questions: What is a logical construction? and
What are sense-data? At the risk of repeating an excessively familiar story, I shall begin with the sense-data.

I believe that the word 'sense-datum' was first used
as a technical term in philosophy by Bertrand Russell:
and he defined sense-data as objects of acquaintance.
But this definition leaves us none the wiser unless we
know what is meant in this context by 'acquaintance'.
In the ordinary way, we talk of being acquainted with
persons, or with places, or even with facts: but this
does not give us a sufficient indication of what it is to be
acquainted with a sense-datum. When someone tells
me that he is glad to make my acquaintance, no doubt
he is also making the acquaintance of sense-data, in
some sense, but the sense in which he is supposed to be
acquainted with them is not the same as that in which
he is acquainted with me. But in what sense, then, is

he acquainted with them? Some technical sense, presumably. But, if so, it needs to be explained: and until it has been explained the term 'sense-datum' has not been satisfactorily defined. Neither do we escape this difficulty by defining sense-data as the objects of 'sensing' or 'direct apprehension' or 'direct awareness', as various philosophers have proposed. For these also are technical terms, and there is no familiar usage of them by reference to which their meaning in this context is to be understood.

This may seem a trivial point, but I think that it is worth making because I suspect that behind these definitions lurks the suggestion that sense-data are objects of knowledge. That is, I suspect, that such artificial expressions as 'direct apprehension' or 'direct awareness', or even the more natural 'acquaintance', as they are used in this context, are euphemisms for the word 'knowledge', which is itself too sacred, or too dangerous, to pronounce. But if sense-data are to be defined as objects of knowledge then I do not think that there are sense-data, because I do not think that there are objects of knowledge. And by this I do not mean that it is just not the case that we know any objects, though we might have known some if we had been luckier or cleverer. Nor, like some philosophers, am I using the word 'knowledge' so strictly that everything that is ordinarily taken for knowledge turns out really not to be so. What I mean is that there cannot be objects of knowledge, because to speak of knowing objects, in the sense here intended, is to commit a type fallacy. Admittedly, the word 'know' is often used as a transitive verb. I may say, for example, that I know a person if I have been in his company, and we recognize each other when we meet: or, in a slightly different sense, I may say that I know him if by being in his company I have learned how he is likely to behave. Again, I may say that I know a place if I have been there ; or perhaps it may be required that I should have been there sufficiently often to be able to find my way about it, or for the various parts of it to be familiar to me. And many other examples could be given, in which the criteria for the proper use of 'know' as a transitive verb would be found to cover a fairly extensive range. But it is not this sort of thing that philosophers have in mind when they say, or imply, that there are objects of knowledge. The sense of 'know' with which they are concerned is the sense in which we speak of knowing that something or other is the case. And in this sense it is meaningless to speak of knowing objects. Failure to realize this has contributed, I think, to a famous piece of philosophical mythology, the act-object analysis of sensation. For once it is assumed that having a sensation involves knowing an object, then it may seem reasonable to apply to this case the principle that what is known must be independent of the knowing of it : and so we come to the fashionable refutations of Berkeley which consist in distinguishing the act of awareness, as a mental entity, from the object, not necessarily mental, which is the accusative of the act. But what are these acts of awareness supposed to be ? No doubt sentences of the form 'A is aware of X', or 'A is conscious of X', are often given a meaning which is such that the propositions which they then express are found to be true : but it does not follow from this that the expressions 'being aware of' or 'being conscious of' are names for anything. And, indeed, not only do I not find any referents for such names when I analyse my sensations empirically, but I do not know what they are supposed to stand for. I do not know what it would be like to come upon an act of awareness. Consequently, if sense-data were defined as the objects of such acts, I should remain unconvinced that there were sense-data.

Professor Price, who has made himself the guardian of sense-data — he is not their parent but it is he who has chiefly interested himself in their welfare: it is to him more than anyone that they owe their present position of honour in the philosophical world — has another method of defining them. He says that when I look at a physical object, for instance a tomato, there is much that I can doubt. I can doubt whether it is not a reflection, or a cleverly painted piece of wax, or even a complete hallucination. But, he goes on to argue, there remains something that I cannot doubt. I cannot doubt that 'there exists a red patch of a round and somewhat bulgy shape, standing out from a background of other colour-patches, and having a certain visual depth, and that this whole field of colour is directly present to my consciousness'. And it is this object whose existence I cannot doubt that he proposes to call a sense-datum. But why can I not doubt it? What prevents me? It is not a question of my psychology. It is not just that I cannot now bring myself to doubt the existence of this bulgy patch, because that leaves open the possibility that I might. If I schooled myself in doubting, I might achieve it. But clearly this is not what Price means. He wants to say that the existence of what he calls the sense-datum is objectively beyond doubt: so that if anyone managed to deny it, he would necessarily be wrong. Thus, there is a sense in which, having accepted the premisses of a valid deductive argument, I cannot doubt the conclusion,

though there is also a sense in which I can doubt it,
since I may not be sure that I have drawn the inference
correctly. Similarly, I may be unsure of the truth of an
analytic proposition, but there is also a sense in which
it may be said that I cannot doubt it, if it is necessarily
true. It is not in this sense, however, that I cannot
doubt the existence of the bulgy patch. For it would
not be self-contradictory to say that no such object
existed. But perhaps what is meant when it is said that
I cannot doubt the existence of the patch is that it does
not make sense to say 'I doubt if this patch exists'. It
may be suggested that the reason why I cannot doubt
it is that one cannot properly speak of doubting in such
a case. But the trouble with this is that there is a
perfectly good sense in which it can be said that I
doubt if this bulgy patch exists. If I were not sure
whether the appearance of the patch in question was
not a constituent of a dream, it would be entirely
proper to describe my situation by saying that I doubted
whether the patch existed. Accordingly, one has to go
on to explain that the sense in which it is meaningless
to say 'I doubt if this patch exists' is the special sense
that is appropriate to sense-data and not to physical
objects. And thus we are once more brought back in
a circle.

All the same, it is not very hard to see what Price
and the other philosophers who talk about sense-data
are getting at. For suppose that I am having an
experience which it would be natural for me to describe
by saying that I was holding a match-box in my hand
and looking at it. In that case, assuming the experience
to be veridical, there is a familiar sense of the words
'see' and 'touch' in which what I am now seeing and
touching is simply 'this match-box'. And there is also

a familiar sense of the words 'see' and 'touch' in which what I am now seeing and touching is not the whole match-box but only a part of its surface. Now, in both these senses, if it should happen that the match-box does not exist, if I am dreaming or having an illusion, then either I am seeing something, or a part of something, other than a match-box, something that I mistake for a match-box, or, in the case of a total hallucination, I am not seeing or touching anything. But it is also possible to use the words 'see' and 'touch' in such a way that even if I am dreaming or having a complete hallucination, so that there is no physical object there, it can still be said that there is some object that I am seeing or touching, and further, that this object really has the characteristics that the physical object, which I mistakenly think that I am seeing or touching, in the other senses of the words 'see' and 'touch', appears to me to have. And what I am seeing in *this* sense may perhaps be a certain patch of colour, 'standing out from a background of other colour patches and having a certain visual depth', though I am inclined on psychological grounds to doubt whether this would be an accurate description of any normal visual experience. Let us then call the whole of what everyone sees in this sense at any given moment, his 'visual sense-field'. Then a visual sense-datum may be defined as anything that is the constituent of a visual sense-field. And, in general, a sense-datum may be defined as anything that is the constituent of a sense-field.

At this point it may be objected that I have not got away from the act-object analysis of sensation. For I have explained the use of the word 'sense-datum' in terms of a special use of words like 'touch' and 'see' and these are transitive verbs. But the answer is that there is no need to assume that such words as 'seeing' and 'touching', in this usage, are names for mental acts. If the word 'sensing' be used to designate the experience of which seeing, touching, and the rest, in this usage, are the various modes, then to say of something that it is sensed need be taken to imply no more than that it is sensibly present, or, in other words, that it appears : and to specify that it is seen or touched is merely to indicate what manner of appearance is in question. We might therefore say that to be seen is to appear visually, that to be touched is to appear tactually, and so on, though we should still have to distinguish different senses of 'appear' as correlates of the different senses of 'touch' and 'see'. Thus what we obtain by introducing the term 'sense-datum' is a means of referring to appearances without prejudging the questions what it is, if anything, that they are appearances *of*, and what it is, if anything, that they appear *to*. And here it may be advisable to make the familiar point that the use of this term 'sense-datum' is not intended to carry any factual implications about the character of these appearances. It is not designed, for example, to beg the question in favour of an atomic as opposed to a *Gestalt* theory of sensation. Thus, when philosophers like Professor Stout make it an objection to 'the sense-datum theory', and so to phenomenalism, that what is sensibly 'given' is something more substantial than a mere sense-datum, their argument is beside the mark. It is an empirical question whether the contents, say, of a visual-field are more accurately to be described as patches of colour or coloured 'objects'. But even if it is decided, on empirical grounds, that what is seen is, in some sense, a coloured 'object', it will still be a sense-datum, according to our usage.

Now if the word 'sense-datum' is understood in this way, then if it is ever true that a physical object is being perceived, it must also be true that some sense-datum is being sensed. If, for example, it is a fact that I am seeing a match-box, in the appropriate sense of the word 'see', then it *follows* that, in the appropriately different sense of the word 'see', I am seeing some sense-datum. But the converse does not hold. I believe that I am now perceiving a match-box and this belief is directly based on the evidence of my senses. But from the fact that I am sensing the sense-data that I am now sensing it does not *follow* that I am perceiving a match-box. For if we disregard all the other evidence available to me, including the evidence of my memories, my having the sense-experiences that I am now having is compatible with there being no such match-box there; it is compatible with my being the victim of an illusion. Thus, when I say, truly as it happens, that I am now perceiving a match-box, part of what I am saying is that I am sensing sense-data of a certain kind; but only part. I am saying that and something more. But what more? That is our problem. And the phenomenalists' answer to it is that the more that I am saying is that further sense-data of the appropriate sort would, in the appropriate conditions, be obtainable.

If this answer is correct, then it seems to follow that the statement that I am perceiving this match-box, or whatever other physical object may be taken as an example, must be equivalent to some set of statements about sense-data. And since to say that I am perceiving a match-box entails saying that the match-box exists, the statement that this match-box exists must also, in that case, be equivalent to some set of statements about sense-data. And to say, as phenomenalists do, that physical objects are logical constructions out of sense-data is merely another way of expressing this. It does not mean that physical objects are literally composed of sense-data, or that physical objects are fictions and only sense-data real. It means simply that statements about physical objects are somehow reducible to statements about sense-data, or, as it is sometimes put, that to say anything about a physical object is to say something, though not necessarily the same thing, about sense-data. This, then, is the claim that we have to discuss.

2

The first point to be made is that if we confine ourselves to actual sense-data, this claim can evidently not be upheld. For to revert to our example, this match-box is not continuously perceived either by me or by anybody else. And yet at times when no one is perceiving it, that is, when there are no sense-data that are directly relevant to its existence, the match-box may still exist. In other words, it is not self-contradictory, though it may in certain cases be false, to say both that a given physical object exists in a certain place, and throughout a certain period of time, and that during that period of time no one was sensing any such sense-data as would constitute direct evidence for the existence of the physical object in question. Consequently, if the sense-datum language is to do the work that phenomenalists require of it, it must permit us to refer to possible sense-data. And what this means is that some at least of the statements about sense-data that are supposed to yield the equivalence of statements about physical objects will have to be hypothetical. They will have to state not that any sense-data have occurred, are

K

occurring, or will occur, but that in certain specifiable conditions certain sense-data would occur. The
difficulty, as we shall see, is to specify the conditions.

Now it would seem that the best way for a
phenomenalist to prove his case would be to set about
giving us some examples. We should expect him to
take a statement like 'there is a flower-pot on the
window sill', and give us its equivalent in terms of
sense-data. But this is something that no phenomenalist has ever yet done, or even, to my knowledge, seriously tried to do. We are told that statements about
physical objects must be translatable into statements
about sense-data, but we do not get any translations.
The most we get are more or less vague descriptions
of the sort of way such translations might run. We are
given recipes for making translations; but they seem
to be recipes that no one can ever put into use. One
reason for this, of course, is the poverty of our sensory
language. The vocabulary that we have for describing
colours, shapes, and the rest is not sufficient for our
purpose: so that we are constantly reduced to saying
things like 'the sort of sense-data that you get when you
look at a match-box' or 'the sort of sense-data that you
get when you hear a telephone ring', where the reference
to the physical object is needed to identify the sense-
data in question. But I suppose that a suitable vocabulary could be invented, if some ingenious person
thought that it was worth his trouble: so that if this
were all that stood in the phenomenalist's way he
might be entitled to hold that his programme could be
carried out, 'at least in principle'. But there are more
serious difficulties.

One that is often brought forward is that no statement about a physical object can be conclusively

verified, on the ground that, however much favourable evidence there may be for it, it is always conceivable that further evidence will show it to have been false all along. And from this premiss it is correctly deduced that no statement about a physical object can be equivalent to any finite set of statements about sense-data. For each of the statements about sense-data will be a description of a single piece of evidence in favour of the statement about the physical object; and if the evidence is to be sufficient the number of these descriptions must be infinite. I used to accept this argument but now I am inclined to reject it. The assumption is that if, for example, I am looking at my telephone and suddenly see it change into what appears to be a flower-pot, or vanish altogether, or what you will, that proves that it never was a telephone. To put the case more precisely, suppose that a series of visual and tactual sense-data were succeeded 'in the same place', which here may be taken to mean 'in similar spatial relations to similar sense-data', by sense-data characteristic of the appearance of a flower-pot, or that, while the surrounding conditions appear to remain unchanged, there cease to be any sense-data characteristic of the appearance of a physical object in the 'place' where the sense-data characteristic of the appearance of a telephone previously were, that proves that I must have been mistaken in taking these sense-data to be the appearances of a real telephone. But does it? The only way of deciding what it proves is to consider what one would say in such a case, that is, how one would describe such a situation. What I should, in fact, say would be that my present experience was hallucinatory: that the illusion lay not in the long series of my past 'perceptions' of a telephone, but in my present 'perception' of a flower-pot.

But suppose that I applied the usual tests for hallucinations, and that they were negative. Suppose that the object that I seemed to be perceiving felt as well as looked like a flower-pot, and that it went on looking and feeling like a flower-pot, and that when I asked other people about it they said that they perceived a flower-pot too. In that case I should probably give up the idea that I was having a hallucination, though it may be remarked that if the evidence that previously led me to believe that I was perceiving a telephone was not conclusive, then the evidence that I was not subsequently having a hallucination with regard to the flower-pot would not be conclusive either. If no evidence is conclusive all the competing hypotheses remain open. But suppose that the evidence is such that I do, in fact, rule out the hypothesis that my 'perception' of the flower-pot is a sustained illusion. I *might* then say that I had been deceived all the time about the telephone. I might even start to distrust my memory, and wonder whether it had not always been the case that I perceived a flower-pot, though here the testimony of others would be a check. But what I think I *should* say is : ' It *was* a telephone and all of a sudden it changed into a flower-pot'. I should think this odd, certainly. I should probably write to the newspapers about it. And then if the ensuing correspondence showed me that other people had had similar experiences, I should begin to feel more comfortable. ' It has to be admitted ', I should say, ' that physical objects do sometimes undergo these abrupt changes. I wonder what the scientific explanation is.'

No doubt this example sounds excessively fanciful, but not long ago I did have a fountain pen that suddenly vanished. At one moment I was looking at it, touching it, writing with it, and the next moment it had

disappeared. I could not find it any more and never
have found it to this day. Of course, I do not really
believe that it vanished. 'Pens do not just vanish', I
say, in default of stronger evidence that they do. But
still less do I believe that it never was a pen. I do not
say: 'The run of favourable evidence has come to an
end as I was always warned that it might. My belief
that it really was a pen that I was perceiving implied
that the run of favourable evidence would continue
indefinitely. Consequently my belief was false.' What
I say is: 'There must be some explanation. Perhaps
I turned my back on it for an instant, though I do not
remember doing so, and somebody crept in and took it.
Or, more probably, it dropped somewhere and I have
not searched for it hard enough.' And from this I
conclude that when I said, as I often have in the past,
like other philosophers, that however strongly one's
sense-data may support the hypothesis that one is
perceiving a physical object of a certain sort, further
experience may show one to have been mistaken, I was
not serious. For when a situation arose which, on the
face of it, supported this view, I did not interpret it in
that way at all. I did not even seriously consider the
possibility that what I had for so long been taking to be
a pen never really had been a pen. Neither do I think
that I am peculiar in this respect. I think that the
explanation that it never really was a pen is one that,
in the circumstances, nobody would consider seriously.

What bearing has this upon the phenomenalist's
claim? As I said before, no single sense-experience,
taken by itself, ever proves that a physical object exists.
From the bare fact that I am sensing *these* visual sense-
data it does not follow that this is a match-box. Nevertheless the occurrence of these visual sense-data, taken

in conjunction with what I remember, fully justifies the
statement that this is a match-box, and would justify
it, I should now maintain, even if the 'match-box' were
to vanish the next instant. By itself the occurrence
of just these sense-data would not be sufficient, but
in conjunction with previous experience it is. This
previous experience may consist of previous perceptions
of the physical object in question, that is, previous
sensings of the appropriate sense-data, but it need not.
In certain circumstances I might be fully justified in
believing in the existence of a physical object that I had
never before perceived : and in such cases the strength
of the evidence would lie in the general character of my
previous experience. For my belief that *this* is a physical object, and a physical object of a certain sort, is not
based solely on the occurrence of sense-data which are
manifestations of *this* : it is derived also from a more
general belief that I live in a world of physical objects
of which things that look like this are specimens : and
this belief is supported by a mass of past experiences.
So much so that if this assumption were to break down
altogether, if, from this moment on, sense-data were
to arrange themselves, as Price once suggested they
might, in an eurhythmic rather than a thing-like order,[1]
I should not say : 'I was wrong all the time : there
never were any physical objects'. I should say : 'The
world has changed : there used to be physical objects,
but now there are none any more'.

Does it follow then that at any rate some statements
about a physical object can be translated into statements about sense-data, namely into those statements
which describe the sense-data, past and present, the
occurrence of which fully justifies us, on the occasions

[1] Vide *The Terminology of Sense-data*, p. 104.

when we are so justified, in asserting that the physical object exists? Not necessarily. For in that case the truth of the statements referring to sense-data would be both a necessary and a sufficient condition of the truth of the statement about the physical object. And while I have argued that in certain cases it may be sufficient, I have not shown, nor do I think that it can be shown, that it is also necessary. No doubt the truth of some statement or other about sense-data is always a necessary condition of the truth of any statement which implies the existence of a physical object: but I do not think that it is ever possible to discover a finite set of statements about sense-data of which it can truly be said in a particular case that precisely these are necessary. In other words, though you may be able to discover sets of sufficient conditions, you cannot list them exhaustively. You cannot say, for example, exactly how much experience, nor exactly what type of experience, a child must have had in order to be fully justified, on the evidence available to him, in saying: 'This is a ball'. In a concrete case you can safely allow that he has sufficient evidence. But you cannot rightly say that it is necessary, because there will always be an indefinite number of other sensory experiences that would have done just as well. Thus, it makes no difference whether his general belief in the existence of physical objects is derived from the sense-data he has obtained when playing with rattles or when playing with teddy-bears: it makes no difference whether he punches the ball or strokes it, whether the angle from which he sees it makes it appear round to him or oval, whether the light is such that it seems to him to be red or orange. The sense-data that are sufficient, in conjunction with his previous experience, to establish the existence of the ball must all fall within a certain range : a sense-datum characteristic of the appearance of an alarm-clock would not fit the case : but the number of possible sense-data that fall within that range is indefinite, while the previous sensory experiences that may go to make the present evidence sufficient not only are indefinite in number, but themselves fall within a range that is extremely wide. And this is one reason why it is impossible to translate a statement about a physical object into any finite set of statements about sense-data. It is not, as has sometimes been suggested, that the physical object is eternally on probation, so that to try to establish its existence by sense-perception is like trying to fill a bottomless well. The reason is that all statements about physical objects are indefinite. The well can be filled, but there are an infinite number of ways of filling it. Consequently, the comparatively definite statements that one makes about sense-data, to the effect that such and such sense-data are being or have been obtained, or that in such and such conditions such and such sense-data would be obtained, cannot be exact translations of the indefinite statements that one makes about physical objects. And by this I mean not, of course, that a statement about a physical object is necessarily indefinite at its own level, but that it is necessarily indefinite at the level of sense-data.

3

If this be admitted, what becomes of the phenomenalist's case ? What is there left for him to claim ? It has been suggested that he should claim no more than that the direct evidence for the existence of a physical object is always the occurrence of some sense-

datum. But if this were all there would be nothing to
discuss. For, as I have already shown, the term
'sense-datum' may be defined in such a way that if
anyone is perceiving a physical object it *follows* that he
is sensing a sense-datum: and not only that but that
all that his senses reveal to him is the presence of
sense-data. This does not mean that his sensory
experiences must be of the sort that we are all familiar
with: they might be very queer indeed: but however
queer they were they would still be experiences of
sense-data. Now it is not to be disputed that the direct
evidence for the existence of physical objects is sensory
evidence: for any evidence that was not sensory would
not be called direct. And clearly if you decide to call
obtaining such evidence 'sensing sense-data' it will
follow that you can obtain such evidence only by sensing
sense-data. The only question then is whether you
agree with the proposal to use the *word* 'sense-datum'.
But surely those who have taken, or accepted, the title
of phenomenalists have thought that they were doing
more than extending their patronage to a word.

Yes, but what more? What is the point of introducing the sense-datum vocabulary? The idea is that
it helps you to learn something about the nature of
physical objects, not indeed in the way that doing
science does, but that you come to understand better
what is meant by propositions about physical objects,
what these propositions amount to, what their 'cash
value' is, by restating them in terms of sense-data.
That is, the fact that you *can* restate them in this way,
if you can, tells you something important about them.
Furthermore, it is claimed that if you talk in terms of
sense-data you are somehow getting deeper than if you
are content to talk, as we all do in everyday life, in terms

of physical objects. The naïve realist is not in error. Naïve realism is not a false theory of perception : it is a refusal to play this sort of game. And if a man will not play he cannot lose. But one is inclined to say that the naïve realist is missing something by refusing to play : that he is not getting to the root of the matter. And the justification for this is that there is a sense in which the sense-datum language is logically prior to the physical-object language. For it is impossible that a physical object should be perceived without its being true that some sense-datum is being sensed : but it is not impossible that any number of sense-data should be sensed without its ever being true that any physical object is perceived. For the relations between sense-data in virtue of which we are justified in claiming that we perceive physical objects are contingent : they might conceivably not have obtained.

But now it turns out that for the reasons I have given, statements about physical objects cannot be translated into statements about sense-data. Consequently, the phenomenalist is obliged to give up his original position. But he need modify it only slightly. He cannot show precisely what you are saying about sense-data when you make a given statement about a physical object, because you are not saying anything precise about sense-data. Nevertheless, he will maintain, what you are saying, though vague, still refers ultimately to sense-data and does not refer to anything other than sense-data. Consequently, he can hope to give a suitably vague translation. It should be possible to indicate at least what sort of thing we are saying about sense-data when we make a statement like 'there is a match-box on the table'. And if the phenomenalist can do this he may be allowed to have proved his case.

The *a priori* argument for supposing that this must be possible is that if we are not referring to sense-data, and exclusively to sense-data, when we talk about physical objects, it is difficult to see what we can be referring to. 'Physical objects', is the unkind answer; and, of course, it is a correct answer, correct but unhelpful. For if we use the sense-datum language — and we have not found any good reason why we should not use it; it has not been shown that it necessarily involves any assumptions that are either logically or empirically mistaken — then it looks as if we are using it as a substitute for the physical-object language. The world does not contain sense-data *and* physical objects, in the sense in which it contains chairs *and* tables, or in the sense in which it contains colours *and* sounds. One is inclined to say, therefore, that phenomenalism must be true, on the ground that the only alternative to it, once we have agreed to use the sense-datum terminology, is the iron-curtain theory of perception: that physical objects are there sure enough but we can never get at them, because all we can observe is sense-data: and surely this theory at least can be shown to be untenable.

4

All the same, there are difficulties in the way of the phenomenalists. One, which I shall now try to meet, concerns the question of causation. Regarded by Professor Stout as a fatal objection to phenomenalism,[1] it led Professor Price to postulate, as the owners of causal properties, a set of unobservable entities to which he gives the name of 'physical occupants',[2] a piece of

---

[1] G. F. Stout, 'Phenomenalism', *Proceedings of the Aristotelian Society*, 1938–39.   [2] H. H. Price, 'Perception', chaps. ix and x.

mythology which I understand that he has since repudiated — and it has recently been restated with force and clarity by Mr. W. F. R. Hardie.[1] The difficulty is this :

Our perceptions are fragmentary. We do not perceive all the physical objects that there are all the time : and yet we believe, and often have good reason to believe, that some of them exist when no one is perceiving them. And not only this, but we often have good reason to believe that they are causally efficacious when no one is perceiving them. An example that Price gives is that of a concealed magnet which causes the observed deflection of a compass needle. Now it may be held that what are described as causal relations between physical objects, or physical events, are analysable in terms of regularities among sense-data. But the trouble is that in a great many cases in which we postulate causal relationships, the required sensory regularities are not observed. Assuming that I perceive the deflection of Price's compass needle, then I am sensing certain visual sense-data, and the occurrence of these sense-data may, it is said, be described as an event. But the existence of the magnet throughout the relevant period of time is not an event in the same sense. For *ex hypothesi* no sense-data 'belonging to' the magnet are occurring. You may analyse the statement that the magnet exists into a hypothetical statement to the effect that if certain conditions were fulfilled, sense-data characteristic of the appearance of the magnet would be obtained. But since the conditions in question are not in fact fulfilled, the statement that the magnet exists does not, when analysed in sensory terms, describe any

[1] W. F. R. Hardie, 'The Paradox of Phenomenalism', *Proceedings of the Aristotelian Society*, 1945–46.

actual event. It does not, when so analysed, say that
anything exists, but only, to quote Mr. Hardie, that
given certain conditions something would exist which
actually does not. But this is to fall into the absurdity,
as Stout calls it, of supposing that 'actual occurrences
depend upon mere possibilities'. For surely it is self-
evident that actual events have actual causes. A mere
possibility cannot be a cause.

Let me try to state this objection more clearly. The
argument may be set out in the following way. It
makes sense to say that physical objects exist and are
causally efficacious at times when no one is perceiving
them. There may, therefore, be unobserved physical
events and they may stand in causal relations to other
unobserved events, or to observed events. Now, if the
phenomenalists are right, an unobserved physical event
is reducible to a set of possible sensory events. But on
an 'agency' view of causation this is incompatible with
its being the cause, since a mere set of possibilities
cannot *do* anything. And the same is true even on a
'regularity' view of causation : for a possible sensory
occurrence is not an event in the sense in which
an actual sensory occurrence is an event, and the
regularities must be assumed to hold between events
of the same type. It is impossible, therefore, for the
phenomenalists to explain how unobserved physical
events can be causes. Consequently phenomenalism
is false.

As Mr. Hardie has pointed out to me, the argument
may be made independent of the empirical premiss that
our perceptions are fragmentary, or, in other words, that
some physical events are unobserved. For whether or
not a physical event is observed, the observation of it is
not logically necessary to its occurrence. That is to say,

the statement that it occurs does not entail the statement that it is observed to occur. Consequently, the
phenomenalist's analysis of a statement which describes
the occurrence of a physical event need refer only to
possible sense-data, though actual sense-data may have
to be brought in if the statement at the physical level
itself involves a reference to a percipient. Furthermore,
the causal properties of physical objects adhere to them
whether they are observed or not. If, therefore, the
phenomenalist is to allow that any physical events are
causes he must maintain that a set of possibilities can
be a cause. And this, in the eyes of those who raise this
objection, is a manifest absurdity.

This argument has convinced many people, but I
think that it is fallacious, and that the fallacy lies partly
in a confusion over the use of the word 'cause', and
partly in an ambiguity in the use of the word 'event'.
I am perfectly willing to admit that an actual event, if it
has a cause at all, must have an actual cause, though
even here there is a play on the word 'actual', since in
many cases what is called the cause will be a past event,
and so, in a sense, no longer 'actual'. Still I will grant
that, if an event has a cause, that cause must itself be an
event which is 'actual' in the sense that it either is
actually occurring or has at some time actually occurred.
But in this proposition the word 'event' is being used
as a term at the physical level. I do not mean by this
that an event, in this sense of the word, must be physical: it may also be mental: but it is at the physical
level inasmuch as it occupies a position in physical
time, as opposed to sensory time, and inasmuch as it
occupies a position in physical space, as opposed to
sensory space, if it is spatially located at all. In this
sense both the deflection of the needle, to recur to

Price's example, and the state of the magnet are actual events, whether they are observed or not. The magnet actually exercises the causal properties in virtue of which the needle is deflected : that is to say, the deflection of the needle can be explained by reference to the properties of the magnet. But this is in no way incompatible with the phenomenalist's view that a proposition asserting the existence of the magnet and describing its causal properties is equivalent to a set of purely hypothetical properties about sense-data. Again, the actual event which is my observing the deflection of the compass needle also has actual causes, including certain processes in my nervous system, which are not themselves observed. Or, in other words, the truth of the proposition that I am observing a compass needle is connected by a well-established theory with the truth of certain other propositions, themselves not directly verified on this occasion, which refer among other things to processes in my nervous system. These propositions are all at the physical level. They are categorical, and consequently they describe actual events, in the appropriate sense of 'event'. But once more this is perfectly compatible with their being analysable into hypothetical propositions about sense-data. Only — and this is the important point — the sense-datum propositions, even those that are categorical, do not describe events in the same sense of the word 'event'. The 'events' that they describe are not in physical time or in physical space. And it is only at the physical level that causal relations hold between actual events. It is indeed only at the physical level that events can properly be said to have causes at all.

This being so, the trouble arises when, instead of asking what is the cause of my observing the compass needle, which is a legitimate question, or even what is the cause of my sensing sense-data 'belonging to' the compass needle, which is still a legitimate question, so long as 'my sensing the sense-data' is taken as the description of a process which takes place in physical time, we ask what is the cause of the sense-data themselves. For this is a nonsensical question. It is nonsensical because the sense-data are not events in the sense in which the deflection of the needle is an event, so that the term 'cause' which is understood as a relation between events at the physical level, does not apply to them. Unfortunately phenomenalists, among whom I must here include myself, have usually failed to see this and so have fallen into the trap of meeting the question 'What is the cause of these sense-data?' with the answer 'Other sense-data'. And in this way they have gratuitously laid themselves open to the sort of objection that Stout and Hardie raise.

To make it clear that such objections are invalid, we may restate the phenomenalist's answer as follows: There are well-established theories, or hypotheses, which connect different propositions at the physical level. There is, for example, a well-established theory of electro-magnetics through which a proposition describing the deflection of a compass needle can be connected with a proposition describing the state of a magnet; that is, the proposition referring to the needle will, given certain conditions, be deducible from the proposition about the magnet in conjunction with the propositions of the theory. When this is so, then, if the hypotheses in question are of certain specifiable types, we say that the event described by one of these propositions is a cause of the event described by the other. This is not by any means the only sense in which

we use the word 'cause', but it is the sense that is
relevant to the present argument. Both events are
actual, in the sense that the propositions which describe
them are categorical, but these propositions, which
are categorical at the physical level, are reducible to
hypothetical propositions about sense-data. This may
be expressed by saying that the physical events in
question are analysable into sets of possible sensory
occurrences; but these sensory occurrences are not
events, in the same sense of 'event'; neither can they
have, or be, causes in the same sense of 'cause'. It is
therefore misleading to say that sense-data depend
upon one another: for this suggests that they can
possess causal properties in the same way as physical
objects, which is not the case. They can, however, be
correlated with one another, and it is only because they
can be so correlated that we have any reason to believe in
the existence of causal connections between physical
events. Indeed to say that there is a causal connection between physical events is, in the last analysis, to
make a very complicated statement about correlations
between sense-data. The sense-data which are correlated may be actual, but they need not be. For
the basis of the correlation is always a hypothetical
proposition to the effect that a sense-datum of a certain
sort occurs if in certain conditions a sense-datum of a
certain other sort occurs, and it is not necessary for the
truth of such a proposition either that the protasis or
that the apodosis should be actually fulfilled. Thus a
proposition of the form 'if, if p then q, then, if r then s'
may very well be true even though p, q, r, and s are all
false. Consequently in the case of sense-data, there is
no absurdity in making actual occurrences 'depend
upon' mere possibilities: for there is no absurdity in

L

saying that a categorical proposition would not be true unless some hypothetical proposition were true. This hypothetical proposition states that such and such an event would occur if certain conditions were fulfilled, and there is no absurdity in holding that it may still be true even if the requisite conditions happen not to be fulfilled. But this is all that the 'dependence' of actual upon possible sense-data comes to. What makes it seem an absurdity is the misleading terminology of 'causes' and 'events'.

5

So far, I hope, so good: but the conception of 'possible sense-data' still involves certain difficulties. It is usually illustrated by some such example as 'the "family" of sense-data which constitutes the table in the next room is possible in the sense that if I were there I should be sensing one of its members': and with that we are supposed to be content. But I do not think that we should be content with anything so simple as that. To begin with, the choice of such an example covers two very important assumptions. It is assumed both that the introduction of myself as an observer would not affect what I am supposed to observe, and that the conditions would be such as to allow of my observing: and neither of these assumptions will be justified in all cases. Consider, for example, the proposition that Dr. Crippen murdered his wife in his house in Camden Town in the year 1910. Now the suggestion is that this means that if I had been there at the appropriate time I should have sensed certain sense-data, namely, such as would constitute a sensory manifestation of a man, answering to the description of Dr. Crippen, engaged in murdering his wife. But even allowing that there is a sense in which I logically *could* have been there, although in actual fact I was not yet born, the answer is that even if I had been there I almost certainly should not have sensed anything of the kind. It is most unlikely that Dr. Crippen would have murdered his wife while I was looking on. But here it may be objected that the word 'I' in this context does not refer explicitly to me. It is a variable, not a constant. What is meant is that if *anybody* had been there, he would have sensed the requisite sense-data. But it is most unlikely that Dr. Crippen would have murdered his wife while anybody, other than an accomplice, was looking on. Besides why do we have to say 'If anybody had been there'. Somebody *was* there. Dr. Crippen was. And he must have sensed a host of sense-data while he was murdering his wife and subsequently dismembering her. So, up to a certain point in the story, did his wife. So why should we not just say that a number of interesting sense-data occurred in such and such a part of Camden Town on such and such a day in the year 1910 ? We shall see later on why this will not do either.

Again, take the proposition that the sun, though it may look no larger than a man's hand, is really very large indeed, so many thousand miles in diameter. Does this mean that if I were very close to it I should see it stretching out enormously in all directions, or that if I laid measuring rods along it of the requisite sort I should sense the required coincidences of sense-data ? But if I were very close to it I should not see anything at all, I should be shrivelled up : and my operation with the measuring rods could not be carried out. Of course it is possible to carry out some operations with a view to determining the dimensions of the

sun : for how else should we, in fact, determine them ?
But these operations are ordinarily thought to provide
only indirect, and not direct, evidence for the conclusions that they establish. Whereas what the phenomenalist is seeking to describe is an observation that
would constitute direct evidence : and the objection
is that in the conditions that he postulates such direct
evidence may not be physically obtainable.

Professor Price has suggested to me that these
difficulties can be overcome by making suitable assumptions about the character of the observer. Thus it is
not necessary, he supposes, that the hypothetical
witness of Dr. Crippen's act should be a human being ;
it might be a mouse. Or, if a human being be insisted
upon, the observer might be assumed to be looking
through the keyhole, or surveying the proceedings
from afar through a telescope. Or it might be made a
supplementary condition that Dr. Crippen should be
affected with psychic blindness, so that he would have
gone about his business just as if no intruder had been
there, in exactly the way, in fact, in which he *did*
go about his business, since no intruder *was* there.
Similarly, in the example of the sun, I might credit
myself hypothetically with an uninflammable body, so
that I could make my observations without being
shrivelled up. And in this case it can also be argued
that all that is required is that the observations should
be 'possible in principle' : so that it is not a fatal objection to the analysis that they would not be made in fact.

But if the fact is that the desired observations would
not be made in the stated conditions then the hypothetical propositions in which it is affirmed that they
would be made are false : and since the categorical
proposition of which they are offered as an analysis may

nevertheless be true, the analysis is incorrect. To say that the observations are 'possible in principle' is merely to say that one can conceive of the conditions being such that they would be made : but it is just the specification of the conditions that constitutes our problem. Neither do I think that the difficulty can be met in the sort of way that Price suggests. For, in his examples, the truth of the hypothetical proposition is dependent upon the truth of some physical or psychological law, as that murderers are not deterred by the presence of mice or that gaseous bodies are not shrivelled by great heat : and while these laws may be valid, their validity is not involved in that of the propositions which we are trying to analyse. After all, Dr. Crippen *might* have been put off by the presence of a mouse : it *might* be the case that when Professor Price approached the sun in his gaseous body he still could not make the required observations. But, however this might be, it would remain true that Dr. Crippen *did* murder his wife, and that the sun has the diameter that it has. And this means that even if we recast our hypothetical propositions in such agreeably fantastic forms as Price suggests, they will still not be equivalent to the propositions of which they are supposed to be the analyses.

Neither is this the only difficulty. So far, in referring to the conditions which go to constitute the 'possibility' of sense-data, in any given case, I have used such phrases as 'if I were in the next room', or 'if any observer had been there' : and it is in such terms as these that phenomenalists do usually talk when they try to indicate the sort of way in which they would analyse propositions about unperceived physical objects. Thus Berkeley, for once ignoring God, says that 'the question whether the earth moves amounts in reality to no more than this, to wit, whether we have reason to conclude from what has been observed by astronomers, that if we were placed in such and such circumstances, and such or such a position and distance, both from the earth and sun, we should perceive the former to move'.[1] But to speak of 'my' or 'our' being in a certain position is to speak about a physical object, namely a human body, and to speak of its position involves a reference to other physical objects, in Berkeley's example the earth and the sun. No doubt he is 'speaking with the vulgar': he has to in order to make himself intelligible; so do we all. But how do 'the learned' speak in this case? If the phenomenalist is to make good his claim that categorical propositions about physical objects are reducible to hypothetical propositions about sense-data, it is not enough that he should indicate what the apodoses of his hypotheticals come to in sensory terms: he must do the same with the protases also. But how is this to be done?

Professor Price deals with this point in the fifth chapter of his book on *Hume's Theory of the External World*.[2] He remarks truly that the phenomenalistic analysis of any 'material-object statement' is extremely complex, since it involves in each case an indefinite number of statements to the effect that if someone were at a place P_1, he would be sensing a sense-datum S_1, if he were at place P_2 he would be sensing S_2 . . . if he were at place P_n he would be sensing S_n, and he goes on to consider what the phenomenalist must mean by someone's being at a place P. His answer is that he must mean 'so far from here' and 'in such and such a direction' and that these expressions 'refer to the sensational route, so to speak, which anyone would have to traverse if he were to pass from P, to the place where the speaker is'. 'Thus the phenomenalistic analysis of "x is at P" will be something like the following: "X is sensing a visual or tactual field such that *if* he had replaced it by another spatially adjoined to it, and *if* he had replaced that by another spatially adjoined to it, and *if* he had replaced that in turn by still another, and so on, then eventually he would have been sensing the visual or tactual field which is actually being sensed by the speaker at this moment".' Presumably some reference to kinaesthetic data would be needed to bring out the point that it is the person X that is supposed to be moving: and certainly one would require some description of the contents of the visual and tactual fields 'through' which X is supposed to pass. For otherwise neither his starting-point nor his route would be identifiable.

A similar treatment is given to the question of position in time. The first stage of the analysis will yield hypothetical propositions such as 'If anyone had been at place P_1, at time t, he would have sensed S_1; if anyone had been at place P_2, at time t_2, he would have sensed S_2 . . .' And here 'at time t' will mean, according to Price, 'so many minutes or hours, or days before *now*', which again must be 'analysed in terms of a sensational route'. So, '"X had a sense-experience at a past date t" (*e.g.* 3000 years ago) must be equivalent to something like the following: "he sensed a sense-field such that *if* he had been going to sense a later one spatio-temporally adjoining it, and if he had been going to sense a still later one spatio-temporally adjoining that one and so on, then eventually he *would* have been going to sense the sense-field which is at present being sensed by the speaker"'".

Price goes on to make the further point that the observer must be supposed *really* to travel along his sensational route, both in space and time, and not merely to dream or have a hallucinatory experience of doing so. And this means that the phenomenalist must include in his analysis the possibility of obtaining innumerable bye-series 'branching off from the main one' as a guarantee that the main series is veridical. Accordingly, Price concludes that although he may not have shown that the phenomenalistic analysis is false he has at least shown it to be very much more complex than is usually realized.

But is it only a question of complexity? I think that the analysis which Price attributes to the phenomenalist is open to a far more serious objection. For it implies that the description of any event which is remote in space or time from the speaker contains as part of its meaning not only a description of the sense-field that the speaker is actually sensing, but also a description of a long series of intervening sense-fields. And surely this is incorrect. Suppose, for example, that I make some remark about the South Pole, say that there is a colony of penguins so many miles to the north of it, engaged in some activity or other. It seems clear that this remark will not contain any reference whatsoever either to what I am sensing now or to what I should sense on my way to the place in question. I have, indeed, only a very vague idea of the way to get from here to the South Pole, and a still vaguer idea of what I should observe on my journey, but I do not think that this impairs my understanding of my original proposition. Of course, if I am allowed to take an aeroplane it

will be easier : there will be fewer sense-fields to
traverse and they are likely to be more homogeneous in
content, assuming that the aeroplane does not crash.
But even aeroplanes take time to travel, and by the
time I get to the South Pole the colony of penguins may
have dispersed. So I shall have to make myself start
earlier. 'If I had taken an aeroplane so many hours
ago' — whatever this may come to in sensory terms —
'then I should now be sensing sense-data characteristic
of the appearance of penguins, preceded by sense-
data . . .' and here there follows a step by step description in reverse of all my experiences *en route*. Surely as
an analysis of my original proposition this is most
unplausible.

   Again, it is to be noticed that Price's phenomenalistic
analysis of the proposition about someone's having an
experience in the past ends with the words : 'eventually
he would have been going to sense the sense-field
which is at present being sensed by the speaker'. But
it is characteristic of the sense-field that is now being
sensed by me, the speaker, that it is somato-centric to
my body : and for anyone to sense it he must, as it
were, be 'in' my body. That is, he must be having
sense-data that are identical with those that are now
being obtained 'from' my body. And this adds a
further touch of strangeness to what is already a very
strange fashion of dealing with the past. Consider, for
example, the proposition that Julius Caesar crossed the
Rubicon in the year 49 B.C. Resurrecting Caesar after
the Ides of March, or ignoring the Ides of March
altogether, which we are presumably entitled to do
since the whole of our story will be hypothetical, we
carry him through two thousand years of history,
second by second or minute by minute, according to

our estimate of the average duration of a sense-field,
and finally bring his wanderings to an end by making
him occupy my body. I cannot believe that when I
say that Julius Caesar crossed the Rubicon in the year
49 B.C. I am implying quite so much as this.

6

These are serious difficulties : and they might well
be thought to be fatal to the phenomenalist, if he were
committed to holding the views that Price attributes to
him : but I do not think that he is. I do not think that
he is bound to claim that the analysis of a proposition
referring to an event which is remote in space or time
from the speaker involves tracing the sensory route from
'there' and 'then' to 'here' and 'now'. There would
in any case be no *one* sensory route to trace. I think
rather that he would hope to describe the 'setting' of
the event directly in sensory terms, without including
what would have to happen for this setting to become
the speaker's own. Thus he would try to reproduce
'being at the South Pole' in sensory terms without
saying anything about *this* sense-field, or about the
other sense-fields that, in a suitably Pickwickian sense
of 'between', may lie between this sense-field and the
sense-field that 'presents' the South Pole. Similarly,
he would try to give a sensory version of 'Caesar crossed
the Rubicon in 49 B.C.', without referring to *this* sense-
field or to the long series of sense-fields that might be
supposed to fill the gap between that time and this.
But how could this be done ? The answer is, I think,
that one would have to describe both places and times
in terms of the local scenery. Thus, it should be
possible to indicate a series of sensory experiences

which were such as would entitle anyone who had them to assert 'I am so many miles north of the South Pole', and in that case the analysis of our proposition about the penguins would be that if such sensory experiences were occurring they would be accompanied by other sense-experiences, which were such as would entitle anyone who had them to assert 'here is a colony of penguins, behaving in such and such a fashion'. It is true, indeed, that not all places are identifiable by obvious landmarks — I imagine, for example, that the South Pole looks very much like the North Pole — so that the descriptions of the 'local scenery' would often have to be rather complicated. In the case of the South Pole I suppose that it would involve a hypothetical reference to the results of making certain measurements. But the fact remains that people do contrive to orient themselves, and that they do so by having certain sense-experiences. Consequently, it seems reasonable for the phenomenalist to set out to define positions in space in terms of the sense-experiences by which they would actually be identified.

There is, however, still a difficulty about time. For the expression 'if such and such sense-experiences were occurring' means 'if they were occurring *now*', and the use of the word 'now' involves a reference to physical time. Consequently, some phrase will have to be added to the effect that these sense-experiences are, or rather would be, sensibly contemporaneous with some standard sense-experiences which fix the moment of time. And this too will be rather complicated : Given such sense-experiences as would entitle anyone who had them to assert that he was looking at a watch, and given such sense-experiences as would entitle anyone who had them to assert that the watch was going

properly, and given such sense-experiences as would
entitle anyone who had them to assert that the watch
showed such and such a reading, and given that these
last experiences were sensibly contemporaneous with
the experiences described in the final apodosis of the
long series of 'if-clauses' involved in the identification
of the place, then (there would be) such sense-
experiences as would entitle anyone who had them to
assert that there was 'there and then' a colony of
penguins, behaving in such and such a fashion. And
even this is a considerable over-simplification since
each of the hypothetical clauses conceals an indefinite
number of subsidiary hypotheticals. But once again
the phenomenalist might appeal to the fact that people
do identify times and that they do so by having certain
sense-experiences. And an analysis of this sort, though
very far from simple, is at any rate not quite so complex
as the analysis in terms of sensory routes.

The same problem arises in the case of propositions
about the past. Take Dr. Crippen again. I suppose
that one could describe a series of experiences which
would be such as to justify the assertion 'this is the year
A.D. 1910', without having to go back to the birth of
Christ, which anyhow is wrongly dated. One might,
for example, invoke calendars or newspapers, though
this would not do so well for such a date as 49 B.C.
Still we do manage to determine dates without having
to refer explicitly to history or astronomy, though there
is a sense in which dating involves both. Consequently, the phenomenalist might try to deal with
Crippen on the following lines. 'If a certain set of
sense-experiences, namely such as would entitle anyone
who had them to assert "this is such and such a room
in such and such a street in Camden Town" had been

sensibly contemporaneous with a series of sense-experiences of such a character as would entitle anyone who had them to assert "this is such and such an hour of such and such a day in the year 1910", they would have been accompanied by a series of sense-experiences of such a character as would entitle anyone who had them to assert "here is a man called Dr. Crippen engaged in murdering his wife".' But the defect of this formulation is that it provokes the question : *When* would all this have happened ? to which the only answer is that the question is illegitimate. For all the wheres and whens are supposed to be included *in* the sensory story : so that there can be no where and when *of* the story. It was for this reason that in dealing just now with my example of the penguins at the South Pole I introduced the conditional clauses with the word "given" instead of the customary "if". My object was to avoid the use of verbs which, by reason of their tenses, would have referred unwarrantably to physical time.

Another defect of the formulation : 'If a series *A* of sense-experiences had been sensibly contemporaneous with a series *B*, they would have been accompanied, or followed, by a series *C*' is that in certain cases it may be that they *were* so accompanied, so that it is idle to say that they *would* have been. Thus, in the Crippen example, it may be objected, as I remarked before, that it is silly to say '*if* anybody were to have had certain experiences' when we can reasonably assume that somebody, namely Crippen himself, *did* have them. But the answer to this is that it is a mistake to say either that certain sense-experiences *were* obtained, or that they would have been obtained, if this is understood, as it naturally would be, to involve a reference to physical time. The protasis of our hypothetical is supposed to describe, in sensory terms, the 'setting' of the event of which the apodosis contains the sensory description. Consequently, there is no need to put the setting itself into space and time : and not only is there no need to do this, but the attempt to do it leads to a vicious confusion of the physical and sensory levels of language.

A similar confusion arises if it is said, or implied, that the sense-data, which supply the phenomenalist with the materials for his analyses, are, or would be, sensed *by* anyone, whether it be myself, the speaker, or anybody else. For not only does this involve an illegitimate reference to physical bodies, and so to physical space and time, but it leads also to the difficulties which I mentioned earlier, concerning the possibility of physical interaction between the observer and the event that he is put there to observe. The way to meet these difficulties, I now suggest, is not to choose some apparently inoffensive observer, such as a mouse, or a man with a telescope, but to exclude from the analysis any reference to an observer at all. Admittedly, it is necessary, in practice, to refer to an observer in order to explain what is meant by a sense-datum : for it is only in terms of what is relatively familiar that an unfamiliar term can be understood. But once the sense-datum language has been accepted as basic, then observers, like everything else at the physical level, must be reduced to sense-data. For to allow them to stand outside 'having' or 'sensing' the sense-data would be to bring sense-data themselves up to the physical level and so vitiate the whole phenomenalistic programme.

That no explicit reference to a physical body should occur in the phenomenalist's analysis would be generally

admitted : but it seems usually to have been thought
that an observer of some sort must always figure in the
protases, not indeed baldly as his physical self, but in
the correct sensory disguise. It does not appear to me,
however, that this is necessary. I do not see, for
example, why the phenomenalist's version of such a
proposition as 'there is a book-case in the dining-room'
should contain the description of any sensory manifestation of a human body. It has to identify the dining-
room in question and also to specify some period of
time, but that should be enough. It may, indeed, be
argued that unless some human body were present no
sense-experiences would occur at all. But the analysis
does not state that any sense-experiences do occur :
only that given certain sense-experiences, then . . .
certain others. That no experiences at all would be
'given' unless there were an observer is indeed a
physical fact : but there is no reason why that physical
fact should be prefixed to every sensory analysis. On
the contrary, the phenomenalist must hold that it is
itself to be analysed in purely sensory terms. The only
cases, therefore, in which the analysis will contain a
sensory description of an observer are those in which
there is some reference to an observer in the proposition
which is to be analysed. In such case the observer will
figure *in* the sensory story, but in no case will there be an
observer *of* the story. The phenomenalist's tale does
not include the author : it is, in that respect, a tale that
tells itself.

7

I suggest then that the phenomenalist's analysis of
a simple proposition about a physical object, say a
proposition to the effect that there exists a physical

object of a certain sort in a certain place throughout a certain period of time, should take the following form. A protasis, which will itself include a number of subsidiary hypotheticals, describing such sense-experiences as would be sufficient to identify the place and time in question, or in other words, to put the physical object in its proper setting: followed by an apodosis which would describe such sense-experiences as would be sufficient to verify the presence of the physical object in question: and this apodosis will also have to contain a number of subsidiary hypotheticals to rule out the possibility of an illusion. If this were done, the truth of the whole hypothetical might, I think, pass as a sufficient condition of the truth of the proposition which it was intended to analyse. It would not, however, be a necessary condition, because of the relative indefiniteness of the proposition at the physical level. But as has already been shown, to formulate a sufficient condition in purely sensory terms is the most that the phenomenalist can reasonably hope for: and I cannot claim to have done more than give a very rough sketch of the way in which this might be achieved.

The fact is that so long as he confines himself to giving a *general* account of the way in which physical objects are 'constructed' out of sense-data, or a *general* account of the way in which physical space and time are 'constructed' out of sensory spaces and times, the phenomenalist does not appear to meet any insuperable obstacles. But directly he tries to reduce any particular statement about a physical object, even the simplest, to a statement, or set of statements, about sense-data, he runs into difficulties which, however he may make light of them in theory, in practice overwhelm him. The reason for this may lie only in the extreme com-

plexity of his undertaking. But I think that there may
be a more serious reason. I think that it might be
argued that he was setting himself a task that could not,
by its very nature, be satisfactorily fulfilled. For the
language in which we refer to physical objects has its
own logic. Now the sensory language to which the
phenomenalist seeks to reduce the other must also have
its logic, and this logic must be either the same as that
of the physical language or different. If it is made
the same — if, for example, the phenomenalist allows
himself to speak of 'sensibilia' having a continued and
distinct existence in space and time — then we are
inclined to say that he has not carried out his programme, because these sensibilia are only physical
objects, or attenuated physical objects, in disguise.
But if the logic of the sensory language is different,
then we are inclined to say that the statements which
are expressed in it are not perfect translations of the
statements at the physical level, just because their logic
is different. So what is the phenomenalist to do ?

If this line of argument is correct, then the solution
of the 'problem of perception' may be to treat our
beliefs about physical objects as constituting a theory,
the function of which is to explain the course of our
sensory experiences. The statements which are expressed in terms of the theory may not then be capable
of being reproduced exactly as statements about sense-
data ; that is, it may not be possible wholly to rewrite
them as statements about sense-data. Nevertheless,
they will function only as means of grouping sense-data :
and it will be a contingent fact that sense-data are so
organized that the theory is valid. It may then be
required of the philosopher to make clear in what this
organization consists : that is, to show in a general way

M

what relations must obtain between sense-data for the demands of the theory to be met. Thus, to echo Kant, he may be represented as trying to answer the question How is the physical-object language possible ? And to this question the phenomenalist has, I think, the makings of a satisfactory answer.

7

STATEMENTS ABOUT THE PAST

IT is characteristic of philosophers that they exercise their scepticism not so much upon particular statements or beliefs, as upon whole classes of them. They are, indeed, inclined to dispute the particular statements that are made by other philosophers; but apart from these special cases they are interested in particular statements only as examples. The weaknesses which they detect in them are those that they are supposed to share with all the members of the class of which they are taken as typical representatives. And it is this lack of discrimination that gives to philosophic doubt both its frivolity and its strength. A scientist may come to doubt some general hypothesis because the evidence for it does not meet his requirements, but his standards are not so rigorous that no hypothesis can satisfy them. It is left to the philosopher to put in question the validity of any generalization whatsoever, to cast doubt upon a general statement not because of any special weakness of its own but simply because it is a generalization. In their relations with one another men often display a lack of understanding; one does not always know what another person is thinking or feeling. But neither does one always live in an atmosphere of mystery. Not all human beings are equally inscrutable, any more than they are equally perspicacious : a man who can conceal his thoughts or feelings on one occasion may not be able to conceal them on another. But the philosophical sceptic ignores these distinctions. He invokes the doubt whether any two people, irrespective of their character or situation, can ever know what is going on in one another's minds. Again, it sometimes happens that people are deceived by their senses ; not all perceptions are reliable : some account must be taken of the conditions in which they are made. But the philosopher is interested in the general question whether perception ever gives us 'knowledge of an external world'. His scepticism bears not upon the truth of some perceptual judgements as opposed to others, but upon the truth of any perceptual judgement whatsoever.

It is sometimes claimed by those who wish philosophers to be considered useful that the study of philosophy teaches people to weigh evidence. But the weighing of evidence is governed by accepted standards of proof. What the philosopher is doing, in the examples I have given, is to call in question the standards of proof themselves. And it is in this way also that the existence of the past becomes a philosophical problem. Here again, the philosopher's scepticism is not discriminating. He is not impugning any special set, or type, of historical beliefs. The question that he raises is whether we have sufficient ground for accepting any statement at all about the past, whether we are even justified in our belief that there has been a past. It is not a matter of sifting historical records. What is put in question is our right to regard anything as a record ; the suggestion is that there is nothing in the character of what we take as records, whether they have the form of memories or any other, to justify the assumption that they point back to a past.

The first stage in such a sceptical argument, in this

as in the other cases I have mentioned, is to show that the conclusion on which doubt is being thrown goes beyond any possible evidence that we can have for it. Thus, to quote Russell,[1] 'it is not logically necessary to the existence of a memory-belief that the event remembered should have occurred, or even that the past should have existed at all. There is no logical impossibility in the hypothesis that the world sprang into being five minutes ago, exactly as it then was, with a population that "remembered" a wholly unreal past. There is no logically necessary connection between events at different times: therefore nothing that is happening now or will happen in the future can disprove the hypothesis that the world began five minutes ago. Hence the occurrences which are *called* knowledge of the past are logically independent of the past; they are wholly analysable into present contents, which might, theoretically, be just what they are even if no past had existed.' Russell himself goes on to say that he is 'not suggesting that the non-existence of the past should be entertained as a serious hypothesis. Like all sceptical hypotheses, it is logically tenable, but uninteresting.' Uninteresting, presumably, because although it cannot be refuted, there is equally no reason to believe it. But to say this is to miss the point of the sceptic's procedure. He is not denying that the past existed, any more than a philosophical solipsist is contending that he himself is the only person in the world. He is not putting forward any hypothesis at all. One may say that he is making a profession of agnosticism: but this too is of no interest in itself. What is of interest is the view, or rather the reasons given for the view, that no other position is logically defensible.

[1] *Analysis of Mind*, pp. 159-160.

The second stage in the argument is to show that not only does the evidence not entail the conclusion which is being subjected to doubt; it does not even in any way support it. If physical objects are not directly 'given' to perception, how can the acquisition of sense-data make it even in the least degree probable that any physical object exists? If all that one person ever observes of another is his overt behaviour, how can he have the slightest reason for believing in the existence of the thoughts and feelings which the behaviour is supposed to overlie? If there is no returning to the past, how can a set of present experiences be in any way a ground for believing in the existence of a past event? That A's and B's have constantly been found in conjunction might, if it could ever be known, be a ground for attaching some probability, given the observation of an A, to the existence of an unobserved B, though even this would be queried by those who raise the problem of induction. But how can the accumulation of A's give any support whatever to the hypothesis of a B's existence, if all the B's themselves are inaccessible?

Not all philosophers are sceptics, but perhaps it is the mark of a philosopher that he takes this sort of scepticism seriously. And one way of taking it seriously is to try to rebut it by denying the premises on which it is based, that is, by finding a way of access to what has been declared inaccessible. This process takes two forms. Either one extends the range of the evidence so that it comes to cover the conclusion in dispute, or one reduces the conclusion to the level of the admitted evidence. Thus it may be claimed on the one hand that physical objects are themselves directly 'given', and on the other that they are nothing but constructions out of sense-data; that one can in certain circumstances experience what is going on in another person's mind, or else that all talk by others about a man's inner life is equivalent to talk about his actual or possible behaviour; and in the case of the past, either that it is possible to be directly acquainted with past events, or that statements about the past are translatable into statements, mainly hypothetical, about the present and future. The choice of either alternative in every case repels the sceptic, in so far as it is then no longer a matter of our having to justify an inference from what can be observed to what is, in principle, unobservable. The trouble, in the case of the past at least, is that neither alternative is acceptable.

The claim that the past is somehow literally preserved in memory is to be distinguished, at least provisionally, from the claim, which is indeed more frequently made, that one can know, through memory or otherwise, that certain statements about the past are true. This apparently weaker claim also rebuts the sceptic, since it cannot be the case both that someone knows a given statement to be true and that he is not justified in accepting it. His knowledge, if he has it, constitutes a justification. But the defect of this rebuttal, for our present purposes, is that ,it represents a refusal to play the sceptic's game. We shall, indeed, find that the final recourse against him is simply to maintain that what is taken to be good evidence really is good evidence. And one way of doing this is to insist that we do in fact know what he holds it to be impossible that we should know. But to say this is not to meet the sceptic's arguments. It is only if the contention that memory is a form of knowledge is construed as implying the possibility of direct acquaintance with the past that it constitutes, what we are now discussing, an attempt to defeat the sceptic on his own chosen ground.

But how are we to interpret this suggestion that people are directly acquainted with the past? In one sense, indeed, it may be said that one is seldom, if ever, acquainted with anything but the past : for light and sound and nerve impulses notoriously take time to travel : so that one perceives physical objects not as they are at the time at which one perceives them but only, at best, in the state in which they were some time before. We may even in this way come to perceive physical objects which no longer exist. But this itself is one of the considerations that have induced philosophers to say that physical objects are not things with which anyone can be directly acquainted. It would seem, therefore, that they construe direct acquaintance in such a way that it can have for its object only the content of a present experience. But, on this interpretation, the claim to have direct acquaintance with the past becomes self-contradictory. What is suggested is that something which is the content of a present experience may be literally identical with the content of a past experience. But how is it possible, within the same terms of reference, that anything should be both present and past ?

Professor Broad, who discusses this question at some length,[1] maintains indeed that the contradiction is easily avoided. We are directly acquainted only with what is presented to us : but what is presented need not necessarily be present. He has his own objections to the identification of memory images with past sensa, including the objection, which he regards as the most serious, 'that we can recognize a *general* qualitative

[1] In *The Mind and its Place in Nature*, pp. 249 ff.

difference between any image and any sensum, and
specific differences in detail and in determinate characteristics between a memory-image and the remembered
sensum',[1] but the 'metaphysical objection' is not
among them. Past events, in his view, do not cease to
exist, they 'are always "there" waiting to be remembered'. And since they are always 'there' there is no
reason *a priori* why one should not enter into cognitive
relations with them.

But by what criterion are we to decide whether past
events do or do not exist? If we make it a rule that
only what is 'there' can be veridically remembered,
then it will indeed follow that some past events exist if
any memories are veridical; for being 'there', in the
sense required, is held to entail existing. But does this
come to any more than that some events are past and
that, being past, they are candidates for being remembered? It is not suggested that there can be any
grounds for saying that a past event 'eternally exists'
other than the grounds that there may be for saying
that it once occurred. And this being so, it makes
no difference whether or not we say that a past event
continues to exist. We are equally at liberty to lay
down the rule that what is remembered is not 'there'
at all. It is simply a matter of how widely we wish to
extend our use of the word 'existence'. There is no
serious harm in talking about the existence, or even
about the eternal existence, of a past event. But
nothing is thereby asserted that could not just as well
be expressed by simply making some historical statement, or by saying of such a statement that it was true.

Thus, when a philosopher, like Samuel Alexander,
says that 'the pastness of (a remembered) object is a

[1] *Op. cit.* p. 263.

datum of experience, directly apprehended', or that
'the object is compresent with me as *past*',[1] he is not
putting forward a theory about the operation of
memory. Or if it be regarded as a theory, it is not a
theory that explains anything. In so far as this statement is anything more than an affirmation of the
psychological fact that memories ostensibly refer to
the past, it merely makes the claim that they are
veridical. Now it is open to anyone to use expressions
like 'directly apprehend' in such a way that if an event
is veridically remembered it is directly apprehended and,
what is more, directly apprehended as past. There is
as much, or as little, justification for this as there is
for saying that the past states of physical objects are
directly apprehended, where there is no question of
anything's being remembered. The usage, in either
case, is philosophically somewhat unconventional, but
not outrageous. Let it then be granted that if any
event is veridically remembered it is directly apprehended. It still remains to be proved that any memory
is veridical. And for this purpose it is no use putting
forward the statement that some past events are directly
apprehended as past; for the fact that some memories
are veridical is required as a proof of it. Thus the
claim that one can be directly acquainted with the past
turns out to be no stronger than the claim that one can
know that certain statements about the past are true,
and it does as little to meet the sceptic's arguments.

At this point, it may be objected that the claim that
memory yields knowledge of the past, whether or not it
takes the form of saying that one is sometimes directly
acquainted with past events, is not reducible to the bare
statement that some memories are veridical, or even to

[1] *Space, Time and Deity*, vol. 1, p. 113.

the conjunction of the statements that some memories are veridical and that one is fully justified in assuming that they are. What is being asserted, it may be said, is that there are memory experiences which guarantee their own validity. But how can this possibly be so? Whether a memory experience is veridical or fallacious is not a question which is settled by the intrinsic character of the experience itself. The experience is veridical if and only if the event of which it is ostensibly a memory actually occurred. Even if our memories never did deceive us, the fact that they never did would not be deducible from any mere description of their content. It is indeed only by consulting our memories, assisted by other records, that we come to have any knowledge of the past; but this does not mean that the possibility of error is ever logically excluded. Of course, if a statement which is based on a memory experience is known to be true, then it does follow logically that the memory is veridical: but then it does not follow from anything in the character of the memory experience that the statement which is based on it is known to be true. One is apt to be misled here by the picture of states of knowing as searchlights which can pick out objects in the present or in the past, or, if precognition be admitted, in the future; when it comes to mathematics or to morals it may even be held that the rays penetrate beyond the natural world; and so, when it is a matter of knowing the past or the future, it is thought that the objects of such knowledge must still, or already, be in some way present: for how else could the searchlight discover them? In this way remembering, like precognizing, comes to be singled out as a way of directly knowing, whereas other methods of obtaining information about the past, or future, are regarded as indirect, because they depend on inference. But in this matter there is no reason to separate memories from other types of record. A document or a fossil may also bear the stamp of authenticity: so may a witness's spoken report. Admittedly, the decision that such records are reliable, that they do give valid information about the past, implies the acceptance of certain general hypotheses or laws; in this sense, the knowledge, or beliefs, to which they give rise are inferential. But this is also true of memories. In the case of memories, there is a tacit acceptance of general hypotheses which correlate certain past events with subsequent memory experiences. And to this it is no objection that the exercise of memory may be psychologically unlike anything that is ordinarily regarded as a process of inference.

A further reason why philosophers have wished to hold that memory somehow turns the past into the present may be that they have thought it the only way of accounting for our having even a notion of the past. Starting from the assumption that our ability to conceive of past events is due to our having memory experiences, they may have held this to entail, not merely that some of these experiences were veridical, but that they somehow actually took in the past. For how else could they even seem to refer to past events? How, if our memory experiences are 'wholly analysable into present contents', could even a false belief in the existence of past events ever have arisen from them? It is all very well to talk about feelings of familiarity. They may perhaps serve to account for our referring certain memory images to the past, once we have acquired the notion of pastness. But we could not have acquired it from them. For they themselves are qualities, or accompaniments, of present contents. And it is impossible to see how any purely qualitative feature of a present experience could in itself give rise to the idea that other experiences were past.

But could not the same argument be used to prove that we were directly acquainted with the future? If there is nothing in a 'present content' that intrinsically points back to the past, neither is there anything that intrinsically points forward to the future. Yet no one has made it an argument for precognition that it is a necessary condition of anyone's understanding what is meant by a future event. Not even their staunchest champions have maintained that precognitive experiences, interpreted as implying direct acquaintance with the future, were actually enjoyed in infancy by all those who have learned correctly to employ the future tense. The explanation of this may be that it is thought that the notion of the future can be derived from that of the past. We conceive of future events as being those that stand in the same relation to events in the present as these do to events in the past. But then it is also possible in this way to derive the notion of the past from that of the future. And from this it follows that it is not essential for obtaining an idea of the past that anything should be, or even seem to be, remembered. If there were beings who were as liberally endowed with precognitive experiences as we are with memory experiences, they could, on this showing, perfectly well conceive of the past, even though they had no memories at all.

I have thought it worth while to make this point because philosophers have tended to be as critical of precognition as they have been uncritical of memory. There may be good empirical grounds for mistrusting reports of precognitive experiences, but logically they are no more suspect than memory experiences; or, putting it the other way to please the sceptic, memory is logically no less suspect than precognition. The fact is, however, that to account for our ability to conceive of the past and future neither memory nor precognition is needed, still less the mysterious assumption that these are modes of direct knowledge. If one knows what it is for one event to precede another then one may conceive of the past as consisting of all and only those events that immediately or remotely precede some present event, and of the future as consisting of all and only those events that are immediately or remotely preceded by some present event. I do not offer this as a psychological account of the way in which people in fact acquire the notion of the past and future, but only as a proof that these concepts can be analysed in such a way as to meet the requirements of even the most strict empiricist. For I take it that instances of the relation of temporal precedence are sensibly given in our experience.

But this, it may be objected, is to allow that one can after all enjoy direct acquaintance with past, and perhaps even with future, events. For if relations of temporal priority are to be sensibly given they must fall within the specious present: and either the specious present terminates in the momentary event which alone is strictly present, in which case it is almost wholly past; or, as William James held, it is like a saddleback extending beyond the strictly present event in both directions, so that it contains in itself a section both of the past and of the future. On either assumption, it follows that at best only one of the events which are related by temporal precedence can be strictly present: but if the relation is directly apprehended, so must be both its terms. To which I answer that if one decides to use the words 'past' and 'future' in such a way that they apply to sections of the specious present, then it will indeed be the case that events which are past or future, in this sense, can be directly apprehended; their being directly apprehended will just be a matter of their being observed to occur within the specious present. But at best this disposes only of the psychological problem of the way in which we come by the conception of the past and future. It in no way establishes our right to postulate the existence of events beyond the specious present; and it is this that the sceptic puts in question when he raises doubts about the past. Furthermore, I do not see why it should be held that for an event to be present, in other than a specious sense, it must be instantaneous. Suppose that I am asked at this moment to delimit the class of events which are strictly present; I think it would be perfectly correct for me to reply that they are all and only those events that lie within the temporal boundaries of this gesture; the gesture of my hand's moving across the paper. Of course, the choice of this particular event as a standard of reference is arbitrary. Any other event that I could have indicated as then occurring would have done as well. And here I must lay stress upon the use of the word 'indicate'. If the event which is taken as the standard of reference is described as one that is now occurring, the way is laid open to a charge of circularity. One seems to be saying that the class of present events is composed of those that are simultaneous with some present event. But there is no circularity if the event to which reference is made is identified, as it easily may be, in some way that does not involve describing it as present. What I shall have to say about the use of tenses will, I hope, make this clear. The point for which I am now arguing is that what is taken as a standard example of a strictly present event may very well have duration. This is not to say, however, that all the events that it is legitimate to take as standard examples must have the same duration. The choice of shorter events confines the present within increasingly narrow boundaries, and no doubt they can be made as narrow as we please. But, so far as I can see, there is no advantage to be gained by this process of compression, nor any warrant for it in ordinary usage. The most, I think, that can be legitimately required of us is that the events which we allow to set the standard should be specious; that is, that they should not be so long that they are not ostensible.

Professor Broad, who has discussed this question also, objects to the reduction of the attributes of past, present, and future to relations of precedence on the ground that it leaves out of account 'the transitory aspect of time'.[1] The picture which it creates, in his opinion, is that of a static world, a world in which nothing happens. Events are spread out in a panorama, eternally standing to each other in the same relations of precedence. There is nothing in this model to represent the flow of time, the moving finger, the fact that events continuously come into being and pass away. But the answer to this is that it is just these relations of temporal precedence and succession that constitute the flow of time. To speak of an event as coming into being, persisting, and then ceasing to be, is to refer to times at which it was not, is, and is no longer; that is, to events which precede, accompany, or succeed it. What is confusing is that these verbs themselves have

[1] *Examination of McTaggart's Philosophy*, vol. ii, Part I, p. 307.

tenses; so that one may be asked when these events succeed one another, or at what rate, or for how long, and if one takes these questions seriously one may find oneself, like Mr. Dunne, attributing to time an infinite series of dimensions, or, like McTaggart, denying its reality altogether. But in fact these questions should not be taken seriously; they should not be admitted at all. To ask when, or at what rate, certain events succeed one another may indeed be legitimate if what is wanted is some further specification, that is a reference to other events and the relations of accompaniment, precedence, overlapping, inclusion, or whatever it may be, that they bear to the events originally specified. But to ask when, or at what rate, or for how long, events in general accompany or succeed each other is just nonsensical. It is because events succeed one another that we can significantly speak of temporal processes: but their being so related is not itself a temporal process; and only metaphysical confusion can result from treating it as if it were.

But how is it then that this elimination of tenses in favour of relational predicates gives rise to the impression that we are substituting a static for a dynamic world, that the fluidity of time is thereby analysed away? The answer is that it is because the picture, thus created, of events standing non-temporally in temporal relations contains no indication that it is taken from any special point of view. It is only from a special point of view, the point of view of some earlier event, that an event comes into being: it is only from a special point of view, the point of view of some contemporaneous event, that it persists: and it is only from a special point of view, the point of view of some later event, that it ceases to be. Now the use of tenses, or of the

N

attributes of past, present, or future, implies a point of view ; but to speak of events as being simultaneous, or as being earlier or later than one another, does not ; for here the copula is introduced only out of consideration for grammar ; it is not to be construed as being in the present tense. Consequently, when we speak in this way, we seem to be divesting time of its character of process. But, since the process of time consists in the fact that events are temporally related, this impression is fallacious. What is left out in our representation is the element of becoming, the arrival and departure of events : for this can be represented only by taking up a position within the series. Even so, it is still a matter of events preceding and succeeding one another. Its peculiarity lies only in the implied selection of some particular event as a point of temporal reference.

Nevertheless, it will be objected, this element of becoming is an essential feature of our experience. In imagination, we may adopt any point of view that we please ; we may even, as has just been shown, contrive to picture the world *sub specie aeternitatis*, in detachment from any point of view whatsoever ; but in actual fact we are not free to choose our point of view. In actual fact one occupies at any given moment a definite position in time, and this position continually changes. There is, again to quote Professor Broad, a ‘steady movement of the quality of presentedness along the series (of one’s experiences) in the direction from earlier to later’.[1] How is this to be accounted for ?

In spite of what is often said, I do not think that this presents us with any very serious difficulty. To say that a person occupies, at any given moment, a definite position in time is just to say that at least one of the

[1] *Examination of McTaggart’s Philosophy*, vol. ii, Part I, p. 308.

class of simultaneous events which constitutes the moment in question is an event in that person's history. The fact that a certain series of events constitutes his history fixes his temporal standpoint. To ask whether he could have had a different standpoint is to ask whether a difference in the temporal relations of the events, which constitute his history, to other events, and perhaps also a consequential difference in the character of his history itself, is consistent with his remaining the same person; and the answer to this depends upon what we choose to understand by 'being the same person'. That one's temporal position continually changes is simply the fact that the events which collectively are one's history stand to each other in relations of temporal succession. The direction of the series is irreversible only in the trivial sense that if a is later than b, and neither a nor b can re-occur, b is not later than a. Considering only the character of the events in question, one can imagine them as occurring in any order: but if their individuality is made to depend, as in fact it is, upon the temporal relations that they bear to one another and to other events, then it will follow, from the fact that they are the events that they are, that they occur in the order that they do. There is no 'movement of presentedness along the series' of one's experiences, apart from their successiveness. It is the fact that they are successive that constitutes this so-called steady movement. The continual recession of events out of the future, through the present, and into the past is, as we have seen, only the reflection of a continual shift in the temporal standpoint from which they are viewed. And the fact that this shift is actually displayed in our lives is again an immediate consequence of the fact that they consist in a succession of experiences.

To assign to anyone a point of view in time as the point of view that he in fact occupies is, then, to relate a particular element of his history to certain other events : and this is just the work that tenses do in any language that contains them. The use of the present tense indicates, without necessarily stating, that the event to which the statement refers is contemporary with its formulation : the use of the past tense indicates that it is earlier, and the use of the future tense indicates that it is later. Tensed verbs are situational in the sense that they reveal the speaker's temporal standpoint relatively to the events that they are used to describe : and the same is true of the attributes of past, present, and future when they are used in conjunction with the non-temporal copula. This point may seem excessively obvious, but it is one that philosophers have sometimes overlooked : and the fact that they have overlooked it helps to account for some of the mistakes that they have made in writing about time.

To find an illustration of this we need only turn to what I described earlier on as the second way of meeting the sceptic's doubts about our knowledge of the past ; the identification of statements about the past with statements about the present and future. The conclusions at which one arrives by taking this course are not indeed formally refutable. If anyone chooses to say, as I once did, that any given statement about a past event is formally equivalent to a set of statements about the favourable evidence that is, or might become, available for it, I do not know how he can be answered except by the production of counter-examples ; and these, if he is obstinate, he may refuse to recognize. At the same time, this is not a position that anyone is likely to hold except as the outcome of a philosophical argument; so that we can at least attack it indirectly by exposing the fallacies on which it appears to be based.

In this case, they are not difficult to find. The mistake arises, in the first instance, from an abuse of the principle of verifiability. Instead of equating the meaning of a statement with the best evidence that could conceivably be had for it, that is, ideally, with a set of statements to which it stands in a relation of mutual entailment, one may fall into the error of equating it with the best evidence that some particular person is in fact in a position to obtain; and since those who are situated at a later time can obtain knowledge of earlier events only through the traces that they leave, the inference may be drawn that statements about these earlier events must, if they are to be significant at all, be equivalent to statements about their actual or hypothetical traces; for it is only through the identification of it with subsequent records that the past event becomes accessible to observation. But it is just this conception of the past as intrinsically inaccessible that betrays the philosopher's misunderstanding of the function of tenses. On the legitimate assumption that what is observed is present, from the point of view of the observer, there is, indeed, a sense in which the past is inaccessible, and the future also : for it is logically true that if one event is earlier, or later, than another, the two of them are not contemporaries. But from the fact that a given event is preceded or succeeded by other events it does not follow that it is unobservable. The most that follows is that it is unobservable from the temporal standpoint of the earlier or later events. But it does not enter into the description of an event that the person who describes it happens to occupy an earlier or later standpoint.

A person who is living in 1951 cannot, at that time, verify statements about the events of 1950 in all the ways that they can, perhaps, be verified by a person who is living in 1950, and a person who is living in 1949 cannot verify these statements in all the ways that they can, perhaps, be verified either by the person who is living in 1950 or by the person who is living in 1951 : but the fact that certain persons may be more or less advantageously placed to observe them has no bearing whatsoever upon the events of 1950, considered in themselves. It may be that the dating of an event always involves relating it to certain other events, but it certainly does not involve relating it to the event which is the formulation of the statement in which this relation is made.

The use of tenses always serves to indicate the temporal situation of the speaker relatively to the event which he is describing, but it does not, I think, always make it explicit. Thus, I am inclined to say that there is no difference in meaning between the statements, 'George VI was crowned in 1937', 'George VI is being crowned in 1937', and 'George VI will be crowned in 1937'. They differ in the indications that they respectively give of the temporal point of view from which they are made, but not, I think, in their factual content. If the world had come to an end with this coronation, the statement that George VI was crowned in 1937 would still be true. What would be false would be the indication given by the past tense that someone occupied a later temporal position : and because of this, the statement could never properly be made in this form. I do not, however, wish to press this point, since there certainly are cases in which events are dated only by the use of tenses, as in the statements 'it is raining' or 'he will come back', and here it is obvious that a change in tense would make a difference in meaning. When used in this way, tenses may be classified with such demonstrative expressions as 'yesterday', 'now', 'next month', 'soon', 'long ago'. It is characteristic of these expressions that they both indicate the event which is the occasion of their use and explicitly locate other events by reference to it. Like other demonstratives, they are not straightforwardly equivalent to descriptions. That it rained yesterday does not formally entail that it rained on November 4th, 1951. But their use conveys no information that could not be conveyed by the use of descriptive phrases which were neutral with respect to any speaker. The substitution of such descriptions for them does not affect the truth-value of the statements in which they occur.

The existence of these temporal demonstratives deserves to be noted: but it does not affect the argument. To whatever extent the relative temporal positions of the speaker and the events which he is describing are made explicit, the result, as regards our present problem, is the same. If I now say, for example, that William the Conqueror landed near Hastings in 1066, my use of the past tense indicates that this event precedes my utterance; and it may be inferred that my statement is one that I am not myself in the most advantageous position to verify. If, on the other hand, I say that the event of William's landing is now past, I may reasonably be taken to be saying that it is earlier than my utterance of this statement, or than some event with which this utterance is contemporary: and here it is my use of the demonstrative 'now' or 'this' that, for anyone who is in a position to interpret it, identifies my temporal situation, and so permits the inference

that it is not so favourable as it might be for the verification of the implied statement about the earlier event.
And if, becoming more explicit still, I replace the
demonstrative by a description, and say of what I then
describe, whether it be my own utterance or some other
contemporary event, that it is later than William's
landing, then there is nothing in my statement to
warrant the inference that the earlier event is in any
way inaccessible to my observation. This inference
may still be drawn by someone whose knowledge of the
context in which my statement is made enables him
to situate me as its author. But from a statement which
consists in a description of two events as standing in
some temporal relation to one another nothing whatsoever can be deduced about the temporal situation of
the person by whom the statement is made, nor, consequently, about the opportunities that he may have for
verifying it.

It follows that there is no such thing as a class of
statements about the past, in the way that there are
classes of statements about numbers, or about people,
or about physical events. There are ways of indicating,
as by the use of tenses or other temporal demonstratives,
that the point of view in time from which a statement
is made is later than the event which it describes, but
no statement says of itself that it is made from any
particular point of view. When such indications are
made explicit, what is stated is just that certain events
stand to one another in certain temporal relations, all
of which are definable in terms of the relation of precedence : and these statements are unaffected by the
temporal position of those who make, interpret, or try
to verify them. It may be required of them that they be
verifiable, but not that they be verifiable by this or that

particular person. And it is only from the point of view of someone who happens himself to occupy a later position that any statement comes to be about the past.

If this is correct, I think it also gives a clue to the stubborn philosophical problem of our knowledge of other minds. Just as no statement is, as such, about the past, so, I suggest, no statement is, as such, about another's mind. What is stated is that someone who satisfies a certain description has certain thoughts or feelings : and from this it does not follow, with respect to any person who may make or understand the statement, either that he satisfies the description or that he does not. It may be indicated by the context, or by the use of demonstratives such as 'you' or 'he', that the speaker is not himself the person whom he is describing, and it may be then inferred that he is in a relatively disadvantageous position for verifying the statement that he makes. But no more in this case than in the case of statements about the past does it enter into the analysis of the statement that this or that person is in a better or worse position to pronounce upon its truth.

Nevertheless, the sceptic is not defeated. We may deny his right to raise general questions about 'one's knowledge of other minds' or 'one's knowledge of the past', but he can meet us by making his questions more specific. What grounds can A, who is not, in fact, identical with B, have for believing any statement about B's thoughts or feelings ? What grounds can a person who is living in the twentieth century have for believing any statement about the nineteenth ? It depends, we may reply, upon the statement chosen. Give us a particular example, and then we will state our reasons. But when we have stated them he may still protest that they are not good reasons. And then we may find ourselves reduced to replying simply that they are. It is not as if, in a case where we had come to believe that p, the sceptic was prepared to give us any reason for believing that not-p. It is rather that he refuses to admit that any of the reasons that we are in a position to give, on either side of the question, can possibly be good. From the fact that someone has to rely on records to establish the existence of some earlier event, it follows, according to the sceptic, that he is not entitled to rely upon them. But historians do have canons of evidence; and it is no criticism of these canons that they do not require for their satisfaction a logical impossibility; that someone, being at the point of time at which he is, should also be at a point of time at which he is not. The sceptic makes his position secure by refusing to recognize as proof anything less than what is logically impossible. But this is itself a reason why we should not follow him.

8

ONE'S KNOWLEDGE OF OTHER MINDS

LET us see how there comes to be a problem about one's knowledge of other minds. Consider the following propositions :

(1) When someone, other than myself, says that he is thinking about a philosophical problem, or that he has a headache, or that he has seen a ghost, what he is saying about himself is the same as what I should be saying about myself if I were to say that I was thinking about a philosophical problem, or that I had a headache, or that I had seen a ghost.

(2) When I say of someone other than myself that he is thinking about a philosophical problem, or that he has a headache, or that he has seen a ghost, what I am saying about him is the same as what I should be saying about myself if I were to say that I was thinking about a philosophical problem, or that I had a headache, or that I had seen a ghost.

(3) When I say that I am thinking about a philosophical problem, or that I have a headache, or that I have seen a ghost, my statement is not equivalent to any statement, or set of statements, however complicated, about my overt behaviour.

(4) I have direct knowledge of my own experiences.

(5) I cannot have direct knowledge of anyone else's experiences.

(6) Consequently, the only ground that I can have for believing that other people have experiences, and that some at least of their experiences are of the same character as my own, is that their overt behaviour is similar to mine. I know that certain features of my own behaviour are associated with certain experiences, and when I observe other people behaving in similar ways I am entitled to infer, by analogy, that they are having similar experiences.

There are philosophers who accept all these propositions, and to them the question how one is to justify one's belief in the existence of other minds presents no special difficulty. If they are concerned with it at all, they are interested only in the choice of premises for the argument from analogy. Thus they may maintain that the basis of the argument is not so much that there is a physical resemblance between other people's behaviour and one's own as that other people also use language or that they behave purposefully. But none of this raises any serious question of principle.

To many philosophers, however, this argument from analogy appears too weak for its purpose ; some of them indeed, for reasons into which we shall enter later on, maintain that it is altogether invalid, or at least that it cannot be valid if the other propositions which I have listed are true. But this leaves them rather at a loss to justify their belief in the existence of minds other than their own. Some take the view that the sixth proposition is incompatible with the fifth. They hold that the argument from analogy can be valid only if it is possible, at least in principle, for one person to have direct knowledge of the experiences of another. Others, who will not allow this to be possible, try to resolve the difficulty by denying the second proposition on my list. Their contention is that while the statements that one makes about one's own experiences need not be equivalent to statements about one's overt behaviour, this does not apply *mutatis mutandis* to the statements that one makes about the experiences of others; to say of someone other than oneself that he is having such and such an experience is, on this view, always to describe his actual, or potential, behaviour. But this asymmetry in the analysis of statements which appear so very similar arouses objections on the score of common sense. A way of removing it is to deny my third and fourth propositions, with the result that all statements about experiences, whether one's own or anybody else's, are interpreted as statements about behaviour; and there are philosophers who take this heroic course. Finally, there are those who, rejecting the sixth proposition but accepting the other five, find themselves inadequately defended against solipsism. Let us try to see where the truth lies.

We may take as our starting-point the propositions that I can have direct knowledge of my own experiences and that I cannot have direct knowledge of anyone else's. What does it mean to say that I have direct knowledge of my own experiences? Presumably the knowledge claimed is knowledge that something or other is the case, that I have a headache, or that I am thinking about a philosophical problem: and the point is that if the statement which expresses what I claim to know refers only to my present experience, I am in the best possible position to decide its truth. If I judge it to be true, it is on the basis of an experience which conclusively verifies it, inasmuch as it is the experience which the statement describes. Let it be granted that others besides myself can come to know that such a statement is true. Even so, their knowledge will not be direct. For it can be founded only upon experiences of their own, and however strongly these experiences favour the truth of the statement about my experience, they do not establish it conclusively. It remains at least conceivable that these experiences should occur and the statement in question be false. But no such possibility of error arises when an experience testifies only to itself. Thus the warrant for saying that I can have direct knowledge of my own experiences but not of anybody else's is just that my experiences are exclusively my own. The reason why I cannot directly know the experiences of another person is simply that I cannot have them.

But is it true that I cannot? There is a good and familiar sense in which two different people may be said to perceive the same object, hear the same sound, feel the same feeling, and from this it follows that they do have the same experiences. But, it will be answered, even though they may perceive the same objects or hear the same sounds, they do not sense the same sense-data : the sense-data which they respectively sense may be qualitatively similar but they cannot be numerically the same. And if it be asked why they cannot, the answer is that sense-data are made private by definition ; they are characterized in such a way that the statement that one person has another's sense-data describes no possible situation. Similarly, if one person is afraid and another shares his feeling, it will still be said that there are two feelings of fear and not one. To say that the feeling is shared is to say that the two feelings are qualitatively similar and that they have the same ostensible object : it is not to say that they are numerically identical. But how are they differentiated ? It is not to be supposed that one can number people's feelings as one can number the things that they may carry in their pockets. The answer is that we are to say that there are two feelings and not one, just because there are two persons. It is made a convention that any feeling that one has is an experience which is private to oneself. And so it becomes a necessary truth that one person cannot have, and therefore cannot strictly know, the experiences of another.

In this sense, then, to wish that one directly knew the thoughts and feelings of others is to demand a logical impossibility. It is not surprising, therefore, nor should it be a matter for dissatisfaction, that the wish cannot be gratified. The situation, however, is normally not so simple as this. In the end one may be in the ridiculous position of deploring a necessary truth; but at the outset the complaint that one does not know what others are thinking or feeling may very well have its source in empirical fact. It may in fact be the case that other people baffle or deceive me. I have some evidence to show what they are really like, but it is not sufficient for me. Even though they tell me, with every appearance of honesty, what is going on in their minds, I may still doubt whether they are telling me the truth. How can I ever be sure, in such a case, that I am not mistaken? A question of this sort frequently expresses a felt anxiety.

But how is this anxiety to be allayed? If someone finds himself in this position, what can be required to reassure him? Perhaps only that he should get to know other people better, and this he may achieve; it is at all events a practical problem. Perhaps he needs something out of the ordinary, like telepathy, which he may not in fact be able to achieve. But even if he were

to achieve it he would be doing no more than add to his
current methods of communication. What is strange
about telepathy is that a message is transmitted, apparently without the employment of any physical means.
But to be informed of another's feeling telepathically
is not to share it; and even if it were to share it,
there would be exactly the same grounds here as in the
case of any other shared feelings for saying that there
were two feelings and not one. There is the experience of the person who makes the communication and
the experience of the person who receives it. These
experiences are necessarily different, since they are the
experiences of different persons, and this remains true
no matter how the communication is made. In this
respect telepathy is no better than the telephone.

The reason why telepathy is apt to be appealed to
in this context is that it is regarded as a possible means
of bridging the gap between one person and another.
But if the gap is empirical in character, if it is a question
of practical ignorance or misunderstanding, then there
are surer ways of bridging it than by telepathy. And
if the gap is logical, nothing can bridge it. It is suggested that in order really to know what another person
is thinking or feeling, I have literally to share his
experiences; and then it turns out that to share his
experiences, in the sense required, is to have his experiences, and that in order to have his experiences I
have to be that person, so that what is demanded of me
is that I become another person while remaining myself,
which is a contradiction. The contradiction is masked
when the requirement is put in the form of my needing
to know another person's experiences in the way that
I know my own. For this may not seem too much to
expect, until it is realized that the way in which I am

supposed to know my own experiences is by actually having them, and that the reason why I cannot in this way know the experiences of others is that my literally having their experiences has been made a logical impossibility.

Just as the factual complaint that other people are opaque is carried to the point where the knowledge sought is made logically unobtainable, so there is a tendency to try to overcome this logical impossibility by making it only factual. No doubt telepathy is not enough, but if I were co-conscious with another person, then perhaps I should really know his experiences in the way that I know my own : I should really then succeed in being two persons at once. Now there is no reason why we should not describe certain paranormal phenomena by speaking of co-consciousness : and if someone who complains that other minds are closed to him is complaining only that he does not have such unusual experiences, his problem is still practical ; he may hope to find some means of acquiring them. But even in an instance of co-consciousness it may still be argued that the gulf between persons remains. For either there is only one person involved, in which case all that is in question is his knowledge of himself, or there are two or more, and in that case there are as many sets of experiences as there are people. Each person has his own experiences, and no one can have those of any other person. The gap is not bridged, and never can be bridged, because, for someone who argues in this way, nothing is ever going to count as one person's having the experiences of another.

It is the crossing and recrossing of the line between the empirical and the logical that makes this a text-book problem in the theory of knowledge. The undoubted

o

fact that one sometimes does not know what other people are thinking and feeling gives rise to the suspicion that one never really does know; the next step is to pass from saying that one never does in fact know what goes on in another person's mind to saying that one never can know, and interpreting this statement in such a way that it is necessarily true. But this appears to concede too much to scepticism, and so a move is made in the reverse direction. It is suggested that even if we never do in fact know what goes on in the minds of others, there might be circumstances in which we should. The assertion of our ignorance is thus reconstrued as empirical but, like an alien without a valid passport, it is constantly liable to deportation. As soon as an attempt is made to treat it seriously as an empirical statement, it tends to change back into a necessary truth. At this point it is tempting to lose one's patience with the problem. It is simply, one may say, a matter of what one chooses to understand by knowledge. If in order to know what another person is thinking or feeling I have literally to share his experiences, and if at the same time nothing is going to count as my literally sharing his experiences, then plainly nothing is going to count as my knowing, really knowing, what he thinks or feels. But the moral of this is just that if we interpret 'knowing' in so strict a fashion we deprive ourselves of the right to use it in this context. All that one has to do to defeat the sceptic is to give up the stipulation that in order to know what goes on in another's mind one must literally share his experiences; or, if the stipulation is to be retained, we must interpret it in such a way that it is at least theoretically capable of being met; one must allow it to be possible that experiences should, in the relevant sense, be common to different persons. In either case the question whether we can know what goes on in the minds of others becomes, what it ought to be, a question of empirical fact.

But this solution of the problem is too simple. The philosopher who raises doubts about our knowledge of other minds is not primarily concerned with questions of linguistic usage. He may readily admit that there is a sense in which different people can be said to share the same experiences: he may admit even that, as words are ordinarily used, it is perfectly legitimate to speak of a person's knowing what goes on in someone else's mind. Nevertheless he will insist that there must still remain a sense in which it is necessarily true that experiences are private, and necessarily true also that one cannot know the thoughts and feelings of others in the way that one knows one's own. Consequently, he will maintain, the statements that one makes about the experiences of others stand in need of justification in a way in which the statements that one makes about one's own experiences do not. The fact, if it be a fact, that it is socially correct in certain circumstances to speak of knowing such statements to be true is beside the point. The question at issue is what such claims to knowledge can be worth.

Even so, it may be said, the sceptic's difficulties are illusory. Let us allow it to be necessarily true that I cannot know the experiences of others in the way that I know my own. It by no means follows that I cannot have good reasons to believe in their existence. Such reasons will indeed be supplied to me by experiences of my own, just as the reasons which someone else may have for believing in the existence of my experiences must ultimately be supplied to him by experiences of

his own. But they may be good reasons none the less.
Even if knowledge is defined so strictly that one can
never rightly claim to know what others think or feel,
it will still be true that we can attain to states of highly
probable opinion. It may well be thought perverse to
insist on speaking of highly probable opinion in cases
where attention to ordinary usage should lead us to
speak of knowledge ; but this is not a point of any
great importance. What is important is that many of
the statements which one makes about the experiences
of others are fully justifiable on the basis of one's own.

But once again this manner of disposing of the
problem is too simple. We are still left with the question how these statements can be justified and how the
insistence that they shall be justifiable conditions their
interpretation. There is here an instructive parallel
to be drawn with the case of statements about the
past. Thus, just as it is necessarily true that I cannot
have the experiences of another person, so is it necessarily true that I cannot now experience a past event.
Accordingly, if I am asked what reason I have to
believe in the truth of any statement which refers to the
past, the best answer that I can make is to produce a
record, whether in the form of memory or some other.
And with this most people would be satisfied. Even
though no form of record be infallible, when different
records agree they are willing to rely upon them. But
philosophers are not so easily satisfied. They point out
that it is logically possible that all the records should be
false and, what is more, that it is logically impossible to
test them, since that would require returning to the past.
Then some attempt to elude the logical necessity by
claiming that in remembering an event we actually
return to the past, a view which they express less

crudely by saying that memory is, or may be, a form of direct knowledge, that when an event is remembered it may be literally re-experienced. And others argue that since our reasons for believing a proposition about the past always come down to our having some experiences in the present, or expecting to have some experiences in the future, propositions about the past are really propositions about the present or the future in disguise. But both are mistaken. Propositions about the past are not about the present or future: they are about the past. And if an event is past in the sense which is here in question, its occurrence is logically independent of any present experience, even if the present experience is a memory of it and the memory is veridical. In the same way my knowing, or believing, that some other person is having an experience of a certain sort is not my having his experience; and in saying, on the basis of certain evidence, that he is having this experience, I am not merely giving a redescription of the evidence.

But if my statement is not just a redescription of the evidence, then one is inclined to say that it must be an inference from it. And this brings back the question whether, and how, the inference is justified. To which, as we have seen, the usual answer is that it is justified by an argument from analogy. But here we come upon the difficulty that the argument, at least as it is commonly presented, is not like any ordinary argument of this type. In the ordinary way, an argument from analogy is a substitute for direct observation. Suppose that the symptoms of two diseases are similar in certain respects and that I have discovered that one of the diseases is caused by a microbe of a certain sort: I may infer by analogy that the other disease also is caused by a microbe which I have not so far observed, and I may

then set about trying to detect it. Had I already
detected it, I should not need the argument from analogy
to establish its existence. But what is the direct
observation for which the argument from analogy is a
substitute in the case of other minds ? There is nothing
describable as detecting the thoughts and feelings of
another apart from adding to the premisses of the
argument, that is, collecting further information about
his behaviour. And it is for this reason that many
philosophers hold that the argument from analogy is
invalid in this case. Yet surely part at least of my
reason for ascribing thoughts and feelings and sensations to others is that I have them myself. Suppose that
someone tells me that he has had a tooth extracted
without an anaesthetic, and I express my sympathy, and
suppose that I am then asked, 'How do you know that
it hurt him ?' I might reasonably reply, 'Well, I know
that it would hurt me. I have been to the dentist and
know how painful it is to have a tooth stopped without
an anaesthetic, let alone taken out. And he has the
same sort of nervous system as I have. I infer, therefore, that in these conditions he felt considerable pain,
just as I should myself.'

Now here I do argue by analogy and up to a point
the argument proceeds like any other. By analogy
with what I have observed of other people and what I
have learned about myself, I infer that someone with
the relevant sort of nervous system, when operated on
in such and such conditions, will show signs of pain,
signs that I may well be able to detect if I watch him
closely enough. But then I want to go further and
argue from the existence of these signs to the existence
of his actual feeling of pain, which *ex hypothesi*, since it
is not my feeling, I cannot detect. And at this point

some philosophers will object. 'You want to infer from the shadows on the blind to the existence of the people inside the room; but the parallel does not hold. For there is nothing which corresponds in this case to going into the room and meeting the people. It is rather as if you were to look for the invisible fairy that you supposed to animate your watch. You are succumbing to the myth of the ghost in the machine.'[1] Nevertheless I maintain that my feeling pain when the dentist operates on me does supply me with a reason for believing that my friend feels pain when the dentist operates on him; and that when I say that my friend feels pain, I do not mean merely that he shows signs of pain. I mean to ascribe to him a feeling of the same sort as I have myself. But what, it may be asked, are we to understand by this?

This question takes us back to the first of the propositions which I began by listing, 'When someone other than myself says that he has a headache, what he is saying about himself is the same as what I should be saying about myself if I were to say that I had a headache'. A shorter and more familiar form of this proposition is: 'When someone other than myself says "I have a headache" what he means is the same as what I mean when I say "I have a headache"'. But when it is put in this way, there is clearly a sense in which the proposition is false. For when he says 'I have a headache' he means that he has a headache, and when I say 'I have a headache' I mean that I have a headache, and since we are two different persons our meanings are not the same. There is, however, a sense in which they are the same. For if he is using the

---

[1] Cf. John Wisdom, *Other Minds, passim,* and Gilbert Ryle, *The Concept of Mind.*

English language correctly, he uses the words 'I have a headache' to state that he has a headache and not, for example, to state that he has a toothache or that he has seen a ghost; and I too, if I am using the English language correctly, use the words 'I have a headache' to state that I have a headache, and not that I have a toothache or that I have seen a ghost. Rules can be given for the correct use in English of expressions like 'I have a headache', and these rules are intersubjective in the sense that not only I but anyone can follow them. Thus the reason for saying that what my friend means when he says that he has a headache is the same as what I mean when I say that I have a headache is that our use of the expression 'I have a headache' conforms to the same rules.

The next question to consider is whether, when I say of him that he has a headache, what I am saying about him is the same as what I say about myself when I say that I have a headache. And here again the answer is that it is the same in so far as the use of the expression 'he has a headache' is governed by the same rules as the use of the expression 'I have a headache'. There are, indeed, peculiarities about the use of personal pronouns, especially in the first person, which make these two expressions function somewhat discrepantly; but there is still a sense in which they may properly be said to conform to the same rules. Thus, the statement that he has a headache is not entailed by 'he says he has a headache', or by 'he groans and clutches his head', or by any combination of such statements, any more than the statement that I have a headache is entailed by any statements about what I say, or about my overt behaviour, or by any combination of such statements. And just as my saying that I have a headache and my

behaving in certain ways is good evidence in favour of
my having a headache, and none the less good because
I myself do not require it, so his saying that he has
a headache and his behaving in certain ways is good
evidence in favour of his having a headache, and none
the less good because he does not require it.   But the
evidence, though good, is not conclusive.   It does not
constitute the meaning of the statement whose truth it
supports.   What it means to say of any person, whether
myself or any other, that he has a headache is that he has
a headache, that his head is hurting him, that he feels
pain in his head.   It does not mean that he says he has
a headache, or that he gives any outward signs of pain.
But his saying that he has a headache, or his showing
signs of pain, may be the best evidence that those who
are not the person in question ever in fact have for
concluding that he really is in pain.

But now some philosopher may say: 'Is it really
good evidence?   Prove to me that it is good evidence.'
To which one might answer, 'He is a truthful sort of
person, and people do commonly tell the truth in these
circumstances unless they have special reason not to,
and he seems to have no motive for lying to us in this
instance'; or 'When people behave in this sort of way
they generally do have headaches'.   'But how do you
know that they do?'   'Well, I do for one, and So-and-so
says that he has a headache when he behaves in this
way, and he usually tells the truth.'   'But how do you
know that he is truthful?'   And then I give the evidence.   'But perhaps he is truthful about the things
that you can test, but not about his own thoughts or
feelings.   How do you know that this is not so?   Can
one ever really know anything about the thoughts and
feelings of another?'

This threatens to bring us back to the point from which we started. Let us see if we cannot now find a way of escaping from the circle. It would seem that this is one of the cases in which the denial that knowledge is attainable has its source in the fact that those to whom it is denied are regarded as being in some way underprivileged. We cannot really know what happened in the past because we cannot go back and look. The best evidence that we can now obtain is not the best conceivable; this follows simply from the fact that we are not contemporary with the events in question. So, if really knowing is to be equated with having the best evidence conceivable, it becomes, as I have said, a necessary fact that one cannot really know the truth of any statement about the past. In the same way, we cannot really know what is going on in some other part of space. This seems a smaller deprivation than the other because of the possibility of visiting the place in question. If we cannot visit it, it is for a practical and not a logical reason. Even so, it takes time for us to travel, and by the time we get to the distant place the event will be past. Our evidence for its occurrence will not be so good as it could be, as it might have been if we had been at the right place when the event was still present. But it is impossible, logically impossible, that, being where we are, we should also be somewhere else. Once more we are necessarily underprivileged, given our actual situation. It is not necessary that we should be in this situation, but it is necessary that if we are in this situation, then we are not also in some other which is incompatible with it. One might have lived at a different time, though it is arguable that this is not to be admitted without qualification. To say of someone living now that he might have lived many million years ago provokes at least the query whether he could, in that case, still be the same person : on the other hand, it appears to make quite good sense to say that one might be a few years older or younger than one is. And clearly one might at any given moment be in a different place from that in which one happens then to be. A statement which mis-describes a person's spatial position is false but not self-contradictory. But if the best possible evidence for the truth of a statement is to be obtained only by those who are in a spatio-temporal situation which happens not to be ours, it does follow necessarily that we cannot obtain it. And if it is, by definition, only the privileged, the eyewitnesses, who can really know the fact in question, then, given that we are not among them, it is necessarily true that we can never really know it.

It does not follow, however, that we are reduced to scepticism. So long as we hold it to be theoretically conceivable that we should be in the privileged situa-tion, the fact that we are not is not regarded as con-demning us to utter ignorance. We are not inclined to say that the evidence we can obtain is good for nothing at all just because it is not, and in the circumstances cannot be, the best possible. Thus, when it is a ques-tion of knowing about events which are remote from us in space, we are quite ready to accept inductive arguments. For, in such cases, the handicap from which we suffer, though logically insuperable, is easily overcome in our imagination. It seems to us that we might very well be privileged, even though we are not ; that in some straightforward sense we could be there among the eyewitnesses, rather than here where we are, in fact. And this assumption that direct evidence is theoretically accessible to us is all that we require to make us content with indirect evidence, provided, of course, that this is good of its kind. When the handicap is due to our position in time, it does indeed appear more serious. We find it less easy to conceive of ourselves as occupying a different position in time than as occupying a different position in space; and this difficulty, as I have remarked, increases as the time envisaged is more remote. The doubt arises whether events occurring at a distant time are even theoretically accessible to us, whether there is any sense in saying that we might have been in the best possible position to observe them; and this in its turn throws doubt upon the validity of the evidence that we are in fact in a position to obtain, however good of its kind it may appear to be. Nevertheless this doubt does not, as a rule, take serious hold even upon philosophers. The fact that some at least of the events which are now remote from us in time have been, or will be, offered to our observation secures their admission into the category of those that are theoretically accessible, and the warrant is then extended to the other members of the class. In this way we credit ourselves with having the required support for our inductive arguments.

When it comes, however, to the case of other minds, the fact of our being underprivileged appears, at first sight, very much more serious. For here it might seem not only that we were necessarily handicapped, given our actual situation, but that the handicap itself was necessary. To be privileged is to be the other person. Only he really knows when he thinks and feels. I do not and cannot because I am myself and not he. But is it even conceivable that I should be he? It is plainly a contradiction that I should both remain myself and be someone other than myself: yet this is exactly what here seems to be required.   In the other cases which we have considered, the fact that one was under-privileged was the outcome of one's situation, the position that one happened to occupy in space and time ; and it could be remedied, at least in theory, by the situation's being changed.   But how could a change in my situation make me someone else ?   Unless I keep something of myself, that is, some characteristic which is peculiar to me, I have not just changed my situation, I am abolished altogether.   But if I do keep something of myself, I have not attained the privileged position, I am not identified with the other person.   Thus it seems that the thoughts and feelings of others are inaccessible to us, not merely because we happen to occupy the relatively unfavourable position that we do, but because we are respectively the persons that we are. The privileged position, in any given instance, which is that of being the person who has the thoughts and feelings in question, is one that only he could occupy. It would appear, therefore, that we are debarred from 'really knowing' one another's inner experiences in a more radical way than we are debarred from 'really knowing' events which are remote from us in space or time.   For while we are underprivileged in these cases also, it is at least conceivable that we should not have been.

   This reasoning is plausible but I do not think that it is sound.   Admittedly, to say that an experience is not one's own but someone else's is to imply that one is not, and could not be, in the best possible position to know that it exists.   But equally, to say of an event that it is remote in time or space is to imply that one is not, and could not be, in the best possible position to know that it exists : for the description of the event as occurring somewhere else, or as being future or past, already carries the implication that one is under-privileged. This does not follow from a mere description of the event, or even from a description of its place and date, so long as it contains no reference to the position of the speaker; and it is for this reason that it can be held to be contingent that the speaker's actual position is not the best possible. But equally, the implication that one is underprivileged is not contained in any mere description of an experience, or even in a description of the person whose experience it is, so long as no reference is made to the identity of the speaker. The use of pronouns like 'he' and 'they' and 'you' shows that the speaker is not himself the person whose experiences are in question, and consequently that he is not in the most favourable position to know about them, just as the use of tenses or of words like 'miles away' shows that the speaker's spatio-temporal position is not privileged. But the implied, or explicit, reference to the situation, or identity, of the speaker is logically irrelevant to the facts which he describes. When these demonstratives are replaced by descriptions it becomes an open question whether the speaker is, or is not, in the best possible position to verify his statement. Suppose that the statement does in fact refer to the experience of some other person. Even so, what is stated is just that some-one who answers to a given description is having such and such an experience, and from this it does not follow, with regard to any person who is not actually identified as one who does not answer to the description or is not having the experience, that he is not the person in question. It does not follow, therefore, that the description is not satisfied by the speaker himself. Once it is stated that an experience is the experience of someone other than myself, the possibility of its also being my experience is indeed ruled out. But so long as the statement contains no explicit or implicit reference to me, it can be no part of its descriptive content that I am relatively ill-equipped to verify it. In a sense, therefore, there are no such things as statements about other minds. There are many statements which do in fact refer to the experiences of persons other than the speaker. But they do not themselves state that this is so. Considered only with respect to its descriptive content, no statement says anything about the point of view from which it is made.

What is asserted, then, by a statement which in fact refers to the experience of someone other than myself is that the experience in question is the experience of someone who satisfies a certain description : a description which, as a matter of fact, I do not satisfy. And then the question arises whether it is logically conceivable that I should satisfy it. But the difficulty here is that there are no fixed rules for determining what properties are essential to a person's being the person that he is. My answer to the question whether it is conceivable that I should satisfy some description which I actually do not, or that I should be in some other situation than that in which I am, will depend upon what properties I choose, for the occasion, to regard as constitutive of myself. Ordinarily one does not regard one's spatial position as constitutive of oneself, and so can readily conceive that, apart from casual obstacles, one might at any given moment be in a different place from that in which one is. Neither does one regard as constitutive the property of living at the precise time at which one does. On the other hand, the property of living at about that time does tend to be regarded as constitutive of the person : and this is the explanation of the fact, which we have already noticed, that while one can easily imagine oneself to be a year or two older or younger than one is, the picture of oneself as living many million years ago has about it an air of contradiction. But it is contradictory only if one chooses to make it so. It is logically, although not causally, possible that having the character I have, nothing else being regarded as essential, I should have lived in the ice age. It is logically possible even that I should under this condition have had my actual memories, though of course they would in that case all have been delusive. In general, it would appear that one can imaginatively deprive a person of any particular property that he possesses without falling into contradiction, but that as this procedure is continued there comes a point where he ceases to be the same person. But the determination of this point, that is, the decision to regard a certain set of properties as being indispensable, is very largely arbitrary. So long as some are kept constant, all the others can be varied, and with the choice of a new set of constants the ones that were previously held constant can be varied in their turn.

Let us now see what bearing this has upon our present problem. The analogy between two persons is never perfect : this follows simply from the fact that they are two different persons. Neither can one suppose it to be perfect ; for to suppose it perfect would be to merge the two persons into one. At the same time, it may be very extensive, and it can always be conceived as being more extensive than it is. Now when one ascribes some inner experience, some thought or feeling, to another, the rational ground for this ascription consists in one's knowing him to possess some further properties. The assumption is that there is a uniform connection between the possession of these properties and the undergoing of an experience of the sort in question. I infer that my friend is in pain, because of the condition of his tooth, because of his nervous system, because of his wincing, and so forth; and the connection of these properties with a feeling of pain is one that I can, in principle, test, one that I may in fact have tested in my own experience. But, it may be objected, the connection may not hold good in his case. How can you tell? But if it does not hold good in his case, this must be because of some other property that he possesses, the addition of which creates a counter-example to the rule. It would not hold good, for instance, if the additional property were that of his having been hypnotized to feel no pain. But with regard to any further property that he possesses it is conceivable at least that I should test the rule so as to find out whether the addition of this property does make a difference. Sometimes I can carry out the test directly by myself acquiring the properties concerned. Of course there are many properties that I cannot acquire. If I happen, for example, to have been born on a Thursday, I cannot directly test the hypothesis that people who were born on a Wednesday do not in these circumstances feel pain. But I have no reason to suppose that this is a relevant factor, and good indirect evidence that it is not. And, if our argument is correct, there will be no properties that I am in principle debarred from testing, however many there may be that I cannot test in fact. But even if my friend has no properties which make him an exception to the rule about feeling pain, may he not still be an exception just as being the person that he is? And in that case how

P

can the rest of us ever know whether or not he really does feel pain ? But the answer to this is that nothing is described by his being the person that he is except the possession of certain properties. If, *per impossibile*, we could test for all the properties that he possesses, and found that they did not produce a counter-example to our general hypothesis about the conditions in which pain is felt, our knowledge would be in this respect as good as his : there would be nothing further left for us to discover.

To sum up, it is necessarily true that, being the person that I am, I am not also someone else. It is necessarily true that I could not conceivably satisfy all the descriptions that some other person satisfies and still remain a distinct person. And if this is made the requirement for my really knowing what he thinks or feels, then it is necessarily true that this is something that I can never really know. On the other hand, with regard to any given property, which I may or may not myself in fact possess, there seems to be no logical reason why I should not test the degree of its connection with some other properties : and what I am asserting when I ascribe an experience to some other person is just that the property of having it is co-instantiated with certain others. The inference is not from my experi-ence as such to his experience as such, but from the fact that certain properties have been found to be conjoined in various contexts to the conclusion that in a further context the conjunction will still hold. This is a normal type of inductive argument ; and I cannot see that it is in any degree invalidated by the fact that, however far one is able to extend the positive analogy, it always remains within the compass of one's own experience.

9

ON WHAT THERE IS

IN this paper I begin by considering some remarks of Professor W. V. Quine's on what he calls 'the onto-logical problem'.[1] Professor Quine holds that from the fact that a sign has meaning it does not, in general, follow either that there is anything that it stands for, or that there is anything that it denotes. This applies, in his view, not only to words like 'red' which are some-times thought to stand for properties, but also to words like 'Pegasus' which are commonly regarded as names; for he argues that it is always possible to convert such names into descriptions, and then analyse out the descriptions in the way that Russell has suggested. Moreover, even in the case where an expression does denote something, it does not follow that what it means is identical with what it denotes; for, as the example of 'the morning star' and 'the evening star' shows, two expressions may denote the same object without having the same meaning. Whether in such cases, or indeed in any others, Professor Quine would wish to say that an expression named, or stood for, what it denoted, is not clear to me; nor is it clear to me whether he thinks that there are any signs, such as demonstratives or pronouns, which are meaningful only if there is something which they denote. But these points are not important for

[1] W. V. Quine, 'On What There Is', *Review of Metaphysics*, vol. ii, no. 5. Reprinted in *Supplementary Proceedings of the Aristo-telian Society*, vol. xxv, appendix.

his argument. What he is concerned to prove is that it is true of all general terms and of a great many, if not all, singular terms that one can use them meaningfully without thereby committing oneself to the existence of anything whatsoever. That is to say, one can use them to make significant, and not merely formal, statements which are such that it does not follow from them that anything exists.

At the same time, one may very well wish to make assertions from which it does follow that something exists; and to the extent that we do make such assertions we are, according to Quine, committed to an ontology. To say that one is committed to an ontology is, indeed, just his way of saying that one affirms that something or other exists. Suppose now that we introduce the convention that when we wish to state that something exists we are to use an existential quantifier. Then the objects which we suppose to exist will be all and only those that are values of the variables which are bound by such existential quantifiers. The range of our ontological commitments may, however, be reduced by our ability to recast some of our existential statements in such a way that variables which take a certain type of value disappear from them. We may, for example, be able to dispense with abstract entities by showing that existential statements in which the bound variables have abstract entities for their values can be transformed, without alteration of meaning, into statements in which there are no bound variables but those allowing as values only concrete entities. This is, indeed, the programme of nominalism, as Quine conceives it. To the extent that we are unable to carry through this programme we are, in his view, admitting abstract entities into our ontology :

and, in general, we are obliged to recognize the existence of the values of any type of variable that we are unable to eliminate from those of our statements that can be existentially quantified.

But how are we to decide which are the statements that admit of existential generalization? Is it always the case that when we assert that ϕa we imply that there is an x such that ϕx? Certainly there are many instances in which this implication is not thought to hold. If I say that the ghost of Miltiades was seen by the Benthamite, I do not necessarily imply that there was anything that was both a ghost and what the Benthamite saw. It would be quite consistent for me to believe the story about the Benthamite and disbelieve in the existence of ghosts. The Benthamite had an hallucination: he saw what was not there. Or again, to take an example of Quine's own, from the statement that appendicitis is dreaded it need not follow that there exists something which is dreaded.[1] The motive for refusing to draw this conclusion might be that which Quine envisages, an unwillingness to allow that there are diseases, as distinct from things which are diseased; but the same refusal might be made by someone who did not at all mind saying that there were diseases but thought that appendicitis was not a disease that anybody ever had. In either case it is maintained that to be feared is not necessarily to exist; but there is a difference, perhaps not sufficiently marked by Quine, between denying that something exists on the ground that nothing of that kind can exist and denying that something exists on the ground that the sufficient

---

[1] W. V. Quine, 'Designation and Existence', *The Journal of Philosophy*, 36, 1939. Reprinted in *Readings in Philosophical Analysis*, ed. Feigl and Sellars.

conditions for its existence are not in fact fulfilled. There is, in other words, a distinction to be drawn between the cases in which one rejects an existential claim on empirical grounds and those in which it is rejected as a matter of principle: and it is only the second class of cases that has a philosophical interest.

Now I am sure that Quine would agree that in asserting ϕa we do not always imply that there is an x such that ϕx. But he might still wish to say that the assertion of ϕa carried with it some ontological commitment, that even if it did not entail that there was anything that satisfied ϕ, it did entail that there was something that satisfied ψ, where ψ was a different predicate, perhaps a predicate of a different order, from ϕ. There was no ghost for the Benthamite to see, but there was at least a sense-datum, the appearance of a ghost, which he sensed. Or, if we do not care to admit sense-data into our ontology, there was at least the Benthamite's body which was in such and such a pathological state. At all events, something happened; we are affirming a fact of some sort, however we may choose to describe it. The ways in which we do choose to describe such 'facts' will depend upon our conceptual system; and it is, according to Quine, the choice of a conceptual system that determines one's ontology.

Quine himself says that 'the only way in which we can involve ourselves in ontological commitments (is) by our use of bound variables'.[1] But this is misleading, as it stands. For it seems to suggest that we could rid ourselves of these commitments altogether merely by changing our notation. Since the function of the bound variable, as Russell uses it, is to assign to predicates a range of application, it would be better to

[1] *Op. cit.* pp. 31-32.

say that we are involved in ontological commitments only to the extent that we use predicates which are alleged to apply to something. And if one is asked what it is that they apply to, the only answer one can give is that it is whatever satisfies the predicates in question; to describe what they applied to would at best be to adjoin other predicates to them, leaving the objector free to ask what it is that these predicates apply to; and no doubt if one were sufficiently resourceful one could continue this game for some time. But there is no point in continuing it. For in using a predicate we already describe what it applies to. If I use the English word 'woman' correctly, I use it to talk of women. It can indeed be said that I use it to talk of adult human females, but the only point of this would be to explain the use of the word 'woman' to someone who did not understand it but did understand the use of 'adult human female'. It is true that merely by understanding the use of the word 'woman', or some predicative expression which is equivalent to it, we do not know what it applies to, in the sense of being able to list all the women that there are. But if names can be converted into descriptions, then listing the members of a class will simply be a question of adding further predicates; to say that the class contains at least two members will be to say that the predicate by which the class is defined is an ingredient in at least two compound predicates, each of which has application. Perhaps Mr. P. T. Geach has something of this sort in mind when, in the course of criticizing Quine, he speaks of 'exists' as a second-level predicate: [1] he may be proposing that instead of talking of objects existing we

[1] P. T. Geach, 'On What There Is', *Supplementary Proceedings of the Aristotelian Society*, vol. xxv, p. 131.

should talk of properties being instantiated. To this Quine takes exception on the ground that he does not accept a view which implies that predicates stand for something.[1] But to say of a predicate that it applies to something, or to make an equivalent statement in the object language by coupling the predicate with an instantiation symbol, which is all indeed that Russell's 'Ⅎx' comes to, is not necessarily to imply that there are properties, as opposed to what instantiates them. On the contrary, if to say that an object exists is to say that a property is instantiated, then to say that this property exists will be to say that some other property is instantiated, namely, some property which this property instantiates. And from the fact that a property ϕ is instantiated it certainly does not follow that there is anything that it instantiates.

The conclusion, then, which we appear to reach as a result of following Quine's argument, is that if we use a predicate in such a way as to assert or to imply that it has an application, we affirm the existence of anything by which the predicate is satisfied. But again we come upon the difficulty that not all the predicates that we use are regarded as being capable of applying to anything. For a formalist who does not admit numbers into his ontology, the expression 'being a prime number between 7 and 13' may have a meaning, but he will not allow that there is something to which it applies. But how, except in the case of negative existential statements, where it is actually asserted that a predicate applies to nothing, are we to distinguish between those predicates that are to be taken as applying to something and those that are not? The answer which Quine

---

[1] W. V. Quine, 'On What There Is', *Supplementary Proceedings of the Aristotelian Society*, vol. xxv, p. 156.

seems to give, when he is dealing with the problem of nominalism, is that we must always take them as applying to something unless we are able to replace them by other predicates; and here the criterion for one predicate's being replaceable by another is the possibility of translating the statements in which it figures into statements which do not contain it but do contain the other. Thus, the formalist aims to get rid of numbers by construing statements about numbers as statements about signs. This is a bad way of putting it since, if he is right, there can be no such thing as 'a statement about numbers', but it should be clear what is meant. And he succeeds only if of all the mathematical statements that he wishes to put forward there are none that he cannot reformulate as statements about signs.

There is, however, another example of Quine's in which he seems to use a different method of assessing ontological commitments.[1] When speaking of our freedom to adopt alternative conceptual schemes he gives as an instance the use of a physicalistic or a phenomenalistic scheme to describe what is perceived. He says that if our conceptual scheme is phenomenalistic we shall regard 'the conceptual scheme of physical objects as a convenient myth', and he implies that this view is justified if it suits our 'interests and purposes'. One might therefore expect him to hold that statements about physical objects could be replaced, without alteration of meaning, by statements about sense-data. For if we are committed to abstract entities so long as we are not able to refashion our statements in such a way that none of the bound variables which they contain take abstract entities as values, it would seem that the same should apply to physical objects. We can

[1] Op. cit. pp. 36-37.

dispense with them, on this showing, only to the extent that the statements which appear to mention them are actually translatable into statements which do not. But what Quine in fact says is that 'there is no likelihood that each sentence about physical objects can actually be translated, however deviously and complexly, into the phenomenalistic language'. And yet he holds that we are entitled, if we please, to treat physical objects as merely 'postulated entities'. But if we are unable to eliminate from our discourse the predicates which are understood as applying to physical objects, how is it that we are still free to deny that physical objects exist? By what criterion is it to be decided that something is a postulated entity? Is it simply a matter of refusing to say that it exists?

Quine himself offers no solution to the problem, but I think that the difficulty can be met. Let us say that a predicate ϕ is reducible to a set of predicates κ if it is not logically possible that anything should be experienced which exemplifies or manifests ϕ unless something exemplifies one or more members of κ, but it is logically possible that something should be experienced which exemplifies or manifests a member of κ even though nothing exemplifies ϕ. And let us say that a predicate is basic with respect to a given language if the language contains no predicate, or set of predicates, to which it is reducible. Then we may construe the statement that certain objects are postulated entities as a statement that certain predicates, namely those that ostensibly apply to the objects in question, are not basic. For, on this view, only what satisfies the basic predicates will be admitted to exist.

It is easy to see that this criterion requires much less than the other of those who wish to reduce their ontological commitments. For one predicate may be reducible to others, in the sense defined, without being eliminable in their favour. Reduction does not here imply the possibility of translation. Nor are we left with any problem about ridding ourselves of abstract entities. For even those who wish to say that there are abstract entities do not maintain that we experience anything that they instantiate without thereby experiencing anything that instantiates them. On this view, the question of one's ontology is a matter of how one chooses to describe what is experienced. It does not commit us to phenomenalism, not even to the weakened form of it which is here in question. We can employ a physicalistic language if we choose. But in any language which admits sensory predicates, they will be basic.

But this, it may be said, is a very arbitrary procedure. No doubt we can rid ourselves of abstract entities, or even of physical objects, by so limiting our use of the word 'exists' that we can consistently label them as 'convenient myths', but this does not prove that they really have no being. For what right have we to assume that nothing exists but what can be experienced? If someone wishes to have a more generous ontology, how can we refute him except on the basis of definitions which he is at liberty to reject? May he not even be right?

Let us explain this objection with the help of an example. It is maintained by Geach that 'whatever "redness" may or may not stand for, "red" certainly stands for something when used predicatively; if A and B are both red, then there is something they both are, and "red" stands for this'.[1] To which Quine

[1] *Supplementary Proceedings of the Aristotelian Society*, vol. xxv, p. 132.

replies that 'this step is gratuitous even granted a predilection for abstract entities'.[1] It is quite bad enough to supply entities for abstract singular terms to stand for without making the corresponding predicates stand for entities as well. It seems to me, however, that Quine here misunderstands Geach just as he accuses Geach on many points of misunderstanding him. For Geach explicitly says that expressions like 'the colour that A and B both are' are not to be regarded as names. They are predicative expressions and so, according to him, are expressions like 'what the predicate "red" stands for'. Consequently, to say that there is something that a predicate stands for commits us, on this interpretation, to no more than we are committed by using the predicate. It certainly does not commit us, as Geach himself points out, to holding that what the predicate stands for is an abstract entity, for this would lead, in the example chosen, to the absurd conclusion that some abstract entity was red. No doubt Quine has been misled here, as he well might be, by Geach's use of the expression 'stands for'. He assumes that Geach's 'standing for' is what he himself calls 'naming': but this is a mistake. On the contrary, one of the points that Geach appears most anxious to establish is that there may be something that a predicate stands for even though there is nothing that, in Quine's sense, it names. Why he is so anxious to establish this I do not know. It seems to me that whenever he says that predicates stand for something he could equally well for his purposes have said simply that they had a meaning. And this would have made it clearer that, at least as regards the being of abstract

[1] *Supplementary Proceedings of the Aristotelian Society*, vol. xxv p. 157.

entities, his disagreement with Quine was merely one of
terminology.

But let us suppose that someone wishes, as Geach
apparently does not, to put forward the view that
predicates do name abstract entities. Can it be shown
that he is wrong ? It might be pointed out that since
we can modify our usage in any way we please, the
realm of abstract entities must be remarkably crowded ;
but this may not disturb him. He may be willing to
affirm that there is an abstract entity waiting to be
named by any predicate that anyone can devise. In that
case, the most that can be done, I think, is to show
that his assumption is gratuitous. Suppose, what is
generally the case, that his only ground for believing in
abstract entities of this type is that words have meaning.
Then our task will be to show that the fact that words
have meaning can be explained without this assumption,
and further, that this assumption does not itself explain
it. Once this is achieved, we need not object to anyone's saying that there are universals. For we can
construe it simply as a way of saying that predicative
expressions are meaningfully used and understood.

The question of universals is unrewarding as a
subject for ontology, since nothing turns on it. Once
we have set out the motives for saying that there are
universals and the motives for saying that there are not,
the decision is unimportant. Whichever view is taken,
nothing follows with regard to the truth or falsehood
of any statement in which the predicates which are
supposed to stand for universals are used. In other
cases, however, a disagreement about ontology may
lead to, or reflect, a disagreement about the validity of
the statements in which the expressions giving rise to
the dispute occur. A formalist may reject a section of

mathematics which a realist accepts ; a physicist, who
is attracted to positivism, may object to the introduction
of unobservables into physical theories ; a behaviourist
may be led by his ontology to try to avoid talking about
the unconscious. There is a tendency to pass from
saying that a certain object or class of objects does not
exist to trying to dispense with the expressions that
appear to mention it. Quine himself would like to
forgo making statements in which the bound variables
have abstract entities for values, except when he can
prove their innocence by finding a method of translating
them. But are such purists justified ? Or are their
opponents justified in allowing themselves a greater
latitude ? The trouble with these questions is that
there are no agreed criteria by reference to which they
can be settled. If the purist wishes to deny himself the
use of certain symbols, then let him do so ; it will be
interesting to see how well he manages without them.
Those who decide to retain them will consider it a
sufficient justification that they perform the function
that they do. But there is no way of justifying their
retention other than describing the use to which they
are put. And if someone, in a given case, considers that
this justification is not sufficient, I do not know what
more is to be said.

This shows, I think, how we should deal with such
questions as ' What right have we to assume that nothing
exists except what can be experienced ? ' If we have
settled our usage of the term ' exists ' in such a way that
nothing which is not capable of being experienced can
properly be said to exist, then our ground for making
the statement that nothing exists except what can be
experienced will be that it is necessarily true. But of
course it is open to anyone to adopt a different con-

vention. If he is allowed to use symbols which do not apply to anything observable, he may also be allowed to say that what those symbols stand for nevertheless exists. It may be that in so doing he will come to use the word 'exist' in ways that are not sanctioned by ordinary usage, but that is objectionable only to the extent that it makes it likely that he will be misunderstood. The important question is not whether he chooses to say that his symbols stand for something, or even whether he chooses to say that the things which his symbols stand for exist, but how he uses these symbols. If there is a point in saying that only what can be experienced exists, a statement which is itself not wholly in conformity with ordinary usage, it is to lay down conditions for the legitimacy of descriptive expressions : we are to admit only such expressions as apply directly or indirectly to what can be experienced. A query may then be raised about the justification of this procedure. But that is a matter into which I shall not enter here.

It is tempting to dismiss all talk about ontology as being merely a question of how we use, or how we propose to use, such expressions as 'is real' or 'exists' or 'there is'. But, while I do not wish to say that this procedure is incorrect, I think that there are cases in which it somewhat misses the point. It is true that such a question as 'Are there numbers?' appears strange. We do not normally speak of there being or not being numbers without qualification, but only of there being or not being numbers which fulfil such and such conditions, for example, the condition of lying within a certain range of integers and being a prime. And it is true that when we speak in this way of there being numbers we do not take ourselves to be implying that

they are identical with physical objects, or with other
things that we are prepared to say exist. The use in
these various contexts of such an expression as 'there
are' does not in practice lead to misunderstanding.
But it is not to be supposed that those who raise
questions about the being of numbers would deny any
of this. Their problem is not that they are baffled by,
or even fretful about, the use of ontological phrases.
It is that they find numbers themselves mysterious.
They see that numbers cannot simply be identified with
numerals, and so they take to wondering what sort of
things they are. The pharisaical answer that numbers
are numbers is not likely to set their minds at rest.
What is required, I think, is to show how knowing what
a number is comes down to knowing how to operate
with numerals. The statement that there are numerals
but there are no numbers is literally false; but it is
interesting in so far as it heralds an attempt to explain
things that are apt to puzzle us; what is meant, for
example, by saying that mathematical propositions are
necessary, or how discovery is possible in mathematics
as well as invention. In general, I think it may be said
that the interest of an ontological dispute lies in someone's denying that something is. The denial of being
is, in philosophy, the prelude to an explanation: the
affirmation of being more often a refusal to provide one.

I agree with Quine, as against Geach, that one's
ontology is to some extent at least a matter of choice.
I do not know why Geach supposes that 'certain
concepts like *existence* and *truth* and *thing* and *property*
are inevitably used in all rational discourse whatsoever'.[1]   To take only one example, it seems to me that
instead of talking about things and properties we might

[1] *Op. cit.* p. 136.

very well talk about predicates having application. Moreover, even if Geach were able to show that all those who did not share his ontology were muddled in their analyses of the concept of 'existence', it would not follow that their conceptual schemes were illegitimate, or even in any way defective. There are, for example, various criteria for deciding whether a conceptual scheme is satisfactory in physics : but the physicist's ability to philosophize about existence is not among them.

The only restrictions that I would put upon our choice of predicates is that the making of some observation must count as a test for their being satisfied : for otherwise I do not see how they are to be understood. With regard to basic predicates, it might be suggested that while there were an indefinite number of alternative schemes available, one was superior to the others in as much as it permitted us to give a more complete description of the facts. But here we meet with the difficulty that what is counted as a fact depends in part upon our conceptual scheme. What can be said, I think, is that a scheme A is superior to another scheme B if to everything describable in B as a fact there corresponds something describable in A as a fact, but there are descriptions of facts in A to which nothing corresponds in B. But this does not carry us very far.

I conclude, as Quine does, that questions about ontology can legitimately be interpreted as questions about the choice of conceptual schemes and about the relationship of their various elements, and that in so far as the adoption of an ontology is simply a matter of choosing a conceptual scheme it is to be attacked or defended on pragmatic grounds. But the tolerance to which this should lead is not always easy to maintain.

Q

When Quine and Goodman renounced abstract entities were they thinking only that it would be more convenient to dispense with statements in which the bound variables took abstract entities for values ? [1]   Was there not a suggestion that their reason for renouncing them was that they did not believe in their existence ? Let us say at least that they found abstract entities mysterious. And in this case also the denial of being was a prelude to an explanation.

[1] *Vide* Nelson Goodman and W. V. Quine, 'Steps towards a Constructive Nominalism', *Journal of Symbolic Logic*, vol. xii, 4.

ON THE ANALYSIS OF MORAL JUDGEMENTS

'Most of us would agree', said F. P. Ramsey, address-ing a society in Cambridge in 1925, 'that the objectivity of good was a thing we had settled and dismissed with the existence of God. Theology and Absolute Ethics are two famous subjects which we have realized to have no real objects.' There are many, however, who still think that these questions have not been settled; and in the meantime philosophers of Ramsey's persuasion have grown more circumspect. Theological and ethical statements are no longer stigmatized as false or meaning-less. They are merely said to be different from scien-tific statements. They are differently related to their evidence; or rather, a different meaning is attached to 'evidence' in their case. 'Every kind of statement', we are told, 'has its own kind of logic.'

What this comes to, so far as moral philosophy is concerned, is that ethical statements are *sui generis*; and this may very well be true. Certainly, the view, which I still wish to hold, that what are called ethical state-ments are not really statements at all, that they are not descriptive of anything, that they cannot be either true or false, is in an obvious sense incorrect. For, as the English language is currently used — and what else, it may be asked, is here in question? — it is by no means improper to refer to ethical utterances as statements;

when someone characterizes an action by the use of an ethical predicate, it is quite good usage to say that he is thereby describing it; when someone wishes to assent to an ethical verdict, it is perfectly legitimate for him to say that it is true, or that it is a fact, just as, if he wished to dissent from it, it would be perfectly legitimate for him to say that it was false. We should know what he meant and we should not consider that he was using words in an unconventional way. What is unconventional, rather, is the usage of the philosopher who tells us that ethical statements are not really statements at all but something else, ejaculations perhaps or commands, and that they cannot be either true or false.

Now when a philosopher asserts that something 'really' is not what it really is, or 'really' is what it really is not, that we do not, for example, 'really' see chairs and tables, whereas there is a perfectly good and familiar sense in which we really do, or that we cannot 'really' step into the same river twice, whereas in fact we really can, it should not always be assumed that he is merely making a mistake. Very often what he is doing, although he may not know it, is to recommend a new way of speaking, not just for amusement, but because he thinks that the old, the socially correct, way of speaking is logically misleading, or that his own proposal brings out certain points more clearly. Thus, in the present instance, it is no doubt correct to say that the moralist does make statements, and, what is more, statements of fact, statements of ethical fact. It is correct in the sense that if a vote were taken on the point, those who objected to this way of speaking would probably be in the minority. But when one considers how these ethical statements are actually used, it may be found that they function so very differently from

other types of statement that it is advisable to put them
into a separate category altogether ; either to say that
they are not to be counted as statements at all, or, if this
proves inconvenient, at least to say that they do not
express propositions, and consequently that there are
no ethical facts. This does not mean that all ethical
statements are held to be false. It is merely a matter of
laying down a usage of the words 'proposition' and
'fact', according to which only propositions express
facts and ethical statements fall outside the class of
propositions. This may seem to be an arbitrary
procedure, but I hope to show that there are good
reasons for adopting it. And once these reasons are
admitted the purely verbal point is not of any great
importance. If someone still wishes to say that ethical
statements are statements of fact, only it is a queer sort
of fact, he is welcome to do so. So long as he accepts
our grounds for saying that they are not statements of
fact, it is simply a question of how widely or loosely we
want to use the word 'fact'. My own view is that it is
preferable so to use it as to exclude ethical judgements,
but it must not be inferred from this that I am treating
them with disrespect. The only relevant consideration
is that of clarity.

The distinctions that I wish to make can best be
brought out by an example. Suppose that someone
has committed a murder. Then part of the story consists of what we may call the police-court details ;
where and when and how the killing was effected ; the
identity of the murderer and of his victim ; the relationship in which they stood to one another. Next there
are the questions of motive : the murderer may have
been suffering from jealousy, or he may have been
anxious to obtain money ; he may have been avenging

a private injury, or pursuing some political end. These questions of motive are, on one level, a matter of the agent's reflections before the act; and these may very well take the form of moral judgements. Thus he may tell himself that his victim is a bad man and that the world would be better for his removal, or, in a different case, that it is his duty to rid his country of a tyrant, or, like Raskolnikov in *Crime and Punishment*, that he is a superior being who has in these circumstances the right to kill. A psycho-analyst who examines the case may, however, tell a different story. He may say that the political assassin is really revenging himself upon his father, or that the man who persuades himself that he is a social benefactor is really exhibiting a lust for power, or, in a case like that of Raskolnikov, that the murderer does not really believe that he has the right to kill.

All these are statements of fact; not indeed that the man has, or has not, the right to kill, but that this is what he tells himself. They are verified or confuted, as the case may be, by observation. It is a matter of fact, in my usage of the term, that the victim was killed at such and such a place and at such and such a time and in such and such a manner. It is also a matter of fact that the murderer had certain conscious motives. To himself they are known primarily by introspection; to others by various features of his overt behaviour, including what he says. As regards his unconscious motives the only criterion is his overt behaviour. It can indeed plausibly be argued that to talk about the unconscious is always equivalent to talking about overt behaviour, though often in a very complicated way. Now there seems to me to be a very good sense in which to tell a story of this kind, that this is what the man did and that these were his reasons for doing it, is to give a complete description of the facts. Or rather, since one can never be in a position to say that any such description is complete, what will be missing from it will be further information of the same type; what we obtain when this information is added is a more elaborate account of the circumstances of the action, and of its antecedents and consequences. But now suppose that instead of developing the story in this circumstantial way, one applies an ethical predicate to it. Suppose that instead of asking what it was that really happened, or what the agent's motives really were, we ask whether he was justified in acting as he did. Did he have the right to kill? Is it true that he had the right? Is it a fact that he acted rightly? It does not matter in this connection what answer we give. The question for moral philosophy is not whether a certain action is right or wrong, but what is implied by saying that it is right, or saying that it is wrong. Suppose then that we say that the man acted rightly. The point that I wish to make is that in saying this we are not elaborating or modifying our description of the situation in the way that we should be elaborating it if we gave further police-court details, or in the way that we should be modifying it if we showed that the agent's motives were different from what they had been thought to be. To say that his motives were good, or that they were bad, is not to say what they were. To say that the man acted rightly, or that he acted wrongly, is not to say what he did. And when one has said what he did, when one has described the situation in the way that I have outlined, then to add that he was justified, or alternatively that he was not, is not to say any more about what he did; it does not add a further detail to the story. It is for this reason that these ethical predicates are not factual; they do not describe any features of the situation to which they are applied. But they do, someone may object, they describe its ethical features. But what are these ethical features? And how are they related to the other features of the situation, to what we may provisionally call its 'natural' features? Let us consider this.

To begin with, it is, or should be, clear that the connection is not logical. Let us assume that two observers agree about all the circumstances of the case, including the agent's motives, but that they disagree in their evaluation of it. Then neither of them is contradicting himself. Otherwise the use of the ethical term would add nothing to the circumstantial description; it would serve merely as a repetition, or partial repetition, of it. But neither, as I hope to show, is the connection factual. There is nothing that counts as observing the *designata* of the ethical predicates, apart from observing the natural features of the situation. But what alternative is left? Certainly it can be said that the ethical features in some way depend upon the natural. We can and do give reasons for our moral judgements, just as we do for our aesthetic judgements, where the same argument applies. We fasten on motives, point to consequences, ask what would happen if everyone were to behave in such a way, and so forth. But the question is: In what way do these reasons support the judgements? Not in a logical sense. Ethical argument is not formal demonstration. And not in a scientific sense either. For then the goodness or badness of the situation, the rightness or wrongness of the action, would have to be something apart from the situation, something independently verifiable, for which the facts adduced as the reasons for the moral judgement were evidence. But in these moral cases the two coincide. There is no procedure of examining the value of the facts, as distinct from examining the facts themselves. We may say that we have evidence for our moral judgements, but we cannot distinguish between pointing to the evidence itself and pointing to that for which it is supposed to be evidence. Which means that in the scientific sense it is not evidence at all.

My own answer to this question is that what are accounted reasons for our moral judgements are reasons only in the sense that they determine attitudes. One attempts to influence another person morally by calling his attention to certain natural features of the situation, which are such as will be likely to evoke from him the desired response. Or again one may give reasons to oneself as a means of settling on an attitude or, more importantly, as a means of coming to some practical decision. Of course there are many cases in which one applies an ethical term without there being any question of one's having to act oneself, or even to persuade others to act, in any present situation. Moral judgements passed upon the behaviour of historical or fictitious characters provide obvious examples. But an action or a situation is morally evaluated always as an action or a situation of a certain kind. What is approved or disapproved is something repeatable. In saying that Brutus or Raskolnikov acted rightly, I am giving myself and others leave to imitate them should similar circumstances arise. I show myself to be favourably disposed in either case towards actions of that type. Similarly, in saying that they acted wrongly, I express a resolution not to imitate them, and endeavour also to discourage others. It may be thought that the mere use of the dyslogistic word 'wrongly' is not much of a discouragement, although it does have some emotive force. But that is where the reasons come in. I discourage others, or at any rate hope to discourage them, by telling them why I think the action wrong; and here the argument may take various forms. One method is to appeal to some moral principle, as, for example, that human life is sacred, and show that it applies to the given case. It is assumed that the principle is one that already has some influence upon those to whom the argument is addressed. Alternatively, one may try to establish certain facts, as, for example, that the act in question caused, or was such as would be likely to cause, a great deal of unhappiness; and here it is assumed that the consideration of these facts will modify the hearer's attitude. It is assumed that he regards the increase of human misery as something undesirable, something if possible to be avoided. As for the moral judgement itself, it may be regarded as expressing the attitude which the reasons given for it are calculated to evoke. To say, as I once did, that these moral judgements are merely expressive of certain feelings, feelings of approval or disapproval, is an oversimplification. The fact is rather that what may be described as moral attitudes consist in certain patterns of behaviour, and that the expression of a moral judgement is an element in the pattern. The moral judgement expresses the attitude in the sense that it contributes to defining it. Why people respond favourably to certain facts and unfavourably to others is a question for the sociologist, into which I do not here propose to enter. I should imagine that the utilitarians had gone some way towards answering this question,

although theirs is almost certainly not the whole
answer. But my concern at present is only to analyse
the use of ethical terms, not scientifically to explain it.
  At this point it may be objected that I have been
excessively dogmatic. What about the people who
claim that they do observe ethical properties, non-
natural properties, as G. E. Moore once put it,[1] not
indeed through their senses, but by means of intellec-
tual intuition ? What of those who claim that they have
a moral sense, and mean by this not merely that they
have feelings of approval and disapproval, or whatever
else may go to define a moral attitude, but that they
experience such things as goodness or beauty in a way
somehow analogous to that in which they experience
sounds or colours ? What are we to say to them ? I
may not have any experiences of this sort myself, but
that, it may be said, is just my shortcoming. I am
surely not entitled to assume that all these honest and
intelligent persons do not have the experiences that
they say they do. It may be, indeed, that the differences between us lie not so much in the nature of our
respective experiences as in our fashion of describing
them. I do in fact suspect that the experiences which
some philosophers want to describe as intuitions, or as
quasi-sensory apprehensions, of good are not significantly different from those that I want to describe as
feelings of approval. But whether this be so or not, it
does not in any way affect my argument. For let it be
granted that someone who contemplates some natural
situation detects in it something which he describes as
'goodness' or 'beauty' or 'fittingness' or 'worthiness
to be approved'. How this experience of goodness, or
whatever it may be, is supposed to be related to the

[1] Vide his *Principia Ethica*, chap 1.

experiences which reveal the natural features of the situation has not yet been made clear, but I take it that it is not regarded merely as their effect. Rather, the situation is supposed to look good, or fitting, in much the same way as a face may be said to look friendly. But then to say that this experience is an experience of good will be to say no more than that it is this type of experience. The word 'good', or whatever other value term may be used, simply comes to be descriptive of experiences of this type, and here it makes no difference whether they are regarded as intuitions or as moral sensations. In neither case does anything whatsoever follow as regards conduct. That a situation has this peculiar property, the property whose presence is established by people's having such experiences, does not entail that it is preferable to other situations, or that it is anyone's duty to bring it into existence. To say that such a situation ought to be created, or that it deserves to exist, will be to say something different from merely saying that it has this property. This point is obscured by the use of an ethical term to describe the property, just because the ethical term is tacitly understood to be normative. It continues to fulfil its function of prescribing the attitude that people are to take. But if the ethical term is understood to be normative, then it does not merely describe the alleged non-natural property, and if it does merely describe this property, then it is not normative and so no longer does the work that ethical terms are supposed to do.

This argument may become clearer if, instead of designating the supposed property from the outset as 'good', we refer to it simply as 'X'. The question then arises whether X is identical with good. How is this question to be interpreted? If it is interpreted as merely asking whether X is of a certain quality, whether it exhibits the character for which the word 'good' is being made to stand, then the answer may very well be that the two are identical; but all that this amounts to is that we have decided to use the word 'good' to designate what is also designated by 'X'. And from this no normative conclusion follows. It does not follow that the situation characterized by X has any value, if its having value is understood as implying not merely that it answers to a certain description but that it has some claim upon us, that it is something that we ought to foster or desire. Having appropriated the word 'good' to do duty for X, to serve as a mere description of a special tone or colouring of the situation, we shall need some other word to do the normative work that the word 'good' did before. But if 'good' is allowed to keep its normative sense, then goodness may indeed be attributed to X, but the two cannot be identified. For then to say that X is good is not just to say that 'X' stands for a certain property. It is to say that whatever has this property is to be valued, sought, approved of, brought into existence in preference to other things, and so on. Those who talk of non-natural qualities, moral intuitions, and all the rest of it, may be giving peculiar descriptions of commonplace experiences, or they may be giving suggestive descriptions of peculiar experiences; it does not matter which view we take. In either case we are left with the further question whether what is so described is to be valued; and this is not simply equivalent to asking what character it has, whether natural, or non-natural, whatever that may mean. Thus even if an intuitionist does have experiences that others do not have, it makes no difference to the argument. We are still entitled to say that it is misleading for him to use a value-term to designate the content of such experiences; for in this way he contrives to smuggle a normative judgement into what purports to be a statement of fact. A valuation is not a description of something very peculiar; it is not a description at all. Consequently, the familiar subjective-objective anti-thesis is out of place in moral philosophy. The problem is not that the subjectivist denies that certain wild, or domesticated, animals, 'objective values', exist and the objectivist triumphantly produces them; or that the objectivist returns like an explorer with tales from the kingdom of values and the subjectivist says he is a liar. It does not matter what the explorer finds or does not find. For talking about values is not a matter of describing what may or may not be there, the problem being whether it really is there. There is no such problem. The moral problem is: What am I to do? What attitude am I to take? And moral judgements are directives in this sense.

We can now see that the whole dispute about the objectivity of values, as it is ordinarily conducted, is pointless and idle. I suppose that what underlies it is the question: Are the things that I value really valuable, and how can I know that they are? Then one party gives the answer: They are really valuable if they reflect, or participate in, or are in some other mysterious way related to an objective world of values; and you can know that they are by inspecting this world. To which their opponents reply that there is no such world, and can therefore be no such inspection. But this sort of argument, setting aside the question whether it is even intelligible, is nothing to the purpose. For suppose that someone did succeed in carrying out such an inspection. Suppose that he had an experience which we allowed him to describe in these terms. He can still raise the questions : Are these values the real ones ? Are the objects that I am inspecting themselves really valuable, and how can I know that they are ? And how are these questions to be answered ? They do not arise, it may be said. These objective values carry the stamp of authenticity upon their faces. You have only to look at them to know that they are genuine. But, in this sense, any natural situation to which we attach value can carry the stamp of authenticity upon its face. That is to say, the value which is attached to it may be something that it does not occur to us to question. But in neither case is it inconceivable that the value should be questioned. Thus, these alleged objective values perform no function. The hypothesis of their existence does no work ; or rather, it does no work that is not equally well done without it. Its effect is to answer the question : Are the things that I value really valuable ? by Yes, if you have a certain sort of experience in connection with them. Let us assume that these experiences can be identified and even that there is some method for deciding between them when they appear to yield contradictory results. Even so, that someone does or does not have them is itself a 'natural' fact. Moreover, this answer merely lays down one of many possible standards. It is on a par with saying : 'The things that you value are really valuable if they increase human happiness, or they are really valuable if certain persons, your pastors and masters, approve of them'. Then either one accepts the standard, or one raises the question again. Why should I value human happiness ? Why should I be swayed by my pastors and masters ? Why should I

attach such great importance just to these experiences ?
In the end there must come a point where one gets no
further answer, but only a repetition of the injunction :
Value this because it is valuable.

In conducting this argument, I have put the most
favourable interpretation upon my opponents' claims ;
for I have assumed that what is described as the apprehension of objective values may be a different experience from the everyday experience of attaching value
to some natural situation ; but, in fact, I am fairly
confident that what we have here are two different ways
of describing the same experience. And in that case
the answer that the 'objectivists' give to the question :
Are the things that I value really valuable ? is the
'subjective' answer that they are really valuable if you
value them, or perhaps that they are really valuable if
certain other people value them. What we are given is
an injunction not to worry, which may or may not
satisfy us. If it does not, perhaps something else will.
But in any case there is nothing to be done about it,
except look at the facts, look at them harder, look at
more of them, and then come to a moral decision. Then,
asking whether the attitude that one has adopted is the
right attitude comes down to asking whether one is prepared to stand by it. There can be no guarantee of
its correctness, because nothing counts as a guarantee.
Or rather, something may count for someone as a
guarantee, but counting something as a guarantee is
itself taking up a moral standpoint.

All this applies equally to 'naturalistic' theories of
ethics, like Utilitarianism. By defining 'right', in the
way that Bentham does, as 'conducive to the greatest
happiness of the greatest number', one does give it a
descriptive meaning ; but just for that reason one takes

it out of the list of ethical terms. So long as the word
'right' keeps its current emotive force, the implication
remains that what is right ought to be done, but this by
no means follows from Bentham's definition. Nevertheless, it is clearly intended that the definition should
somehow carry this implication; otherwise it would not
fulfil its purpose. For the point of such a definition,
as Professor Stevenson has well brought out in his
Ethics and Language, is not that it gives precision to the
use of a word, but that it covertly lays down a standard
of conduct. The moral judgement is that happiness is
to be maximized, and that actions are to be evaluated,
praised or blamed, imitated or avoided, in proportion
as they militate for or against this end. Now this is not
a statement of fact, but a recommendation; and in the
ordinary way the sense of such a recommendation is
contained in some ethical term. These ethical terms
can also be given a descriptive meaning, but it is not
qua descriptive that they are ethical. If, for example,
the word 'wrong' is simply equated with 'not conducive
to human happiness', some other term will be needed
to carry the normative implication that conduct of this
sort is to be avoided; and it is terms of this kind, which
are not descriptive, that I am treating as distinctively
ethical.

I hope that I have gone some way towards making
clear what the theory which I am advocating is. Let
me now say what it is not. In the first place, I am not
saying that morals are trivial or unimportant, or that
people ought not to bother with them. For this would
itself be a judgement of value, which I have not made
and do not wish to make. And even if I did wish to
make it it would have no logical connection with
my theory. For the theory is entirely on the level of

R

analysis; it is an attempt to show what people are doing when they make moral judgements; it is not a set of suggestions as to what moral judgements they are to make. And this is true of all moral philosophy, as I understand it. All moral theories, intuitionist, naturalistic, objectivist, emotive, and the rest, in so far as they are philosophical theories, are neutral as regards actual conduct. To speak technically, they belong to the field of meta-ethics, not ethics proper. That is why it is silly, as well as presumptuous, for any one type of philosopher to pose as the champion of virtue. And it is also one reason why many people find moral philosophy an unsatisfying subject. For they mistakenly look to the moral philosopher for guidance.

Again, when I say that moral judgements are emotive rather than descriptive, that they are persuasive expressions of attitudes and not statements of fact, and consequently that they cannot be either true or false, or at least that it would make for clarity if the categories of truth and falsehood were not applied to them, I am not saying that nothing is good or bad, right or wrong, or that it does not matter what we do. For once more such a statement would itself be the expression of a moral attitude. This attitude is not entailed by the theory, nor do I in fact adopt it. It would indeed be a difficult position to maintain. It would exclude even egotism as a policy, for the decision to consult nothing but one's own pleasure is itself a value judgement. What it requires is that one should live without any policy at all. This may or may not be feasible. My point is simply that I am not recommending it. Neither, in expounding my meta-ethical theory, am I recommending the opposite. It is indeed to be expected that a moral philosopher, even in my sense of the term, will have his moral standards and that he will sometimes make moral judgements; but these moral judgements cannot be a logical consequence of his philosophy. To analyse moral judgements is not itself to moralize.

Finally, I am not saying that anything that anybody thinks right is right; that putting people into concentration camps is preferable to allowing them free speech if somebody happens to think so, and that the contrary is also preferable if somebody thinks that it is. If my theory did entail this, it would be contradictory; for two different courses of action cannot each be preferable to the other. But it does not entail anything of the sort. On my analysis, to say that something which somebody thinks right really is right is to range oneself on his side, to adhere to that particular standpoint, and certainly I do not adhere to every standpoint whatsoever. I adhere to some, and not to others, like everybody else who has any moral views at all. It is, indeed, true that in a case where one person A approves of X, and another person B approves of not-X, A may correctly express his attitude towards X by saying that it is good, or right, and that B may correctly use the same term to express his attitude towards not-X. But there is no contradiction here. There would be a contradiction if from the fact that A was using words honestly and correctly when he said that X was good, and that B was using words honestly and correctly when he said that not-X was good, it followed that both X and not-X were good, or that X was both good and bad. But this does not follow, inasmuch as the conclusion that X is good, or that not-X is good, itself expresses the attitude of a third party, the speaker, who is by no means bound to agree with both A and B. In this example, indeed, he cannot consistently agree with both, though he may disagree with both if he regards both X and not-X as ethically neutral, or as contraries rather than contradictories in respect of value. It is easy to miss this point, which is essential for the understanding of our position. To say that anything is right if someone thinks so is unobjectionable if it means no more than that anyone is entitled to use the word 'right' to refer to something of which he morally approves. But this is not the way in which it is ordinarily taken. It is ordinarily taken as the enunciation of a moral principle. As a moral principle it does appear contradictory; it is at least doubtful whether to say of a man that he commits himself morally both to X and not-X is to describe a possible attitude. But it may perhaps be construed as a principle of universal moral tolerance. As such, it may appeal to some; it does not, in fact, to me. But the important point is that it is not entailed by the theory, which is neutral as regards all moral principles. And here I may repeat that in saying that it is neutral as regards all moral principles I am not saying that it recommends them all alike, nor that it condemns them all alike. It is not that sort of theory. No philosophical theory is.

But even if there is no logical connection between this meta-ethical theory and any particular type of conduct, may there not be a psychological connection? Does not the promulgation of such a theory encourage moral laxity? Has not its effect been to destroy people's confidence in accepted moral standards? And will not the result of this be that something mischievous will take their place? Such charges have, indeed, been made, but I do not know upon what evidence. The question how people's conduct is actually affected by their acceptance of a meta-ethical theory is one for empirical investigation; and in this case, so far as I know, no serious investigation has yet been carried out. My own observations, for what they are worth, do not suggest that those who accept the 'positivist' analysis of moral judgements conduct themselves very differently as a class from those who reject it; and, indeed, I doubt if the study of moral philosophy does, in general, have any very marked effect upon people's conduct. The way to test the point would be to convert a sufficiently large number of people from one meta-ethical view to another and make careful observations of their behaviour before and after their conversions. Assuming that their behaviour changed in some significant way, it would then have to be decided by further experiment whether this was due to the change in their philosophical beliefs or to some other factor. If it could be shown, as I believe it could not, that the general acceptance of the sort of analysis of moral judgements that I have been putting forward would have unhappy social consequences, the conclusion drawn by illiberal persons might be that the doctrine ought to be kept secret. For my part I think that I should dispute this conclusion on moral grounds, but this is a question which I am not now concerned to argue. What I have tried to show is not that the theory I am defending is expedient, but that it is true.

I I

THE PRINCIPLE OF UTILITY

'THE law-giver should be no more impassioned than
the geometrician. They are both solving problems by
sober calculation.' The quotation is from Jeremy
Bentham's *Deontology*,[1] and it gives a measure both of
his peculiarity and his importance as a moral philosopher. His peculiarity was that he believed that
morals and politics could be made into a branch of
science: his importance lies in the way in which he
worked this theory out.

In its main outlines his system was very simple.
He accepted, apparently without question, the psychological hypothesis that every man acts only with a view
to his own interest; and this self-interest Bentham
identified with happiness. Happiness he defined as
'the possession of pleasures with the absence of pains,
or the possession of a preponderant amount of pleasure
over pain'.[2] These pleasures and pains, which he
laboriously classified, might be of various sorts. In
saying that every man pursued his own happiness,
Bentham did not mean to imply that every man was an
egotist, in the narrow sense of the term. He allowed
the existence of natural human sympathies which
would lead men to promote the happiness of others,
and among the conscious principles of human action

[1] Vol. ii, p. 19 (Bowring's edition).   [2] *Ibid.*

he included 'principles of benevolence'. It was, indeed, one of his main objects to recommend these principles of benevolence: like Bishop Butler, he maintained that to pay attention to the happiness of others was a mark of enlightened self-interest; it was the surest way of securing one's own. But the fact that men were capable of active benevolence did not seem to him to be inconsistent with his assumption that they acted always with a view to their own interest. If someone behaved, as we should say, unselfishly, he thereby showed that the pleasure which he derived, or expected to derive, from his unselfish action, even if it were no more than the pleasure of giving pleasure to someone else, seemed to him greater on balance than the pleasure he would derive from acting 'selfishly', or indeed from acting in any other way than the way in which he did. He might, of course, be mistaken. It might be that the result of his benevolence was 'to confer upon others a smaller portion of happiness than he himself sacrificed',¹ and in that case, Bentham held, his conduct 'would not be virtue — it would be folly'. 'It would not be effective benevolence, it would be miscalculation.' It would, indeed, be 'a course of action which could not intentionally have place'. A man might make a sacrifice of his own happiness to the happiness of others, but 'unless in some shape or other he derived more pleasure from the sacrifice than he expected to derive in abstaining from making the sacrifice, he would not, he could not, make it'.²

¹ An infelicitous quotation. As Mr. C. W. K. Mundle has pointed out in his review of *Jeremy Bentham and the Law* (*Mind*, vol. lviii, No. 229, pp. 119-120), it implies that a man can seek to promote the happiness of others at the expense of his own. But this is inconsistent with Bentham's fundamental thesis that the only possible motive for action is the maximizing of one's own happiness.

² *Deontology*, vol. i, p. 191.

From these psychological premisses Bentham inferred that 'pleasure is in *itself* a good; nay, even
setting aside immunity from pain, the only good'; and
that 'pain is in itself an evil; and indeed, without
exception, the only evil'. 'Or else', he adds, 'the
words good and evil have no meaning.' ¹ The logic of
this reasoning is not very clear, but I suppose that
Bentham, like his disciple John Stuart Mill, conceived
of 'good' as the object of desire and 'evil' as the object
of aversion; and from this, on the assumption that
things were sought only for their tendency to give
pleasure or avoided only for their tendency to give pain,
it would follow that pleasure was a good, and indeed
the only good, and that pain was an evil, and indeed the
only evil. If this was his reasoning, Bentham was more
consistent than Mill. For Mill was inclined to allow
that one pleasure might be qualitatively preferable to
another.² He spoke of 'higher' and 'lower' pleasures
in a way which suggested that he recognized another
standard of value than the mere preponderance of
pleasure. He seemed to imply that there was somehow
more intrinsic value in the enjoyment of a 'higher'
pleasure than in the enjoyment of a 'lower' pleasure to
an equal amount. This may indeed be unfair to Mill.
He may have meant only that what he called the higher
pleasures were the more intense, or possibly that the
total consequences of pursuing them were, in general,
more felicific than the consequences of pursuing
'lower' pleasures. And if he did mean only this his
talk about quality of pleasure, though certainly misleading, was not inconsistent with his principle that

¹ *Introduction to the Principles of Morals and Legislation*, chap. 10,
s. 10 (vol. i, p. 40, in Bowring's edition of *Works*).
² *Vide* J. S. Mill, *Utilitarianism*, and G. E. Moore, *Principia
Ethica*, pp. 77-81.

pleasure alone was good. But whereas Mill's language is ambiguous on this point, Bentham's is quite clear. He held that in comparing the value of two pleasures the only relevant consideration was the quantity of pleasure involved in either case, and this he characteristically brought under seven headings: the intensity of the pleasure, its duration, its certainty or uncertainty, its propinquity or remoteness, its fecundity, by which he meant its chance of being followed by further pleasures, its purity, by which he meant its chance of not being followed by pains, and finally, in cases where a number of persons are involved, its extent.[1] How one of these factors is to be weighed with another is never made clear, but if we allow, what Bentham seems never to have doubted, that there could be some practical method of scoring, then by the terms of his theory the pleasure that obtained the highest score would be the most valuable. Indeed, to say of one pleasure that it was more valuable than another could mean nothing else for Bentham than that when marked by these standards it had obtained a higher score. Naturally, these assessments would vary from person to person, but this would not affect their validity. Bentham's standard of value is objective in the sense that his rule that pleasure is the only good and pain the only evil is supposed to hold equally for all sentient

---

[1] Vide *Introduction to the Principles of Morals and Legislation*, chap. 4 (Bowring, vol. i, p. 16). To enable his readers to memorize these points, 'on which the whole fabric of morals and legislation may be seen to rest', Bentham puts them into verse. Thus

> '*Intense, long, certain, speedy, fruitful, pure*
> Such marks in *pleasures* and in *pains* endure.
> Such pleasures seek, if *private* be thy end :
> If it be *public*, wide let them extend.
> Such *pains* avoid, whichever be thy view :
> If *pains* must come, let them *extend* to few.'

The italics are his.

beings; but, in a derivative sense, it makes different things good for different persons, in so far as in all matters of pleasure and pain, different persons have different tastes. Neither was there any question for Bentham of their not being entitled to their respective tastes. A man might be mistaken in his estimates of what would bring him happiness, and in such a case he might benefit from advice. It might be that the sources of his pleasure were productive of greater pain to others, and then, as we shall see, the legislator might be called upon to intervene. But as regards the value of any actual experience it seemed obvious to Bentham that the person who was having the experience was the best, indeed the only sure, judge of whether it gave him pleasure or not. And in so far as it did give him pleasure it was to that extent good.

Now if it is true that the only object that any person is capable of seeking is his own happiness, then clearly there can be no sense in saying that he ought to seek any other. For any individual such questions as What ought I to do ? What is it my duty to do ? What is it right for me to do ? are all reducible to the question What will make me happiest ? Which of the courses of action open to me will secure for me the greatest preponderance of pleasure over pain ? From the point of view of the individual, therefore, there can be no distinction between morality and expediency. If the most expedient action is defined as that which will in fact procure him the greatest measure of happiness, then it is also the action that he ought to do. To recommend him, on so-called moral grounds, to do any other would be either to deceive him about his chances of happiness, or else to bid him act in a way of which *ex hypothesi* he is psychologically incapable.

The case is different, however, when it is considered not from the point of view of the individual but
from the point of view of the community. Admittedly,
the community is nothing apart from the individuals
who belong to it. As Bentham says, 'the community is
a fictitious *body*, composed of the individual persons
who are considered as constituting as it were its
members', and he adds that what is called 'the interest of
the community' is nothing but 'the sum of the interests
of the various members who compose it'.[1] Nevertheless it does not follow that the interest of any given
member of the community at a given moment will be
the same as that of the community as a whole. It may,
in general, be true that a person consults his own interest
best by consulting the interests of others, but this rule
is not infallible. Occasions may arise in which the
effects of a certain course of action are such as to bring
more happiness to the agent himself than those of any
other course of action that was open to him, but are
not such as to bring more happiness to the total number
of persons who are affected by it. And this is especially
likely to be true in cases where the agent occupies a position of power; for in such cases the other members of
the community have a smaller chance of taking reprisals,
and so rendering his selfishness unprofitable to him.

Consequently, what is right for the individual is not
necessarily right for the community, and it is because
of this that there is in Bentham's system both an open-
ing and a need for a science of morality. The standpoint from which he considered all questions of right
and wrong, justice and injustice, and so forth, was not
personal but social; and it is only when this is understood, as it has not always been by his critics, that one

---

[1] *Introduction to Principles*, etc., chap. 1, s. 4 (Bowring, vol. i, p. 2).

is able to deal correctly with his principle of utility.

The principle of utility is simply this. Let us say that the value of an action is positive if the total quantity of pleasure that it causes to all the persons in any way affected by it is greater than the total quantity of pain ; and let us say that its value is negative if the total quantity of pain that it causes is greater than the total quantity of pleasure. If it causes an equal amount of pleasure and pain it may be said to have neutral value. Then, in any case in which the value of an action A exceeds that of another action B, it may be that both are positive but that the margin is greater in the case of A, or that while A's value is positive B's is neutral or negative, or that A's is neutral and B's negative, or that while the value of both is negative the margin is greater in the case of B. In all these cases let us say, for the sake of brevity, that A produces a greater quantity of happiness than B. Now the principle of utility is that of any two actions which differ in value, by these criteria, the more valuable is to be preferred. In other words, that action is to be chosen which will cause the greater quantity of happiness in the sense defined. And if the amount of happiness that they will respectively cause is equal, then there is no reason for choosing one of them rather than the other.[1]

Thus the principle of utility is defined in terms of happiness, which is itself defined by Bentham in terms of pleasure and pain. But since the word 'utility' does not in itself convey any very strong suggestion of happiness or pleasure, Bentham often preferred to speak explicitly of 'the greatest-happiness principle';

---

[1] This formulation of Bentham's principle is more precise than any that he actually gives himself. I am largely indebted for it to G. E. Moore. *Vide* his *Ethics*, pp. 40-42.

and it is under this title that the principle of utility commonly figures in his later works. He also used the expression 'the greatest happiness of the greatest number', which is the one most frequently quoted. Thus, in his *Introduction to the Constitutional Code*,[1] he wrote, 'The right and proper end of government in every political community is the greatest happiness of all the individuals of which it is composed, say, in other words, the greatest happiness of the greatest number'. The objection to this, however, is that the use in such a context of the words 'the greatest number' may suggest that a new criterion is being introduced, which would not necessarily coincide with the criterion of pleasure. It might be thought that one was required to consider not merely the total quantity of happiness that an action produced but also the way in which that happiness was distributed; so that an action which produced a greater quantity of happiness might not be preferable to one that produced a smaller quantity, if in the case of the less felicific action the happiness was more widely enjoyed. I am fairly sure, however, that this was not what Bentham meant. I think that he held, as he must have held to be at all consistent, that the right action was that which produced the greatest measure of happiness, no matter how it was distributed; and that in speaking of 'the greatest happiness of the greatest number' he intended only to emphasize the point that one of the most important factors by which the total quantity of happiness would be determined was the number of persons whom the action affected, and that no matter who these persons might be the interests of all of them were alike to count.

As I have said, the principle of utility is a social

---

[1] Section 2 (Bowring, vol. xi).

principle; it refers to the interests of individuals only in so far as they combine to constitute the interests of the community. At the same time it is put forward by Bentham as a criterion of morals. Thus he says : 'Of an action that is conformable to the principle of utility, one may always say either that it is one that ought to be done, or at least that it is not one that ought not to be done. One may say also, that it is right it should be done; at least that it is not wrong it should be done; that it is a right action; at least that it is not a wrong action. When thus interpreted the words *ought* and *right* and *wrong*, and others of that stamp, have a meaning : when otherwise they have none.' [1]

At this point, however, a difficulty arises. The object of Bentham's definition is to give words like 'right' and 'wrong' a purely descriptive meaning. It is assumed that there are various possible ways of acting in any given situation, and that one has to decide which of them is right. But this is equivalent to asking which of them produces the greatest quantity of happiness; and this, according to the theory, is a plain question of fact. Thus to say of two alternative actions that one is right and the other is not is simply to describe their respective consequences. It is to assert a proposition which is supposed to be objectively verifiable. Either the one action will produce more happiness than the other or it will not. And this might seem to justify Bentham's claim that he succeeds in putting morals on to a scientific basis. But let us suppose that I am actually faced with a choice of actions, and that of the various actions that I can choose there is one that will in fact produce a greater quantity of happiness than any of the others; and let us suppose, what is evidently

[1] *Introduction to Principles*, etc., chap. 1, s. 10 (Bowring, vol. i, p. 2.).

questionable, that I can know this to be so. Then this action will be right, according to Bentham's definition, and I may know that it is right. But is that any reason for my doing it ? As the word 'right' is ordinarily understood, this might seem a strange question to ask. It might be thought that the fact that I knew the action to be right would be a sufficient reason for my doing it. But this by no means follows from Bentham's argument. According to his principles, the only motive that I can have for doing any action is that I think it will secure my own greatest happiness; and from the fact that an action is right, in the sense that it brings the most happiness collectively to all those who are affected by it, it does not follow that it brings the most happiness to them severally; in particular, it does not follow that it brings the most happiness to me. Consequently, the fact that an action is right, and known to me to be right, is not a ground for my doing it.[1] For, as we have already seen, the only ground that I am allowed to have for doing any action is that I think that it will be in my own best interest, that it will bring the greatest quantity of happiness, not to the world at large, but simply to myself.

To some extent we have already met this objection by distinguishing between the personal and the social uses of words like 'right' and 'wrong', and by pointing out that it is only with the social uses that Bentham is concerned. Nevertheless the difficulty remains that every action, if it is to be done at all, has to be done by some person, and that, on Bentham's principles, it will not be done by any person unless he conceives it to be in his own interest. Consequently, while Bentham

---

[1] Except in so far as the thought that I am doing right may happen to give me pleasure. I recur to this point later on.

may have succeeded in finding a descriptive meaning
for the ethical terms that he uses, it appears to be at the
cost of sacrificing their normative force. If I adhere to
Bentham's system, I shall no longer judge of right and
wrong merely by my own sentiments; I am furnished
with an objective rule. And this is the great argument
that Bentham urges in its favour: that it takes moral
judgements out of the nebulous realm of sentiment, in
which other moral philosophers had placed them, and
brings them under the control of reason. But of what
use is my objective rule if it governs neither my own
actions nor those of anybody else? We shall all
continue to pursue our several interests: there is *ex
hypothesi* nothing else that we *can* do. Consequently,
all that I obtain by my acceptance of Bentham's principles is a new way of *describing* a certain class of actions,
namely those that conduce to the greatest happiness of
my community. I shall now say that these actions are
right, which I might not have said before. But I shall
not thereby be any more inclined to do them, unless I
have reason to believe that the action which conduces
to the greatest happiness of the community is also that
which conduces most greatly to my own.

    Bentham's solution of this difficulty is not so much
theoretical as practical. It is to try to make the interest
of the individual and that of the community coincide.
The point of view which he takes up is that of a law-
giver. He assumes that this law-giver has the power to
enforce his legislation upon the community, and the
question that he raises is, What laws shall he impose?
Now here again it may be objected that, if Bentham is
to be believed, the law-giver will in fact do whatever he
thinks will bring the greatest happiness to himself; so
that the question of what he ought to do is not of any

practical importance. But Bentham skilfully removes
the ground from this objection by assuming that his
legislator is a person who happens to find his own
greatest happiness in promoting the happiness of those
for whom he legislates.[1]   Thus, by psychological
necessity, he will in fact set out to make such laws as
will secure 'the greatest happiness of the greatest
number': he is morally obliged to do so by definition,
though if his psychology were different this would not
count for much; and the only question that remains is,
How is this end to be achieved?

   The answer to this question is complicated in detail:
in one form or another it occupies almost the whole
of Bentham's exceedingly voluminous works. But in
essentials it is simple. On the one hand people must
be encouraged, by precept, by their education, and
by social as opposed to legal sanctions, to find their
sources of pleasure in activities that conduce to, or at
least do not detract from, the happiness of others. And
on the other hand the laws must be so devised that
anti-social activities become unprofitable. There will
probably always be people who are naturally disposed
to take their pleasure in ways that run counter to the
interests of the community: but these dispositions can
be checked if the operation of the law makes the total
consequences of such activities to the agent himself a
lesser source of pleasure than of pain. Such at least
was Bentham's opinion. He assumed, what is not
altogether borne out by experience, that the knowledge
that he stood to suffer by them more than he would
gain would be sufficient to deter the prospective
'criminal' from following out his natural inclinations.
Accordingly, Bentham attached very great importance

[1] Vide *Introduction to the Constitutional Code.*

S

to the question of legal punishment. Since punishment consists in the infliction of pain, he was obliged to
regard it as in itself an evil. The only, but sufficient,
justification for it was that it made his 'offences'
unprofitable to the offender and so deterred both
him and others from repeating them. The problem
then became to find the degree of punishment that
would in every case most economically achieve these
ends. Too great a degree of punishment would
diminish the general happiness by causing an un-
necessary amount of suffering to the criminal; too
small a degree of punishment would improperly favour
the criminal at the expense of the community. But
how to discover the mean? The answer, as Bentham
recognized, would depend to some extent upon the
circumstances of each particular case, but he still
thought it possible to lay down certain general rules,
and in his usual systematic way he set about discovering
them. How near he thereby came to solving his problem is a matter that does not here concern us; but
it may very well be doubted whether the problem, as
Bentham conceived it, is capable of any precise solution.

We have remarked that one of the ways in which the
benevolent legislator operates is by encouraging people
to pursue their happiness in ways that will not conflict
with the happiness of others; and we may now add that
this seems to be the primary purpose of Bentham's
own moral system. And by this I do not mean merely
that he sets out to depict the rewards of benevolence in
such a manner as to make them appear as attractive as
possible. He does do this, but he also pursues his
end in a very much more subtle way. Like all moral
philosophers, he writes for an audience which is already
conditioned to respond in a certain fashion to the use

of moral terms. Thus, most people are brought up in such a way that they like, on the whole, to think of themselves as doing what is right and do not like to think of themselves as doing what is wrong. That is to say, it gives them pleasure to be able to tell themselves that they are acting rightly and pain to feel that they are acting wrongly. Thus the fact that an action is *called* 'right' does provide a motive for doing it, just as the fact that an action is called 'wrong' provides a motive for avoiding it. Now what Bentham does is to appropriate these moral terms for his own purposes. By defining right action as that which promotes 'the greatest happiness of the greatest number', he tries to get people to transfer to this notion of promoting the greatest happiness the feelings that they already have about doing what is right. He does not, indeed, himself appear to be aware that this is what he is doing. He talks of his definitions as if they were purely and simply descriptive, but in fact they are not so much descriptive as persuasive. The principle of utility is not a true, or even a false, proposition; it is a recommendation. Strictly speaking, it is a recommendation to use words in a certain fashion, but the point of it is that by this use of words people may be brought to act in the way that Bentham wishes. If the principle of utility were to be regarded as a true or false proposition, then its validity would turn on the question how words like 'right' and 'wrong' were actually used; and Bentham does in fact maintain that people do very commonly use such words in a way that conforms with his principle. His evidence is that when people dispute about questions of morality the considerations that they adduce, in so far as they are rational at all, are considerations of utility. But sometimes these considerations are not rational. In many cases, as Bentham himself admits, people's use of moral terms does not follow any principle. It merely reflects their more or less arbitrary sentiments of approval or disapproval. Bentham's comment on this is that it does not affect his argument; for, in such cases, the moral terms are being used without any factual meaning. But if his object really were to describe the current use of these terms this answer would be nothing to the purpose. For why should he not conclude, in conformity with the evidence, that words like 'right' and 'wrong' were sometimes used in accordance with the principle of utility, sometimes in accordance with some other, say, some religious principle, and sometimes without any factual meaning at all? The reason is that his object was not to discover exactly how such words are used. His object was to *give* them a meaning, which should be sufficiently in line with ordinary usage to serve the practical end that he had in view. What he was trying to do, whether he was aware of it or not, was to make the best of two worlds; to turn judgements of value into judgements of fact and at the same time to retain their emotive force, so that they would actually cause people to do what they were understood to describe. Unless the use of words like 'right' and 'wrong' was primarily emotive, this aim would not be achieved. And that is why I said that Bentham's definitions were not so much descriptive as persuasive.

Are we then to be persuaded by them? The stock objection to Bentham's system is that it is based upon a false psychology.[1] Not all human action is purposive; and of those actions which are purposive it is

---

[1] For elaborations of this criticism *vide* G. E. Moore, *Principia Ethica*, chap. 3, and F. H. Bradley, *Ethical Studies*, chap. 3.

not true that they are always such as the agent thinks will bring him the most happiness. For the most part people aim at particular objects ; they set out to accomplish certain tasks, to indulge their emotions, to satisfy their physical needs, to fulfil their obligations, to outwit their neighbours, to gratify their friends. These, and many others, are their ends, and while they are engaged in pursuing them they do not look beyond them. It may be that the achievement of these ends will actually give them pleasure, but this does not imply that they have had this pleasure in view all along. It is, indeed, possible to pursue an object, say, that of gratifying a friend, not even immediately for its own sake, but solely for the sake of the pleasure that one expects oneself to derive from its attainment ; but this is a sophisticated attitude, which even in the case of purely selfish action furnishes the exception rather than the rule. Nevertheless, it may be objected, whatever ends a person may in fact pursue, it is surely the case that he would not pursue them unless he liked doing so. And to say that he does what he likes is to say that he acts with a view to his own happiness, whether he be conscious of doing so or not. But now the question is, By what criterion are we to establish that a person is 'doing what he likes' ? If our measure of what a person likes is simply what he does, then to say, in this sense, that every man acts with a view to his own happiness is just to assert a tautology. It is to say no more than that every man does what he does. But if, on the other hand, our criterion of a person's liking one thing better than another is his saying to himself that he will derive more pleasure from it, then the proposition that every man, who acts purposively, does what he likes best is psychologically false ; and so, consequently, is the proposition that every man seeks his own greatest happiness.

I think that this objection is certainly valid against Bentham, but I do not think that it is so fatal an objection as some of his critics have supposed. For one thing, it is still possible to hold that pleasure is the only thing which is good in itself, even if one gives up the contention that it is the only thing which is ever actually desired. One can still encourage people to pursue pleasure, and nothing but pleasure, as an end, even while admitting that there are other ends which they can pursue. But I do not think that many people would be inclined to take this view, unless they also held the psychological doctrine that there could be no other end but pleasure. Once this psychological doctrine was shown to them to be false, I think that they would mostly not take pleasure as their only value. They would say that pleasure was sometimes to be aimed at, but sometimes not; and that some types of pleasure were more worth having than others. There is, however, a more subtle way of preserving the essential part of Bentham's system, and that is to maintain his proposition that every one seeks happiness, not in the way that he maintained it, as a psychological generalization, but as a tautology. Thus, we may agree to understand the word 'happiness' as referring, in this context, not to some particular object of desire, but to any object of desire whatsoever. That is to say, we can identify the 'happiness' of a person with the class of ends that he in fact pursues, whatever these may happen to be. No doubt this is not quite what is ordinarily meant by happiness, but that does not matter for our purpose. Then Bentham's principle of utility becomes the principle that we are always to act in such a way as to give as many people as possible as much as possible of whatever it is that they want. I think that this interpretation preserves the essence of Bentham's doctrine, and it has the advantage of making it independent of any special psychological theory.

A much more serious objection than the one that we have just now tried to meet is that Bentham's criterion is not practically workable. For, in the first place, it is impossible for any one to estimate *all* the consequences of any given action; they may extend over centuries. If Bentham had not written as he did, I should not now be writing this. I do not know in what way my writing will affect the ratio of pleasure to pain that Bentham's actions have so far produced; but presumably it will alter it in some way, if only for its effect upon myself; yet this is not a circumstance that Bentham could conceivably have taken into account. Besides, we are required to consider not merely the actual consequences of our actions but also what would have been the consequences of the actions that we might have done in their place. Ought Brutus to have murdered Caesar? Would someone else have murdered Caesar if Brutus had not? Suppose that but for Brutus Caesar would not have been murdered, what difference would this have made to the history of the Roman Empire? And what further difference would that have made to the history of Europe? Would Shakespeare still have existed? If he had still existed, he presumably would not have written the play of *Julius Caesar* in the form in which he did. And how much difference would that have made to the general happiness? Plainly the whole question succumbs into absurdity.

It is clear then that if we are to make any sense at

all of Bentham's principle we must confine its application to a limited number of the consequences of our
actions, namely to those consequences that the agent
can reasonably be expected to foresee. And, in fact, if
Bentham's principle is to be regarded, as I think that
he himself wished it to be regarded, not as a rule for
passing moral judgements after the event, but as a
practical guide to action, we are bound to interpret it
in this restricted way. For to a man who is considering
how he ought to act the only consequences that can be
relevant are those that he foresees. Even so, when it
comes to the assessment of these consequences, the
problem is by no means so straightforward as Bentham
seems to have assumed. Suppose that I am hesitating
between two courses of action, both of which, so far as
I can see, will affect only five people. And suppose
that I have reason to believe that if I do action A three
of these people will obtain some satisfaction from it,
whereas only two of them will be satisfied if I do action
B. But suppose also that the amount of dissatisfaction
that I shall cause to the remainder is likely to be somewhat greater in each instance if I do action A than if I
do action B. How, even in such a simplified example,
can I possibly work out the sum? In virtue of what
standard of measurement can I set about adding the
satisfaction of one person to that of another and
subtracting the resultant quantity from the dissatisfaction of someone else? Clearly there is no such standard, and Bentham's process of 'sober calculation' turns
out to be a myth.

Here again the answer is that to do justice to
Bentham's principle we must consider it as applying
not to individuals but to a society. The amount of
happiness that is likely to follow from any particular

action cannot be calculated with any nicety, though even so it will often be reasonably safe to judge that one course of action will produce more happiness than another; and in these cases there will be no difficulty in making Bentham's principle apply. But what can be judged with very much greater certainty is that the general observance of a certain set of rules throughout a given society will contribute more to the happiness of the members of that society than will the general neglect of those rules, or the observance of some other set of rules which might be adopted in their place. Our proposition is, in short, that the members of a given community will be more likely to obtain what they want on the whole, if they habitually behave towards one another in certain ways rather than in certain other ways, if they are, for example, habitually kind rather than cruel. And it seems to me that this is a type of proposition that can be practically verified. It is not indeed a question that can be settled by mathematical calculation. Our estimates of what it is that people 'really' want and how far they are satisfied are bound to be somewhat rough and ready. Nevertheless I think that by observing people's behaviour one can become reasonably sure that their general adherence to certain rules of conduct would on the whole promote the satisfaction of their wants. And it is just the discovery and application of such rules that Bentham's principle of utility recommends.

My conclusion is then that, while he did not succeed in setting either morals or politics 'upon the sure path of a science', Bentham did produce a guide for action which it is possible to follow, though not perhaps exactly in the form in which he stated it. Whether one follows it or not is then a matter for a moral decision.

If any one chooses to adopt what Bentham called the principle of asceticism and set about making himself and everyone around him as miserable as possible he can be remonstrated with but, strictly speaking, not refuted. It is, however, unlikely that he would now get very many people to agree with him. Again, it might be urged against Bentham that the question which we have to consider is not what people actually want but what they ought to want, or what they must be made to want; and no doubt there is something to be said for this point of view. But Bentham's attitude is simpler and it is at least arguable that from the practical standpoint it should be preferred.

12

FREEDOM AND NECESSITY

WHEN I am said to have done something of my own free will it is implied that I could have acted otherwise; and it is only when it is believed that I could have acted otherwise that I am held to be morally responsible for what I have done. For a man is not thought to be morally responsible for an action that it was not in his power to avoid. But if human behaviour is entirely governed by causal laws, it is not clear how any action that is done could ever have been avoided. It may be said of the agent that he would have acted otherwise if the causes of his action had been different, but they being what they were, it seems to follow that he was bound to act as he did. Now it is commonly assumed both that men are capable of acting freely, in the sense that is required to make them morally responsible, and that human behaviour is entirely governed by causal laws: and it is the apparent conflict between these two assumptions that gives rise to the philosophical problem of the freedom of the will.

Confronted with this problem, many people will be inclined to agree with Dr. Johnson: 'Sir, we *know* our will is free, and *there's* an end on't'. But, while this does very well for those who accept Dr. Johnson's premiss, it would hardly convince anyone who denied the freedom of the will. Certainly, if we do know that our wills are free, it follows that they are so. But the logical reply to this might be that since our wills are not free, it follows that no one can know that they are : so that if anyone claims, like Dr. Johnson, to know that they are, he must be mistaken. What is evident, indeed, is that people often believe themselves to be acting freely; and it is to this 'feeling' of freedom that some philosophers appeal when they wish, in the supposed interests of morality, to prove that not all human action is causally determined. But if these philosophers are right in their assumption that a man cannot be acting freely if his action is causally determined, then the fact that someone feels free to do, or not to do, a certain action does not prove that he really is so. It may prove that the agent does not himself know what it is that makes him act in one way rather than another : but from the fact that a man is unaware of the causes of his action, it does not follow that no such causes exist.

So much may be allowed to the determinist; but his belief that all human actions are subservient to causal laws still remains to be justified. If, indeed, it is necessary that every event should have a cause, then the rule must apply to human behaviour as much as to anything else. But why should it be supposed that every event must have a cause ? The contrary is not unthinkable. Nor is the law of universal causation a necessary presupposition of scientific thought. The scientist may try to discover causal laws, and in many cases he succeeds; but sometimes he has to be content with statistical laws, and sometimes he comes upon events which, in the present state of his knowledge, he is not able to subsume under any law at all. In the case of these events he assumes that if he knew more he would be able to discover some law, whether causal or statistical, which would enable him to account for them. And this assumption cannot be disproved. For however far he may have carried his investigation, it is always open to him to carry it further; and it is always conceivable that if he carried it further he would discover the connection which had hitherto escaped him. Nevertheless, it is also conceivable that the events with which he is concerned are not systematically connected with any others: so that the reason why he does not discover the sort of laws that he requires is simply that they do not obtain.

Now in the case of human conduct the search for explanations has not in fact been altogether fruitless. Certain scientific laws have been established; and with the help of these laws we do make a number of successful predictions about the ways in which different people will behave. But these predictions do not always cover every detail. We may be able to predict that in certain circumstances a particular man will be angry, without being able to prescribe the precise form that the expression of his anger will take. We may be reasonably sure that he will shout, but not sure how loud his shout will be, or exactly what words he will use. And it is only a small proportion of human actions that we are able to forecast even so precisely as this. But that, it may be said, is because we have not carried our investigations very far. The science of psychology is still in its infancy and, as it is developed, not only will more human actions be explained, but the explanations will go into greater detail. The ideal of complete explanation may never in fact be attained: but it is theoretically attainable. Well, this may be so: and certainly it is impossible to show *a priori* that it is not so: but equally it cannot be shown that it is. This will not, however, discourage the scientist who, in the field of human behaviour, as elsewhere, will continue to formulate theories and test them by the facts. And in this he is justified. For since he has no reason *a priori* to admit that there is a limit to what he can discover, the fact that he also cannot be sure that there is no limit does not make it unreasonable for him to devise theories, nor, having devised them, to try constantly to improve them.

But now suppose it to be claimed that, so far as men's actions are concerned, there is a limit : and that this limit is set by the fact of human freedom. An obvious objection is that in many cases in which a person feels himself to be free to do, or not to do, a certain action, we are even now able to explain, in causal terms, why it is that he acts as he does. But it might be argued that even if men are sometimes mistaken in believing that they act freely, it does not follow that they are always so mistaken. For it is not always the case that when a man believes that he has acted freely we are in fact able to account for his action in causal terms. A determinist would say that we should be able to account for it if we had more knowledge of the circumstances, and had been able to discover the appropriate natural laws. But until those discoveries have been made, this remains only a pious hope. And may it not be true that, in some cases at least, the reason why we can give no causal explanation is that no causal explanation is available ; and that this is because the agent's choice was literally free, as he himself felt it to be ?

The answer is that this may indeed be true, inasmuch as it is open to anyone to hold that no explanation is possible until some explanation is actually found.

But even so it does not give the moralist what he wants. For he is anxious to show that men are capable of acting freely in order to infer that they can be morally responsible for what they do. But if it is a matter of pure chance that a man should act in one way rather than another, he may be free but he can hardly be responsible. And indeed when a man's actions seem to us quite unpredictable, when, as we say, there is no knowing what he will do, we do not look upon him as a moral agent. We look upon him rather as a lunatic.

To this it may be objected that we are not dealing fairly with the moralist. For when he makes it a condition of my being morally responsible that I should act freely, he does not wish to imply that it is purely a matter of chance that I act as I do. What he wishes to imply is that my actions are the result of my own free choice: and it is because they are the result of my own free choice that I am held to be morally responsible for them.

But now we must ask how it is that I come to make my choice. Either it is an accident that I choose to act as I do or it is not. If it is an accident, then it is merely a matter of chance that I did not choose otherwise; and if it is merely a matter of chance that I did not choose otherwise, it is surely irrational to hold me morally responsible for choosing as I did. But if it is not an accident that I choose to do one thing rather than another, then presumably there is some causal explanation of my choice: and in that case we are led back to determinism.

Again, the objection may be raised that we are not doing justice to the moralist's case. His view is not that it is a matter of chance that I choose to act as I do, but rather that my choice depends upon my character.

Nevertheless he holds that I can still be free in the sense that he requires; for it is I who am responsible for my character. But in what way am I responsible for my character? Only, surely, in the sense that there is a causal connection between what I do now and what I have done in the past. It is only this that justifies the statement that I have made myself what I am: and even so this is an over-simplification, since it takes no account of the external influences to which I have been subjected. But, ignoring the external influences, let us assume that it is in fact the case that I have made myself what I am. Then it is still legitimate to ask how it is that I have come to make myself one sort of person rather than another. And if it be answered that it is a matter of my strength of will, we can put the same question in another form by asking how it is that my will has the strength that it has and not some other degree of strength. Once more, either it is an accident or it is not. If it is an accident, then by the same argument as before, I am not morally responsible, and if it is not an accident we are led back to determinism.

Furthermore, to say that my actions proceed from my character or, more colloquially, that I act in character, is to say that my behaviour is consistent and to that extent predictable: and since it is, above all, for the actions that I perform in character that I am held to be morally responsible, it looks as if the admission of moral responsibility, so far from being incompatible with determinism, tends rather to presuppose it. But how can this be so if it is a necessary condition of moral responsibility that the person who is held responsible should have acted freely? It seems that if we are to retain this idea of moral responsibility, we must either

show that men can be held responsible for actions
which they do not do freely, or else find some way
of reconciling determinism with the freedom of the
will.

It is no doubt with the object of effecting this
reconciliation that some philosophers have defined
freedom as the consciousness of necessity. And by so
doing they are able to say not only that a man can be
acting freely when his action is causally determined,
but even that his action must be causally determined
for it to be possible for him to be acting freely. Nevertheless this definition has the serious disadvantage that
it gives to the word 'freedom' a meaning quite different
from any that it ordinarily bears. It is indeed obvious
that if we are allowed to give the word 'freedom' any
meaning that we please, we can find a meaning that
will reconcile it with determinism: but this is no more
a solution of our present problem than the fact that
the word 'horse' could be arbitrarily used to mean
what is ordinarily meant by 'sparrow' is a proof that
horses have wings. For suppose that I am compelled
by another person to do something 'against my will'.
In that case, as the word 'freedom' is ordinarily used,
I should not be said to be acting freely: and the fact
that I am fully aware of the constraint to which I am
subjected makes no difference to the matter. I do not
become free by becoming conscious that I am not. It
may, indeed, be possible to show that my being aware
that my action is causally determined is not incompatible with my acting freely: but it by no means
follows that it is in this that my freedom consists.
Moreover, I suspect that one of the reasons why people
are inclined to define freedom as the consciousness of
necessity is that they think that if one is conscious of

T

necessity one may somehow be able to master it. But this is a fallacy. It is like someone's saying that he wishes he could see into the future, because if he did he would know what calamities lay in wait for him and so would be able to avoid them. But if he avoids the calamities then they don't lie in the future and it is not true that he foresees them. And similarly if I am able to master necessity, in the sense of escaping the operation of a necessary law, then the law in question is not necessary. And if the law is not necessary, then neither my freedom nor anything else can consist in my knowing that it is.

Let it be granted, then, that when we speak of reconciling freedom with determinism we are using the word 'freedom' in an ordinary sense. It still remains for us to make this usage clear: and perhaps the best way to make it clear is to show what it is that freedom, in this sense, is contrasted with. Now we began with the assumption that freedom is contrasted with causality: so that a man cannot be said to be acting freely if his action is causally determined. But this assumption has led us into difficulties and I now wish to suggest that it is mistaken. For it is not, I think, causality that freedom is to be contrasted with, but constraint. And while it is true that being constrained to do an action entails being caused to do it, I shall try to show that the converse does not hold. I shall try to show that from the fact that my action is causally determined it does not necessarily follow that I am constrained to do it: and this is equivalent to saying that it does not necessarily follow that I am not free.

If I am constrained, I do not act freely. But in what circumstances can I legitimately be said to be constrained ? An obvious instance is the case in which I am compelled by another person to do what he wants. In a case of this sort the compulsion need not be such as to deprive one of the power of choice. It is not required that the other person should have hypnotized me, or that he should make it physically impossible for me to go against his will. It is enough that he should induce me to do what he wants by making it clear to me that, if I do not, he will bring about some situation that I regard as even more undesirable than the consequences of the action that he wishes me to do. Thus, if the man points a pistol at my head I may still choose to disobey him : but this does not prevent its being true that if I do fall in with his wishes he can legitimately be said to have compelled me. And if the circumstances are such that no reasonable person would be expected to choose the other alternative, then the action that I am made to do is not one for which I am held to be morally responsible.

A similar, but still somewhat different, case is that in which another person has obtained an habitual ascendancy over me. Where this is so, there may be no question of my being induced to act as the other person wishes by being confronted with a still more disagreeable alternative : for if I am sufficiently under his influence this special stimulus will not be necessary. Nevertheless I do not act freely, for the reason that I have been deprived of the power of choice. And this means that I have acquired so strong a habit of obedience that I no longer go through any process of deciding whether or not to do what the other person wants. About other matters I may still deliberate ; but as regards the fulfilment of this other person's wishes, my own deliberations have ceased to be a causal factor in my behaviour. And it is in this sense that I may be said to be constrained. It is not, however, necessary that such constraint should take the form of sub-servience to another person. A kleptomaniac is not a free agent, in respect of his stealing, because he does not go through any process of deciding whether or not to steal. Or rather, if he does go through such a process, it is irrelevant to his behaviour. Whatever he resolved to do, he would steal all the same. And it is this that distinguishes him from the ordinary thief.

But now it may be asked whether there is any essential difference between these cases and those in which the agent is commonly thought to be free. No doubt the ordinary thief does go through a process of deciding whether or not to steal, and no doubt it does affect his behaviour. If he resolved to refrain from stealing, he could carry his resolution out. But if it be allowed that his making or not making this resolution is causally determined, then how can he be any more free than the kleptomaniac? It may be true that unlike the kleptomaniac he could refrain from stealing if he chose: but if there is a cause, or set of causes, which necessitate his choosing as he does, how can he be said to have the power of choice? Again, it may be true that no one now compels me to get up and walk across the room: but if my doing so can be causally explained in terms of my history or my environment, or whatever it may be, then how am I any more free than if some other person had compelled me? I do not have the feeling of constraint that I have when a pistol is mani-festly pointed at my head; but the chains of causation by which I am bound are no less effective for being invisible.

The answer to this is that the cases I have mentioned

as examples of constraint do differ from the others : and they differ just in the ways that I have tried to bring out. If I suffered from a compulsion neurosis, so that I got up and walked across the room, whether I wanted to or not, or if I did so because somebody else compelled me, then I should not be acting freely. But if I do it now, I shall be acting freely, just because these conditions do not obtain ; and the fact that my action may nevertheless have a cause is, from this point of view, irrelevant. For it is not when my action has any cause at all, but only when it has a special sort of cause, that it is reckoned not to be free.

But here it may be objected that, even if this distinction corresponds to ordinary usage, it is still very irrational. For why should we distinguish, with regard to a person's freedom, between the operations of one sort of cause and those of another ? Do not all causes equally necessitate ? And is it not therefore arbitrary to say that a person is free when he is necessitated in one fashion but not when he is necessitated in another ?

That all causes equally necessitate is indeed a tautology, if the word 'necessitate' is taken merely as equivalent to 'cause': but if, as the objection requires, it is taken as equivalent to 'constrain' or 'compel', then I do not think that this proposition is true. For all that is needed for one event to be the cause of another is that, in the given circumstances, the event which is said to be the effect would not have occurred if it had not been for the occurrence of the event which is said to be the cause, or *vice versa*, according as causes are interpreted as necessary, or sufficient, conditions : and this fact is usually deducible from some causal law which states that whenever an event of the one kind occurs then, given suitable conditions, an event of the other kind will occur in a certain temporal or spatio-temporal relationship to it. In short, there is an invariable concomitance between the two classes of events; but there is no compulsion, in any but a metaphorical sense. Suppose, for example, that a psycho-analyst is able to account for some aspect of my behaviour by referring it to some lesion that I suffered in my childhood. In that case, it may be said that my childhood experience, together with certain other events, necessitates my behaving as I do. But all that this involves is that it is found to be true in general that when people have had certain experiences as children, they subsequently behave in certain specifiable ways; and my case is just another instance of this general law. It is in this way indeed that my behaviour is explained. But from the fact that my behaviour is capable of being explained, in the sense that it can be subsumed under some natural law, it does not follow that I am acting under constraint.

If this is correct, to say that I could have acted otherwise is to say, first, that I should have acted otherwise if I had so chosen; secondly, that my action was voluntary in the sense in which the actions, say, of the kleptomaniac are not; and thirdly, that nobody compelled me to choose as I did: and these three conditions may very well be fulfilled. When they are fulfilled, I may be said to have acted freely. But this is not to say that it was a matter of chance that I acted as I did, or, in other words, that my action could not be explained. And that my actions should be capable of being explained is all that is required by the postulate of determinism.

If more than this seems to be required it is, I think, because the use of the very word 'determinism' is in some degree misleading. For it tends to suggest that one event is somehow in the power of another, whereas the truth is merely that they are factually correlated. And the same applies to the use, in this context, of the word 'necessity' and even of the word 'cause' itself. Moreover, there are various reasons for this. One is the tendency to confuse causal with logical necessitation, and so to infer mistakenly that the effect is contained in the cause. Another is the uncritical use of a concept of force which is derived from primitive experiences of pushing and striking. A third is the survival of an animistic conception of causality, in which all causal relationships are modelled on the example of one person's exercising authority over another. As a result we tend to form an imaginative picture of an unhappy effect trying vainly to escape from the clutches of an overmastering cause. But, I repeat, the fact is simply that when an event of one type occurs, an event of another type occurs also, in a certain temporal or spatio-temporal relation to the first. The rest is only metaphor. And it is because of the metaphor, and not because of the fact, that we come to think that there is an antithesis between causality and freedom.

Nevertheless, it may be said, if the postulate of determinism is valid, then the future can be explained in terms of the past: and this means that if one knew enough about the past one would be able to predict the future. But in that case what will happen in the future is already decided. And how then can I be said to be free ? What is going to happen is going to happen and nothing that I do can prevent it. If the determinist is right, I am the helpless prisoner of fate.

But what is meant by saying that the future course of events is already decided ? If the implication is that some person has arranged it, then the proposition is false. But if all that is meant is that it is possible, in principle, to deduce it from a set of particular facts about the past, together with the appropriate general laws, then, even if this is true, it does not in the least entail that I am the helpless prisoner of fate. It does not even entail that my actions make no difference to the future: for they are causes as well as effects; so that if they were different their consequences would be different also. What it does entail is that my behaviour can be predicted: but to say that my behaviour can be predicted is not to say that I am acting under constraint. It is indeed true that I cannot escape my destiny if this is taken to mean no more than that I shall do what I shall do. But this is a tautology, just as it is a tautology that what is going to happen is going to happen. And such tautologies as these prove nothing whatsoever about the freedom of the will.

INDEX

absolute ethics, 231
acquaintance, 125-126. *See also*
    apprehension *and* awareness
affirmative statements, 36-65
    best way of differentiating between
    affirmative and negative state-
    ments, 45
    describing positive facts, 47
ALEXANDER, SAMUEL, 173
analogy, argument from
    as substitute for direct observation,
    201-214
    whether invalid, 192
analysis of moral judgements
    on the, 231-249
    social consequences of, 248, 249
    see moral judgements
apprehension, direct, 66 f., 74 f., 84 f.,
    101, 103, 126
a priori, 45, 57, 105, 106, 107, 108,
    143, 173
attributes, 2, 8
awareness, direct, 125-126. *See also*
    apprehension

basic predicates
    complementary, 60
    whether incompatible when ap-
    plied to same individual, 59
basic statements
    analysis of, 105-124
    and meaning rules, 123
    false basic statements, 59
    falsification of, 60
    logical independence of, 59
BENTHAM, J., 244, 250 & n., 251-270
BERKELEY, G., 127, 153 f.
BLACK, MAX, 32 f. & n.
BOUWSMA, O. K., 68, 71, 78 f.
BRADLEY, F. H., 38 f. & n., 26 & n.
BROAD, C. D., 77, 91 n., 172, 180, 182
BUTLER, Bishop, 251

CARNAP, R., 5, 59
category statements, 6
causation and phenomenalism, 143-
    150

causation *contd.*—
    and freedom, 271-284
    not to be contrasted with freedom,
    278
certainty
    about matters of fact, 105
    and correct use of words, 121-122
    and good usage, 113
    and meaning rule of the language,
    121-124
    and misdescribing, 116
    and probability, 124
    of *a priori* propositions, 105
    philosophers' ideal of, 105
CHISHOLM, R., 92 & n., 97
classes and predicates, 117-120
complementarity
    definition of, in terms of negation,
    61
COOK WILSON, 52 & n.

demonstratives
    and logically proper names, 12
    as indicators, 23
    precision of, 13
DESCARTES, R., 105
descriptions, Russell's theory of, 17
determinism
    and freedom, 271-284
    and law of universal causation, 272
    and prediction, 273, 283, 284
    presupposed by moral responsi-
    bility, 276
    requires only that actions should be
    capable of being explained, 282
doubt
    empirical, 122
    logical, 105-107
    neurotic, 107, 122
    perpetual, 124
    philosophic, frivolity and strength
    of, 167
    whether one is in pain, 115
DUNNE, J. W., 181

ethical statements
    analysis of, 231-249

285

THE END

PRINTED BY R. & R. CLARK, LTD., EDINBURGH